Popular Songs
and
Ballads of Han China

Popular Songs
and
Ballads of Han China

ANNE BIRRELL

UNIVERSITY OF HAWAII PRESS

HONOLULU

First published in Great Britain by Unwin Hyman,
an imprint of Unwin Hyman Limited, 1988

Paperback edition published
by University of Hawaii Press 1993

Printed in the United States of America

93 94 95 96 97 98   5 4 3 2 1

Library of Congress Cataloging-in-Publication Data

Birrell, Anne.
    Popular songs and ballads of Han China / Anne
Birrell. — Paperback ed.
        p.   cm.
    Includes bibliographical references and index.
    ISBN 0-8248-1548-3
    1. Yüeh fu (Chinese poetry) — Translations into
English.   2.   Yüeh fu (Chinese poetry) — History
and criticism.   3.   Chinese poetry — Ch'in and
Han dynasties, 221 B.C.-220 A.D. — Translations
into English.   4.   Chinese poetry — Ch'in and
Han dynasties, 221 B.C.-220 A.D. — History and
criticism.   I.   Title.
PL2658.E3B57   1993
895.1'12209—dc20   93-18715
                                                CIP

University of Hawaii Press books are printed on acid-free
paper and meet the guidelines for permanence and durability
of the Council on Library Resources

To Hans H. Frankel,
pioneer of yüeh-fu *studies*

Acknowledgements

I wish to thank The British Academy for their generous Fellowship which assisted my research on this book. I would also like to take this opportunity of thanking the University of Michigan for enabling me to commence my degree programme some years ago by awarding me a National Defense Foreign Language Fellowship. I am indebted to my former publisher, Mr. Rayner S. Unwin, now retired, for his helpful advice in producing the first edition.

For this revised edition, I wish to thank sincerely my colleagues whose useful corrections and comments have been incorporated into my text. They are Professor Burton Watson, Professor Jean-Pierre Diény, Professor David R. Knechtges, and Professor Joseph R. Allen. Moreover, I am happy to acknowledge the contribution of Professor Hans H. Frankel in terms of his valuable suggestions and his continuing scholarly research in this field. Finally, I am delighted that the University of Hawaii Press has reissued this book and has allowed a generous number of revisions. Its editor, Sharon F. Yamamoto, has been extremely helpful in arranging for the publication of this new edition.

Contents

Chronological Table

The Age of Culture Heroes and Sage Kings	trad. 2852–2206 BC
Yellow Emperor/Emperor Yao/Emperor Shun	
The Golden Age of the Three Dynasties	trad. 2205–221 BC
Hsia Dynasty (trad. 2205–1767)/Shang Dynasty (trad. 1766–1123)	
Chou Dynasty: Western Chou (trad. 1123–771), Eastern	
Chou: Spring and Autumn Era (722–481),	
Warring States Era (403–221)	
Ch'in Dynasty	221–207BC
Han Dynasty: Former Han (202 BC–AD 8),	202 BC–AD 220
Latter Han (AD 25–220)	
Hsin Dynasty (Interregnum)	AD 9–23
The Three Kingdoms: Minor Han, Wei Dynasty	AD 221–280
(AD 220–265), Wu Dynasty	
Chin Dynasty	265–419
The Period of Disunion (or The Six Dynasties, or The	386–589
Northern and Southern Dynasties): Wu, Eastern	
Chin, Liu-Sung, Ch'i, Liang (502–556), Ch'en	
Sui Dynasty	589–618
T'ang Dynasty	618–907
Five Dynasties	907–959
Sung Dynasty: Northern Sung (960–1126), Southern	960–1279
Sung (1127–1279)	
Yüan (Mongol) Dynasty	1280–1368
Ming Dynasty	1368–1644
Ch'ing (Manchu) Dynasty	1644–1911
Republic of China	1912
People's Republic of China	1949

Foreword

Thanks to the efforts of many translators, the English-speaking world has become fairly well acquainted with the poetic effusions of Chinese men of letters. But another, delightfully different kind of Chinese poetry is still comparatively unknown, namely, anonymous poems that are either true folk songs or modifications or imitations of folk songs.

A translator's choice of folk songs rather than poems by known authors has two advantages: first, biographical criticism with its intricacies and pitfalls is automatically excluded; and second, folk songs are only rarely encumbered with learned allusions, which present so many problems in the poetry of the literati. The universal appeal of folk songs, even to readers of different cultures and epochs, is too obvious to require elaboration.

Dr. Anne Birrell's present selection, translation, and elucidation of folk songs from Han China is distinguished by the same qualities that have made her earlier book, *New Songs from a Jade Terrace* (George Allen and Unwin, 1982, rev. ed. Penguin Books, 1986), so useful and enjoyable. She is one of the few translators able to combine scholarly accuracy with idiomatic fluency and poetic flavor in English.

Dr. Birrell is happily free from the prejudices that have caused traditional scholars (Chinese, Japanese, and western) to overlook, ignore, or distort concepts and images that were incomprehensible or offensive to them. In particular, she succeeds in exposing erotic images that seemed, to traditional scholars, to violate Confucian taboos, and were therefore misunderstood or explained away. While not everybody will go along with Dr. Birrell in her reading of all such passages, she has certainly made a convincing case for less puritanical readings of many poems. For example, she notes the erotic significance of the fish playing hide-and-seek among the lotos leaves in the song *South of the River*.

Unlike many translators, Dr. Birrell conscientiously renders every phrase and every image, rather than skirting difficult passages, 'smoothing over' rough spots, and 'tidying up' poems that seem incoherent. One of the features that I find especially commendable in her translations is that she takes great pains to preserve the word order and syntactic structure of the Chinese as far as possible, without doing violence to English syntax. But while she is uncompromising in her fidelity to the Chinese text, her translations are eminently readable, and will give pleasure and enlightenment to a wide circle of readers for many years.

HANS H. FRANKEL (Yale University)
New Haven, Connecticut,
December 21, 1984

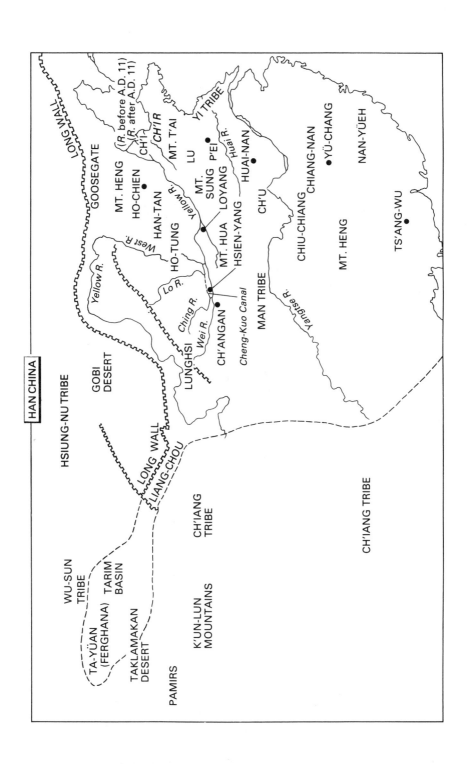

HAN CHINA

HSIUNG-NU TRIBE

LONG WALL

GOOSEGATE

(R. before A.D. 11)
(R. after A.D. 11)

CH'I

CH'I R

MT. T'AI

YI TRIBE

MT. HENG

HO-CHIEN

LU

MT. SUNG

LOYANG

P'EI

Huai R.

HUAI-NAN

CHIANG-NAN

YÜ-CHANG

NAN-YÜEH

HAN-TAN

Yellow R.

CH'U

HO-TUNG

West R.

MT. HUA

HSIEN-YANG

CHIU-CHIANG

MT. HENG

TS'ANG-WU

Yellow R.

Lo R.

MAN TRIBE

Yangtse R.

Ching R.

Wei R.

CH'ANGAN

Cheng-Kuo Canal

LUNGHSI

GOBI
DESERT

LONG WALL

LIANG-CHOU

WU-SUN
TRIBE

CH'IANG
TRIBE

TA-YÜAN
(FERGHANA)

TARIM
BASIN

K'UN-LUN
MOUNTAINS

CH'IANG TRIBE

TAKLAMAKAN
DESERT

PAMIRS

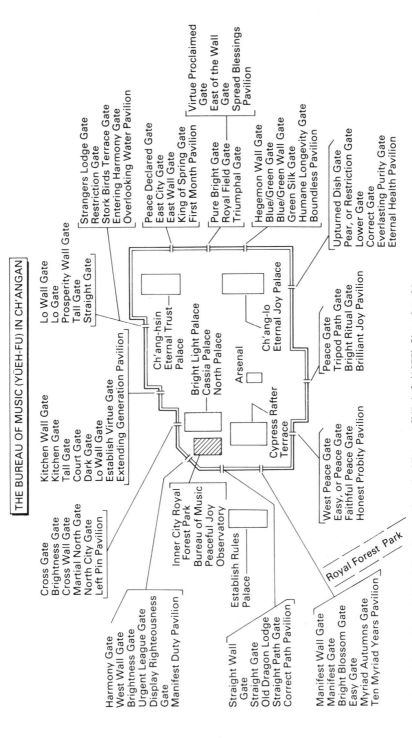

THE BUREAU OF MUSIC (YÜEH-FU) IN CH'ANGAN

Cross Gate
Brightness Gate
Cross Wall Gate
Martial North Gate
North City Gate
Left Pin Pavilion

Harmony Gate
West Wall Gate
Brightness Gate
Urgent League Gate
Display Righteousness Gate
Manifest Duty Pavilion

Kitchen Wall Gate
Kitchen Gate
Tall Gate
Court Gate
Dark Gate
Lo Wall Gate
Establish Virtue Gate
Extending Generation Pavilion

Lo Wall Gate
Lo Gate
Prosperity Wall Gate
Tall Gate
Straight Gate

Strangers Lodge Gate
Restriction Gate
Stork Birds Terrace Gate
Entering Harmony Gate
Overlooking Water Pavilion

Peace Declared Gate
East City Gate
East Wall Gate
King of Spring Gate
First Month Pavilion

Pure Bright Gate
Royal Field Gate
Triumphal Gate

Hegemon Wall Gate
Blue/Green Gate
Blue/Green Wall Gate
Green Silk Gate
Humane Longevity Gate
Boundless Pavilion

Virtue Proclaimed Gate
East of the Wall Gate
Spread Blessings Pavilion

Upturned Dish Gate
Pear, or Restriction Gate
Lower Gate
Correct Gate
Everlasting Purity Gate
Eternal Health Pavilion

Ch'ang-hsin
Eternal Trust Palace

Bright Light Palace
Cassia Palace
North Palace

Arsenal

Ch'ang-lo
Eternal Joy Palace

Cypress Rafter Terrace

Inner City Royal Forest Park
Bureau of Music
Peaceful Joy
Observatory

Establish Rules Palace

Straight Wall Gate
Straight Gate
Old Dragon Lodge
Straight Path Gate
Correct Path Pavilion

Royal Forest Park

West Peace Gate
Easy, or Peace Gate
Faithful Peace Gate
Honest Probity Pavilion

Peace Gate
Tripod Path Gate
Bright Ritual Gate
Brilliant Joy Pavilion

Manifest Wall Gate
Manifest Gate
Bright Blossom Gate
Easy Gate
Myriad Autumns Gate
Ten Myriad Years Pavilion

Adapted from Masuda Kiyohide, *Research on the History of Yüeh-fu* (1975), Chart 2, p. 21.

Introduction

Han Songs and Ballads as Social Documents

The writings of a great civilization may be subsumed under the Great Tradition and the little tradition. To the Great Tradition belong the works of the classical philosophers, historians, poets, scholars, and scientists who form an educated élite of inspired talent. Thanks to the translations of Arthur Waley in England, Burton Watson in the United States, and other sinologists, their writings and those of anonymous classical authors have become familiar to Western readers.[1] Inherent in the word 'classical' is the idea of serious literature from the ancient past written by members of the aristocracy, of court circles, and families whose social status and political position granted them an education.[2] The Great Tradition in China instructed and entertained the generations of men whose destiny was to shape and govern the empire. Significant though its humanistic influence has been, it represents only the most visible stratum of civilization.

The less visible layers are perceived through the little traditions of art, crafts, dance, music, and song, which tell of the lives, thoughts, feelings, and aspirations of the nameless mass of people in rural and urban regions. They are the eloquent, enduring creations of anonymous crafts-men and makers: the magnificent tombs of ancient kings; vessels and ornaments of bronze and jade; paintings; sculpture; woven silk; and lacquerware. These material expressions of creative, but mostly unknown, people form much of the archaeological heritage of ancient China which has been revealed to us in the past few decades.[3] Less tangible is the oral tradition of song, 'a rich and disorderly pattern', which has been fixed in texts and transmitted through the centuries.[4] The folk-songs and ballads in this book belong to the oral tradition of the Han period, when the first great dynasty of China was founded and the empire was formed. They express the hopes and dreams of ordinary people, their routine lives, the tragedies which beset them, their brief moments of happiness, the values and beliefs they cling to. Such utterances from foot-soldiers, farm-hands, servant girls, entertainers, poor wives, orphans, and destitute husbands, many of whom were

1

considered to be outside the traditional social classes, counterbalance the picture we have of Han China derived from the Great Tradition.

These songs and ballads are the legacy of the popular, oral tradition, works of art which have endured because of their simple, honest, and unfailingly human qualities. More importantly, perhaps, they constitute informal social documents which help to illuminate the darker, less familiar existence of the people.

Han Culture

In 202 BC Liu Pang, a commoner, founded the Han Dynasty. The Liu family succession was maintained until AD 220, except for a short interregnum between AD 9–23. During these four centuries, the imperial foundations of China were established and consolidated. Han China inherited a revolutionary sociopolitical structure from the short-lived Ch'in Dynasty which immediately preceded it.[5] The Ch'in, informed by a Legalist and Governmental philosophy, conceived of a new social order in which the people were divided into functional classes and were accountable directly to the State. The Ch'in rulers dismantled the old aristocratic orders, imposing a new state-centred system. The economy came under central control; weights, measures, vehicle axle gauges, and coinage were standardized. The writing system was also made uniform. The people were mobilized for huge projects, such as the construction of the capital city and the building of the Great Wall, and were conscripted into the army. The early Han emperors endorsed the Ch'in institutional innovations, even extending some aspects of state management of the economy, such as state monopolies on salt, iron, liquor, and the marketing of grain.[6]

The Ch'in government had set in motion measures toward political and social cohesion and economic efficiency within its immediate boundaries. Yet because the dynasty was so short-lived (just 16 years), the practical implementation of its radical measures, the complete unification of the many regions of the empire, and the pacification of neighbouring countries or tribal zones were left to Han rulers.

The new social order envisaged by the first Ch'in emperor was posited upon a dynamic, omnipotent role for the emperor: he stood at the apex of society, aided by a meritocratic bureaucracy. The first Ch'in emperor, Cheng, was himself a man of extraordinary ability and energy, and ably fulfilled his imperial role.[7] Similarly, some Han rulers, such as the founder, Emperor Kao-tsu, Emperor Wu, and Emperor Kuang-wu, who restored the Han Dynasty, proved to be shrewd and competent administrators.[8] Such a centralized political system which was dominated by one leader failed, however, when that leader was

2

ineffectual, or was bored by affairs of state. Consequently, although on the surface the four centuries of the Han appear to enjoy cohesion and continuity, there were periods of severe political dislocation and social disorder.

Emperor Wu's long reign of over half a century from the age of 16 to 70 years is a formative era in Han history. He introduced innovation and reform into many spheres of life. On the military front he extended his empire's borders north-east into Korea, south into Yunnan and north Vietnam, east down to Chekiang and Fukien, and west to the Tarim Basin. These areas were colonized and assimilated into Han culture. The emperor's armies also succeeded in expelling the northern enemies of China, the Hsiung-nu, as far away as the Gobi desert, but had to endure persistent and sporadic raids. Han envoys and generals even reached Ferghana to procure the famous horses of the region. In his economic policies, Emperor Wu made radical changes, such as the state appropriation of the lucrative salt and iron industries (previously under private ownership), and established a state mint. He also embarked on a policy of government marketing and trade, ostensibly to provide famine relief and to stabilize prices, but indirectly to ensure huge revenues for the treasury.

This dynamic ruler personally supervized the administration of his expanding empire and participated in the planning and construction of grandiose palaces and halls designed to reflect the glory of the Han. He built lavish mansions and parks. The splendour of his royal park was eulogized by one of his court poets, Ssu-ma Hsiang-ju, in 'Rhapsody on Shang-lin Park'.[9]

Ch'angan, the capital city of the Former, or Western Han, was reconstructed and refurbished in 194 BC. Like many ancient Chinese cities it was formally designed as a rectangle, with its main gate facing south, the source of the cosmic *Yang* principle. At the beginning of the Christian era, the population of Ch'angan and the adjacent rural area was estimated to be about a quarter of a million, with approximately 80,000 inhabitants living within the city's double walls.[10] The rich lived in great luxury in storied, timbered mansions which were profusely carved and decorated in vivid colours. Silks and embroideries softened and brightened the interiors. They wore fine silks, furs, and jewels. At their banquets they enjoyed exotic menus served on dishes ornamented with gold or silver. Their carriages and horses were magnificently arrayed with lacquer, leather, silk, and jewels. Many of the wealthy residents attended court in an official capacity. Apart from their enjoyment of court entertainment, they often had their own orchestras and entertainers, with dancing, acrobatics, juggling, warrior dances with sword-play, cock-fighting, racing, and hunting.[11]

The numbers of people required for the service of the expanding class of *nouveau-riche* in Han China must have been considerable. Coachmen, stablelads, entertainers, cooks, stewards, builders, decorators, tailors, and scores of servants were resident in or near the mansion compounds within the city. Besides this, there were government offices to maintain throughout the city, which enlisted the services of many attendants and slaves.

In the countryside (termed *yeh*, or wilds) beyond the city walls lived the farmers and their hands. As has been the case throughout Chinese history, and in the present, the population was mainly rural. Although the Ch'in founder had inaugurated a system of land re-allocation so that the rural population could own land which previously had belonged to the aristocracy, the concept of an equitable system of land ownership became eclipsed during the Han, especially at the end of the Former Han (*c.* AD 9) and at the end of the Latter Han (*c.* AD 220). The recurring pattern was that due to natural disaster such as flooding, to heavy taxation, corvée duties when men were forced off the land each year for construction work or the army, and to the increase of family numbers owning the original parcel of allocated land, many displaced farmers and hands sold up and became tenant farmers or even serfs on large estates. The traditional contrast between city and country became more pronounced.

In this period, agriculture was the mainstay of the economy. It was a slow and painstaking process, occasionally based on animal-power, but more often on manpower. Very few technical contrivances aided the farmer, and heavy work like irrigation, sowing, harvesting, milling and so forth, were mostly manpower jobs.[12] It was only towards the end of the Han era that some rudimentary mechanization was introduced, such as well-pulleys and milling rollers.

Many aspects of life in the city and country are reflected in the songs. The hymns hint at the pageantry of seasonal religious processions in the outskirts of the city. Political broadsides voice criticism of the government's requisition of farm animals and the removal of men from the land at harvest-time, and the stockpiling of grain by fortune-hunting members of the imperial family. The war songs complain of conscription, inadequate provisions, and the waste of human life in seemingly senseless construction projects far from home. Domestic ballads describe penury in the home, where infants are left to starve and the mother dies of neglect. Rustic fables express the grim and harsh reality of the countryside where death and destruction pose a constant threat. In the *carpe diem* ballads, especially, there appears a generalized sense of spiritual and social malaise; even at a banquet at which rich food and strong liquor are served, a singer sings a troubled piece about the meaning of existence.

In short, these popular ballads provide written evidence of the imbalance between certain sectors of Han society. While we may enjoy the luxuriant exuberance of the Han rhapsody and formal odes eulogizing the regime, the songs and ballads remind us of the people whose labour underwrote the glittering opulence of the city and whose own life was likely to be spent in poverty. The lack of merry, carefree songs and ballads testifies to the ordinary person's miserable lot.

The Bureau of Music: Yüeh-fu

The repertoire of anonymous songs and ballads in the Han is inextricably linked to the establishment and development of the Han Bureau of Music, the *Yüeh-fu*. There is general agreement on the question of when the Han Bureau of Music was abolished: that occurred in the year 7 BC when Emperor Ai acceded to the throne and was convinced of the unethical, unorthodox trends in this government office.[13] There is little agreement, however, on the questions of when and by whom this institution was established. The problem lies in the documentary evidence. Historical texts contemporary with the Han carry contradictory statements on the founder and the foundation date. The Latter Han historian Pan Ku (AD 32–92) states that the Bureau of Music was subordinate to another bureau, the *Shao-fu* or Lesser Treasury, which itself dated from the Ch'in and was responsible for the emperor's personal needs—harem, household, robes, secretariat, missions, parks, arsenal, and so forth.[14] The Former Han historian, Ssu-ma Ch'ien (?145–?90 BC) confirms the early date of the Bureau of Music when he states that the three early Han emperors who reigned between 195–141 BC '. . . neither added nor changed anything in the Bureau of Music; they simply practised ancient custom.'[15] The existence of the Bureau in the early Han is even more definitely fixed by Pan Ku in his 'Treatise on Rites and Music' where he suggests it was active in the year 194 BC.[16] Yet in the same treatise he implies a much later date, stating that Emperor Wu established the Bureau when he instituted new religious ceremonies between 114–113 BC.[17] This text goes on to say that Emperor Wu appointed Li Yen-nien as his Master of Music, and that he often performed musical arrangements of poems and rhapsodies composed by Ssu-ma Hsiang-ju and others.[18] In his biography of Li Yen-nien Pan Ku repeats his statement about the new cults, adding that Emperor Wu '. . . commissioned Ssu-ma Hsiang-ju and others to compose poems.'[19] The problem here is one of chronology: Ssu-ma Hsiang-ju died *c.* 117 BC, about four years before Pan Ku's founding date of between 114–113 BC of the Bureau of Music. Moreover, Li's appointment as the court Master of Music took place at the time when his brother became a general, a promotion which is said to have occurred in 104 BC. A parallel text in the histories of both Pan Ku and Ssu-ma Ch'ien states that Li

Yen-nien persuaded Emperor Wu to introduce music and dance into the service of thanksgiving for victory in Nan-Yüeh in 111 BC, which would indicate that the Bureau was in existence only quite late in the reign of Emperor Wu. Apart from the debate about the Bureau's connection with Ssu-ma Hsiang-ju and Li Yen-nien as late as 114 BC, another group of texts suggests that the Bureau was formed in c. 121–120 BC, a date linked to the reported discovery of a 'horse of heaven'.[20]

The earlier date of 120 BC for the establishment of the Bureau of Music by Emperor Wu is the one which is traditionally accepted. This date has its adherents among modern critics. J. R. Hightower, Burton Watson, and Hans H. Frankel accept that the Bureau was established by Emperor Wu around that year. Takeo Sawaguchi also tends toward this early date, arguing that Emperor Wu must have employed the musician Li Yen-nien at his court in 121 BC. Hellmut Wilhelm argues for a much earlier date, suggesting that the Bureau, '. . . like other institutions of Han times was a Ch'in establishment.' P'eng Li-t'ien favours a pre-Ch'in date, suggesting that the Bureau originated in the late Warring States era. He cites as evidence the archaeological discovery of an inscribed official seal which reads: 'The Seal of the Ch'i State Bureau of Music'.[21] M. Loewe prefers a dating around 114 BC.[22] G. S. Williams, after presenting the most important documentary evidence, declines to settle on a date.[23]

J.-P. Diény, in my view, offers the safest and soundest compromise in this conflict of textual evidence. He thoroughly reviews the texts, pointing out inconsistencies and exposing the flaws in various arguments. He concludes that the Bureau of Music existed from the beginning of the Han and was not created by Emperor Wu or during his reign. On the other hand, Diény points to the year 111 BC, when Li Yen-nien was appointed as Master of Music, as the commencement of a period when Emperor Wu possibly renamed an existing government office of music and, more importantly, completely reoriented the concept, functions, and scope of the office. So radical was this institutional reform, Diény argues, that it must have seemed at the time to be the creation of an entirely new institution.[24] The mainspring of this reform was the introduction of popular elements into religious and secular ceremonies which reflected Emperor Wu's taste for modern music from foreign countries and traditional folk music and dance.

The various texts which mention the Bureau provide some vague information about its functions. Its alleged tasks were to collect popular songs from regions of the Han empire (especially Chao, Tai, Ch'in, and Ch'u) and from foreign countries; to adapt and orchestrate popular songs; to compose new hymns and put them to music; to put existing texts to new, modern tunes; to set to music compositions commissioned from famous poets, such as Ssu-ma Hsiang-ju; to participate in, and perform at, religious and secular functions.[25] Virtually nothing is known

6

of how the Bureau functioned, but its great popularity may be judged from a statistic given at the time it was abolished in 7 BC: no fewer than 829 personnel were employed in its different departments. Their number was reduced by about half and the functions of the Bureau were redistributed among other government offices.[26] In the Latter Han the Bureau seems to have been revived, but it did not survive much beyond the Han.

The Genre of Yüeh-fu Songs and Ballads

In the post-Han literary tradition, certain hymns, songs, and poems acquired the name of the Han Bureau of Music, or *Yüeh-fu*, from which they were believed to have historically emerged. The first literary figure to use the generic term *yüeh-fu* is Shen Yüeh, late fifth century AD. In the 'Autobiographical Postface,' *ch.* 100 of his *History of the Southern Sung*, he enumerates 17 genres in which his older relative, Shen Liang, composed 189 pieces, the ninth genre being *yüeh-fu*. He failed to attach the term, however, to any text in the collection of Han and post-Han songs in the 'Treatise on Music' of his *History*. Therefore, although Shen may be said to be the earliest literary figure to use the term *yüeh-fu* for a composition, he was not the first to apply the term specifically to extant song-texts. The first to apply the term to such texts were Hsiao T'ung and Hsü Ling, compilers of early sixth century imperial anthologies. *Anthology of Literature (Wen hsüan)*, compiled by Hsiao T'ung and others, and *New Songs from a Jade Terrace (Yü-t'ai hsin-yung)*, edited by Hsü Ling, both contain valuable Han *yüeh-fu* material, so named and so dated. A somewhat earlier work of literary criticism, *The Literary Mind and the Carving of Dragons (Wen-hsin tiao-lung)* by Liu Hsieh (d. *c.* AD 523) established the authenticity of the genre of *yüeh-fu* songs and ballads by elevating them to a separate category after *sao*-elegies and *shih*-lyrics but before *fu*-rhapsodies.[27] The terms *yüeh-fu* or *ku* (old) *yüeh-fu*, designating Han pieces from the perspective of post-Han writers and commentators, appear as a sub-section of *shih* poetry in *Anthology of Literature, ch.* 27–28, and independently in *New Songs from a Jade Terrace, ch.* 1. But already in these three post-Han sources the classification of pieces by generic titles began to be confused. For example, the Han Emperor Kao-tsu's song, 'A Great Wind Rises', is classified as a miscellaneous song (*tsa-ko*) in the *yüeh-fu* section of *Anthology of Literature*, but as a plain *yüeh-fu* piece by Liu Hsieh. Similarly, the Han Emperor Wu's song, 'Autumn Wind', is classified as a *tz'u*, or Ch'u elegiac piece in *Anthology of Literature*. Six centuries later, Kuo Mao-ch'ien classified Kao-tsu's song under category 8, 'Song-texts for Lute Pieces', among *ko*-songs and *ts'ao*-lute songs, and Emperor Wu's song under category 11, 'Words for Miscellaneous Ditties', among *ko*-songs.[28]

7

After the sixth century AD, the generic term *yüeh-fu* became fixed and, in the course of time, was attached to an increasing number and variety of songs to be found in Han and post-Han sources. The repertoire of *yüeh-fu* actually surviving from the Bureau cannot be ascertained because songs are not recorded under that generic title in extant Han documents. By the early twelfth century, though, they formed a vast repertoire of, so-called, *yüeh-fu* texts, notably anthologized by Kuo Mao-ch'ien.

The corpus of Han songs has come down in a piecemeal and rather battered fashion. The earliest source is Pan Ku's 'Treatise on Rites and Music' and 'Treatise on the Five Elements'. The former contains Han hymns, the latter, political lampoons. Another treatise by Pan Ku, the 'Treatise on Literature', tantalizingly lists compositions under twenty-eight headings but it does not give the text of the songs. So in cases where his titles correspond with those in the extant repertoire we cannot be sure that his title represents the same surviving text. On the whole, however, his titles do not tally with those of the present repertoire. When Han historians and ritualists discussed music, it was mainly at the level of theory, or else in the form of scattered comments.[29]

The next, and most important, source is the 'Treatise on Music' in the *History of the Southern Sung* by the poet and musicologist Shen Yüeh (AD 441–512), compiled some two and a half centuries after the end of the Han. As was the case with Western ballads, 'It was the literary men who made the ballad a prestigious enough article to be granted the status of [book form] in the course of time'.[30] His 'Treatise' includes a valuable collection of *ku-tz'u* (old songs), some of which he lists under the rubric of *hsiang-ho*, 'Concerted' pieces, defined by him as old songs of the Han era.[31]

Chronologically, the next sources are the previously mentioned *Anthology of Literature* and *New Songs from a Jade Terrace* of the sixth century AD. The source par excellence of anonymous songs and ballads, however, is the *Anthology of Yüeh-fu Poetry (Yüeh-fu shih chi)* compiled by Kuo Mao-ch'ien. Very little may be gleaned about Kuo's biography. He lived most of his life in the Northern Sung era. His grandfather, Kuo Pao, and his father, Kuo Yüan-chung, were both famous officials in Yün-chou (modern Shantung) in the first half of the eleventh century. Kuo Mao-ch'ien, was the eldest of five sons (and five daughters). His courtesy name was Te-ts'an. In about AD 1084 he took up a subordinate official post in the prefecture of Ho-nan. He became a specialist in music. Besides his great anthology, he compiled the *Anthology of Miscellaneous Verse Forms (Tsa t'i shih chi)*, which is no longer extant, and some of his own poetry. It seems likely that he compiled his *Anthology of Yüeh-fu Poetry* by the end of the Northern Sung era, c. AD 1126, because it was already being mentioned by literary critics by the beginning of the Southern Sung, AD 1127.[32]

His anthology comprises nearly all extant *yüeh-fu* texts between the

Han and T'ang to Five Dynasties. Kuo's collection, allowing for some wrong attributions, is now considered to contain the main repertoire of traditional songs and ballads. They are hymns, ceremonial songs, marching songs, folk-songs, dance songs, songs for the lute, miscellaneous airs, 'modern' (*i.e.* Sui-T'ang) songs, and 'new' (*i.e.* T'ang) *yüeh-fu*. Kuo arranged this vast corpus of 5,290 pieces into one hundred chapters, subdivided into twelve categories, for the most part based on the musical setting of the song-texts.[33] Unfortunately, the music has been lost. Kuo also arranged his material in a unique and innovative manner: he presents an original piece, such as an anonymous Han song with its variant text, and immediately after it he places influential imitations of it by known poets of the Han to the T'ang and Five Dynasties. This organizing principle is of great literary value, for it enables the reader to compare the original with its later imitations, and to contrast existing versions of the early text.

One's first response to this vast corpus of songs and ballads is that it manifests generic diversity. Under one so-called genre of *yüeh-fu* are subsumed a variety of other genres or sub-genres, each with its own generic title. For example, *ko* (song), *ko-tz'u* (song-words), *ko-ch'ü* (song piece), *hsing* (suite [?ballad]), *yin* (lay), *yin* (lament), *ch'ü-tz'u* (melodic words), *p'ien* (piece [?folk-song]), *tsa-ch'ü* (miscellaneous piece), *tsa ko-yao tz'u* (words for miscellaneous ditties).[34] By Kuo Mao-ch'ien's time a *yüeh-fu* piece indicated almost any song prior to the Sung Dynasty.[35]

It is interesting to compare the continuing controversy among Western literary critics concerning the origins of the ballad, and what constitutes a ballad, with its Chinese counterpart. In both cases the genre defies an exclusive definition. As A. Bold succinctly defines the Western ballad, 'The ballad can accept any number of epithets, and there are tuneless ballads as well as broadside ballads and popular ballads and literary ballads.'[36] G. H. Gerould's definition of the Western ballad neatly combines the two terms ballad and folk-song: 'A ballad is a folk-song that tells a story with stress on the crucial situation, tells it by letting the action unfold itself in event and speech, and tells it objectively with little comment or intrusion of personal bias.'[37] In generic terms we may define the anonymous Chinese ballad or song of the Han era as follows: it was composed by an anonymous amateur and, until fixed in a text, was in subsequent folk possession and became part of a popular repertoire; originally oral, it was later fixed in texts of varying degrees of literary quality and usually with a number of variant words or phrases; it was set to music which is now lost; it is relatively simple in diction, content, and point of view; it may either tell a story as a narrative ballad, or convey an emotion as a lyrical ballad; it may describe action and feeling with numerous musical devices, such as repetition and refrain; its title usually includes a term relating to song or melody.

9

The twelve categories which Kuo Mao-ch'ien used to order his *yüeh-fu* material did not originate with him. The specialization of types of music is already apparent in Pan Ku's discussion of numerous sub-sections of the Bureau of Music at the time of its radical reorganization under Emperor Ai in 7 BC. Most of these sub-sections were categorized as religious (suburban sacrifice) or regional (Han-tan drumming, Huai-nan drumming, and the like). In the reign of the Han Emperor Ming (AD 58–75) four musical categories of song were distinguished: 1) The Grand *Yü* Music, 2) Music for Classical Odes and Praise Songs, 3) Music for Drumming Songs of the Yellow Gate, and 4) Music for Songs for Short Pan-pipes and *Nao*-bell. Another set of four classes of music for songs in the Han is attributed to Ts'ai Yung (AD 133–92), the statesman, classicist, poet, astronomer, and musician, who is also credited with authorship of the book, *Song Melodies for the Lute (Ch'in ts'ao)*. These four were: 1) Sacred Mysteries of the Suburban and Temple (Sacrifices), 2) Imperial Banquets, 3) Court Entertainments with Archery (Contests), and 4) Songs for the Short Pan-pipes and *Nao*-bell.[38] In the Northern Sung Dynasty, Kuo utilized much of this early system. The first category of the second set became his first category, 'Words for Suburban and Temple Songs'. He combined the second and third categories of the same set to form his second category, 'Words for Banquet and Archery Songs'. He also combined the last two categories of the first Han set, equivalent to the last category of the second set to form his own third category, 'Words for Drumming and Blowing Pieces'. He probably did not derive this material at first hand, but through the T'ang critic Wu Ching (d. AD 749), who will be discussed shortly.

Shen Yüeh, the late fifth-century statesman, historian, and poet, is to be credited with the emphasis on anonymous popular songs of the Han, giving them the cachet of orthodoxy by including them in his 'Treatise on Music' in his *History of the Southern Sung*. He termed them *hsiang-ho*, 'Concerted', and wrote of them: 'All the musical songs that survive today are Han period ditties from the streets and lanes.'[39] We may translate 'streets' as the city, 'lanes' as the country. This group became Kuo's fifth category, 'Words for Concerted Songs'. This contains most of the songs and ballads generally regarded as the repertoire of anonymous Han *yüeh-fu*.

Shen Yüeh's 'Treatise on Music' is a valuable literary document, for it constitutes the earliest source of Han *yüeh-fu* songs and ballads and of information about them. Its four volumes (*ch.* 19–22) comprise the following material: 1) a discussion of song and music from legendary times to Shen's own day, AD 488; 2) an anthology of hymns and praise songs of the Wei, Chin, and Southern Sung Dynasties; 3) an anthology of *ku-tz'u*, old songs, anonymous, popular pieces deriving from the Han, and their imitations by famous poets of the immediate post-Han era; and 4) an anthology of song-texts for miscellaneous named dances and for *nao*-bell pieces.

Shen divided his material into four musical categories: 1) Hymns and Formal Court Pieces, 2) *Hsiang-ho*, 'Concerted' pieces, *Ch'ing-Shang* Pieces in Three Modes, Major Pieces, and Ch'u-mode, 3) Songs for Dances and Dance Melodies, and 4) Drumming and Blowing Pieces.[40] Only with category 4) did he attach the label 'Han' to *nao*-bell songs, making the set of 18 Han Songs for the *Nao*-bell the earliest firmly dated pieces in his collection. (For the list of his categories, showing the Han songs I have translated, see p. 206.) Elsewhere he affixed the label *ku-tz'u*, 'old songs', to certain titles such as 16 *Hsiang-ho* pieces in *ch*. 21. Since he affixed post-Han dynastic labels to all other titles, *i.e.*, Wei, Chin, and Southern Liu-Sung, it may be assumed that by *ku-tz'u* Shen meant songs of the Han era, or even earlier perhaps, in his estimation.

On the other hand, it would be rash to infer that these texts, designated as *ku-tz'u* and Han by Shen, were transmitted intact from the Han to the Southern Sung era. Shen Yüeh frequently states that the recension of the old texts was a preoccupation of several musicians and poets of the Wei court. From his discussion and song collection it is clear that the processes of restoration, reconstruction, reinterpretation, and imitation were initiated by poets and musicians such as Fu Hsüan (AD 217–278), and firmly established by Ts'ao Ts'ao (AD 155–220), Ts'ao P'ei (AD 187–226), Ts'ao Chih (AD 192–232), and Ts'ao Jui (AD 204–239), who were all born in the Latter Han era, some barely surviving the dynasty itself. Moreover, since Shen Yüeh adopted the format of placing some *ku-tz'u* titles after their poetic (not necessarily musical) imitations by the royal Ts'ao poets, it follows that those *ku-tz'u* titles must date at least from the Latter Han, and in some cases possibly earlier.

Shen Yüeh credits eight musicians of the Wei court with the valuable work of the recension and transmission of the texts of the anonymous popular songs of the Han, each specializing in different branches of music: one Mr. Sun, Ch'en Tso, Ho So, Chu Sheng, Sung Shih, Lieh Ho, and Hsün Hsü and his son Hsün P'an ('Treatise on Music', *ch*. 19.559, *ch*. 20.603, *ch*. 19.542). Hsün Hsü is especially commended for his work on old song titles and music, *Hsün's Poetry Notes*. This is no longer extant, but is extensively cited in subsequent *yüeh-fu* literary criticism. Hsün also composed sets of hymns (two sets being preserved by Shen Yüeh in *ch*. 20). Shen also records that ' "*Ch'ing-Shang* Song Poems in Three Modes: Level-mode, Clear-mode, and Zither-mode" are old texts which Hsün Hsü selected and realized' (*ch*. 21.608).

The 'Three Modes' are interesting in so far as they differ from Kuo Mao-ch'ien's later perception of 'mode' (*tiao*). In the first place, Kuo linked the Ch'u-mode, a quite separate modal category in Shen, to form four modes. Secondly, the appellation *Ch'ing-Shang* Kuo divorced completely from the modes, which he restricted to *Hsiang-ho*, 'Concerted' pieces. For Kuo, *Ch'ing-Shang* pieces meant certain post-Han popular songs. Kuo reallocated certain titles within Shen's categories to different mode categories. For example, Kuo transferred several of Shen's 'Major Pieces' titles to the 'Zither-mode' and one to the 'Ch'u-mode'. One possible conclusion to be drawn from this is that the texts of *yüeh-fu*, once they were committed to writing from an earlier oral tradition, were more or less preserved unchanged, whereas the more fugitive form of music, not fully notated, altered through the centuries to suit the prevailing taste in music. Musicians wrote in different modes for the same song-text. Alternatively, during the seven centuries between Shen Yüeh's times and Kuo's, from AD 488 to about AD 1126, the original music of the Han songs was lost and the apprehension of mode *per se* became obscured, resulting in an antiquarian reconstruction of mode categories in the early twelfth century, or earlier, which sometimes proved to be quite faulty.

The next important classification of music is the nine categories of Wu Ching in the T'ang. He eliminated the hymn and praise song category, while up-grading popular songs to first place. In his *Explanations of the Old Titles of Yüeh-fu* he presented nine groups of song titles, indicating after each group to which musical or prosodic category the group belongs. His nine categories are: 1) *Hsiang-ho*, Concerted (pieces), 2) Sweeping Dance Songs, 3) White Hemp Songs, 4) Songs for the *Nao*-bell, 5) Horizontal Flute Pieces, 6) *Ch'ing-Shang* Pieces, 7) Miscellaneous Titles, 8) Pieces for the Lute, and 9) Old Titles and Miscellaneous Titles.[41] Of these the first and fourth have been encountered before. Wu's second and third categories became Kuo's seventh, 'Song-texts for Dance Pieces'. Wu's fifth became Kuo's fourth category, 'Words for Horizontal Flute Pieces'. Wu's sixth remained Kuo's category number six, 'Words for *Ch'ing-Shang* Pieces'. Wu's seventh is probably the equivalent of Kuo's ninth, 'Song-texts for Miscellaneous Pieces', while Wu's eighth remains Kuo's. It is Wu's last category which seems the most deceptive. A valuable source of pre-Han, Han, and post-Han titles, it became Kuo's eleventh category, 'Words for Miscellaneous Ditties'. Thus far, ten of Kuo's categories have been found to derive from pre-existing musical and prosodic categories of song. Kuo's tenth and twelfth categories contain songs and poems dating from the Sui-T'ang to Five Dynasties era.[42]

The clue to Kuo's borrowing from Wu's scheme lies in his uncritical adoption of the first part of Wu's last category, 'Old Titles', as his own eleventh. For in Kuo's day some of these titles were believed to date from hoary antiquity and were alleged to be songs by the legendary Emperor Yao. It would have been more logical for Kuo to have opened his massive anthology with these ancient rimes, following on with the Han hymns and banquet pieces. In fact, a later anthologist of *yüeh-fu*, Tso K'o-ming (14th century), did precisely this when he arranged his *yüeh-fu* pieces in eight categories in *Ancient Yüeh-fu*. Tso began with ancient rimes, omitting hymns and formal ritual pieces; then he followed Kuo's categories up to Kuo's ninth; he omitted Kuo's tenth and last categories. In this scheme Tso was clearly presenting his material in a more or less chronological manner, but he was also attempting to provide an ancient pedigree for the Han *yüeh-fu*, thus rendering them acceptable as orthodox literature. Tso's scheme of the late Yüan was followed in the main by Feng Wei-no of the Ming, but thereafter the musical categories tended to be dropped and *yüeh-fu* merged with poetry in literary criticism. The *yüeh-fu* material was arranged chronologically with *shih*-lyric poetry as with Shen Te-ch'ien, and more recently with Ting Fu-pao and Lu Ch'in-li.[43]

While it appears that Kuo Mao-ch'ien merely adapted his scheme from existing schema from the Han to the T'ang, he may be judged original in the following ways. He introduced the organizing principle of arranging original songs and their later imitations chronologically within each of his twelve categories. He placed versions of the same title next to each other. He presented his categories more or less in sequence as each historically evolved. Also, he was the first to amalgamate the traditional categories of religion and court ceremonial with the more popular, secular musical idiom, although it is true that he was prompted by earlier exemplars of musical classification. Finally, he strove to preserve the remnants of musical information associated with many of his categories, even though by his day the musical accompaniment was largely lost. In this sense he was a true Sung scholar and an antiquarian of the first rank.

Sources of Kuo Mao-ch'ien's Song-texts and Their Contexts

When Kuo Mao-ch'ien compiled his anthology of *yüeh-fu* songs and ballads in around AD 1126, he looked back on a period of over a millennium during which the genre had evolved and matured. In his own day a new song form, the *tz'u* lyric, had displaced the *yüeh-fu* and had become the fashionable medium for poets and song-writers to exercise their talents. Although the *yüeh-fu* had influenced the *tz'u* at its inception in the T'ang Dynasty, by Kuo's time the *yüeh-fu* was regarded as an old-fashioned literary form which had enjoyed its renaissance in the T'ang. In a sense, the *yüeh-fu* was becoming defunct by the end of the eleventh century and was in need of conservation. Kuo admirably performed this task of preserving a vast repertoire of familiar and recherché titles. His was an age of literary compilation on a grand scale. Early in the Northern Sung, Li Fang and his colleagues were commissioned by Emperor T'ai-tsung to compile a compendium of

13

knowledge which resulted in *The Four Books of the Northern Sung* consisting of over 3,500 volumes. One unintended advantage of such compilations was that much fugitive material has been preserved.[44]

To complete his task of gathering virtually every song title prior to the Sung, Kuo referred to over 160 works, either at first or second hand.[45] Even by Shen Yüeh's day the works of certain authorities on *yüeh-fu* were no longer extant, such as Hsün Hsü (d. AD 289). Collections of songs and critical comments were included in treatises on music and literature in the official histories through the centuries, so that by the end of the Northern Sung a considerable amount of research material on old *yüeh-fu* had accumulated. Much of this material Kuo incorporated into the essays prefacing his twelve categories and some sub-categories. The main treatises from the histories, arranged chronologically according to the dates of their authors, are as follows:

Historical Records (Shih chi) ch. 24, 'History of Music' (1st cent. BC)

History of the Han (Han shu) ch. 22, 'Treatise on Rites and Music' (1st cent. AD)

History of the Han (Han shu) ch. 30, 'Treatise on Literature' (1st cent. AD)

History of the Latter Han (Hou Han shu, hsü) ch. 1–3, 'Treatise on Pitchpipes', *ch.* 13–18, 'Treatise on the Five Elements' (3rd–4th cent.)

History of the Southern Sung (Sung shu) ch. 19–22, 'Treatise on Music' (5th cent.)

History of the Southern Ch'i (Nan-Ch'i shu) ch. 11, 'Treatise on Music' (5th–6th cent.)

History of the Wei (Wei shu) ch. 109, 'Treatise on Music' (6th cent.)

History of the Chin (Chin shu) ch. 22–23, 'Treatise on Music' (6th–7th cent.)

History of the Sui (Sui shu) ch. 13–15, 'Treatise on Music' (7th cent.)

Old History of the T'ang (Chiu T'ang shu) ch. 28–31, 'Treatise on Music' (9th–10th cent.)

New History of the T'ang (Hsin T'ang shu) ch. 11–22, 'Treatise on Rites and Music' (11th cent.)

Apart from this material from the histories Kuo made use of a number of works from the Han to the Sung by specialists on music and literature. One third of this material existed only in a fragmentary form (marked with an asterisk in the list below).

Record of Ritual (Li chi), ch. 11 / 19, 'Record of Music' (1st cent. BC)

**'Treatise on Rites and Music,'* ?Ts'ai Yung (2nd cent. AD)

Master Ch'iao's Legal Precepts, Ch'iao Chou (3rd cent.)

**Hsün's Poetry Notes*, Hsün Hsü (3rd cent.)

Record of Things Ancient and Modern, Ts'ui Pao (3rd–4th cent.)

Record of Neglected Data, Wang Tzu-nien (4th cent.)

**Arts Record of Correct Music . . .*, Chang Yung (5th cent.)

*Arts Record of Banquet Music . . ., Wang Seng-ch'ien (5th cent.)
*Procedures for Controlling the Army, Liu Hsien (5th cent.)
Anthology of Literature, Hsiao T'ung et al. (early 6th cent.)
New Songs from a Jade Terrace, Hsü Ling (mid-sixth cent.)
*Record of Ancient and Modern Music, Chih-chiang (late 6th cent.)
*Record of Songs, anon. (pre-T'ang)
Compendium of Literature, Ou-yang Hsün (6th–7th cent.)
Commentary on Anthology of Literature, Li Shan (late 7th cent.)
Notes for Beginning Students, Hsü Chien (7th–8th cent.)
Explanations of the Old Titles of Yüeh-fu, Wu Ching (7th–8th cent.)
Comprehensive Survey of Classical Learning, 'Music' ch. 141–47, Tu Yu
    (8th–9th cent.)
Miscellaneous Records of Yüeh-fu, Tuan An-chieh (9th cent.)
Imperial Survey of the T'ai-p'ing Era, Li Fang (10th cent.)
Prize Blooms from the Garden of Literature, Li Fang (10th cent.)

From these works Kuo derived texts, background information, data on music, theoretical writings on music and literature, and variant texts and readings. To control and organize such a mass of data bears witness to his artistic and scholarly genius.

The Oral Nature of Han Songs and Ballads

Balladry has attracted a great deal of theorizing, sometimes informed by ideology. In eighteenth-century Europe, Johann Gottfried von Herder asserted that ballads originated with the folk and expressed the voice of the people.[46] His theory nicely dovetailed with his desire for a national renaissance in Germany. In China, too, we find in pre-Han and Han texts political theorists, ritualists, and historians arguing that local songs produced by the folk represent the pure expression of the people.[47] These writers insisted that the ruler should receive the songs collected from among the people, and in some cases portrayed the sage ruler as one who personally engaged in this activity. The political benefit was explained in this way: 'Thus the king, without going to the window or leaving the door, knows fully the sufferings of his realm.'[48] In their persuasions to a ruler the theorists would always argue from the standpoint of authority, the authority of the ancient sage rulers. Whether this theory was based on historical fact is subject to doubt, but clearly the theory became a potent political myth, for it promised that public opinion might be divined and even influenced. Several Han rulers, especially in the Latter Han, are reported to have sent officials to collect folk-songs, for example, Emperor Kuang-wu, and Emperors Ho, Shun, and Huan. The political theory of collecting folk-songs in the Han owes its origin to the parallel tradition that Confucius had compiled the *Book of*

Poetry's 305 songs from a collection of 3,000 Chou pieces.[49] Unfortunately, we know as little about the true manner of the compilation of that classic anthology as we do about the provenance of Han ballads.

One historic episode in the life of the founder of the Han perhaps provides some clues about the oral origin of balladic art. In the winter of 195 BC, when Emperor Kao-tsu was on his way back to the capital, he stopped in the countryside at P'ei in the region of former Ch'u state, where he had begun his politico-military career. At a banquet in his honour, overwhelmed by the occasion with its memories of hardship and triumph, he composed a spontaneous song, 'A Great Wind Rises'. Accompanying himself on a stringed instrument he chanted it. Then he formed a choir of some 120 local boys who joined in and repeated his song while the emperor danced, weeping with grief. After his death the choir was charged with performing the song at the memorial temple at P'ei.[50] In this vignette we note several features that might pertain to other Han songs: the emperor was a commoner who had educated himself along the way to victory; he was a composer of simple song; he could play a musical instrument; he could dance, improvising the steps and tempo to suit his own composition; the context of his amateur composition was a banquet where wine (the other muse) flowed freely; the song, dance, and music were spontaneous expressions of profoundly felt emotion; some members of the community learned the piece and repeated it thereafter in the community as a remembered song-text with music and dance; the text was preserved in the official biography of the emperor. With an imperial patron like Emperor Kao-tsu, and later Emperor Wu, it is not surprising that the simple, beautiful art of balladry was nurtured and flourished, particularly in the Han.

When we search the anonymous Han ballads themselves for evidence of orality we may make a few observations. First the children's songs, or *t'ung-yao*, are a sub-category of anonymous Han ballads which were deployed by historians as prophetic utterances, but were traditionally believed to have been produced in the 'streets and lanes', presumably by illiterates. Secondly, if we compare two formal versions of the same poem in the quite different styles of the *ku-shih*, or old poem, and the ballad, *yüeh-fu*, we notice at once that the version in the *ku-shih* style is concise, metrically regular, literary, and polished, while the other version in the *yüeh-fu* style is often prolix, metrically irregular, and without literary polish. This contrast is most clear in the 'West Gate Ballad' and *ku-shih* no. 15 of the 'Nineteen Old Poems'. Clearly, the *ku-shih* version was a literary piece composed by a professional poet, the ballad, or *yüeh-fu*, was an oral piece composed by an amateur.[51] Thirdly, the presence of textual versions among some ballads, that is ballads having two or more versions, one usually longer, suggests, but does not prove

16

their oral origin. Variations on an original ballad continued apace from region to region and from time to time until the oral ballad died or was fixed in print. Conscientious archivists, such as Kuo Mao-ch'ien, happily preserved these alternative versions, even if he did err in the matter of their dating.[52] It so happens that we possess two versions of 'West Gate Ballad'. One is longer, and there are differences in diction and point of view. The long version treats the *carpe diem* theme and bases its point of view on the rejection of religion, philosophy, and drugs; the shorter version treats the same theme, but its point of view is based on the speaker's wretched poverty. A song going by a different title, 'A *Yen* Song, The Whenever Ballad', appears to constitute even a further version on the same theme, and might in fact be the original among the three songs.

Apart from these oral aspects of Han *yüeh-fu*, there are oral features typical of popular songs and ballads, such as colloquialism, direct speech, earthy or folkloric subject matter, a rustic, unlettered point of view, nonsense words, and commonplace expressions.

The oral origin of anonymous Han ballads does not mean that they were invariably produced by illiterate folk. For instance, 'The Ballad of the Prefect of Goosegate', 'The Lament of Liang-fu', 'The Ballad of Breaking Willow', and the hymns are the products of educated composers. Their categorization as ballads rather than as odes or literary hymns must signify their subsequent folk possession rather than their folk composition. Moreover, several ballads contain hints of literariness in diction and content. We know, for example, that the pursuit of immortality through elixirs and cults was originally the province of the ruling classes. Later as the cult of immortality lost imperial patronage it filtered down to the people with its arcane lore and language. In other ballads, the presence of non-folk elements indicates that there was an interaction between popular and literary culture and a creative inter-relationship between city and country.

Many features which characterize the Western ballad are present in most anonymous Han ballads, and it seems useful to summarize them here: universality of point of view; stereotyped characterization, situation, and plot; detachment, impersonality, and objectivity in presentation; no localized action or setting; ahistoricity, or a lack of historical perspective; no analysis; no introspection; commonplace phrases; little plot; weak narrative line; abrupt entry into the balladic story and equally abrupt transitions; understatement; dialogue; nonsense words; alliteration; refrain; repetition; irregular metre; colloquialism; a homely style drawing on familiar material rather than from the literary tradition.

The Han song is storytelling set to music. Although the music can now only vaguely be hinted at, the songs contain striking features which allow them to be enjoyed as literature to be read rather than songs to be heard at a banquet or a party. Without the charm of music and the conviviality of the banquet the ballads and songs lend themselves to a different kind of interpretation and appreciation. Whereas oral art in performance is a fleeting experience, in which the note, once sung, lingers only in the memory, ballads and songs as literature may be savoured more deeply and examined in a more leisurely manner.

The singer of tales is essentially a narrator who introduces us to a crucial situation and shows us how certain characters respond to the crisis. Hans H. Frankel identifies three types of relationship between the narrator and the characters of early narrative *yüeh-fu*: 1) 'objective third-person narration', 2) 'impersonation', and 3) an interchange between objective narration and impersonation. From his analysis of Han and post-Han narrative ballads he finds that the third type is more common. What particularly distinguishes the genre is the 'multiple and shifting role of a single performer as narrator and actor, impersonating one or more characters.'[53] His classification system may be usefully applied to the larger repertoire of Han *yüeh-fu* I have translated.

Because the storyteller is a performer, the narration is enlivened by dramatic techniques. Sometimes we are rushed headlong into the situation when the characters are at a breaking-point: a sick wife lies on her deathbed and begs her husband to care for her infants; a man leaves home to escape bleak penury; a soldier comes home from a lifetime in the army to find his house in ruins and deserted; or a girl finds that the man she hoped to marry has gone off with another woman. The narrator sketches in some details of a character's life prior to the action of the tale, for example, the opening lines 'An orphan boy I was born' and 'At fifteen I joined the army'. Plot is not so much the unfolding of events by action as the revelation of events by the characters' thoughts, words, and feelings. In 'East Gate' we follow a poverty-stricken husband's emotional conflict as he decides whether to leave his wife and family. In 'West Gate' we listen to a man at a banquet as he questions the meaning of life. The endings of the ballads often leave a scene of despair and destruction, with infants wailing, an old man weeping, or an orphan longing to die. There is little character development, for this art form deals with one-dimensional types, as some titles suggest; 'The Ballad of the Ailing Wife', or 'The Ballad of the Orphan Boy'.

The song narrative is characterized by abrupt transitions, a technique identified by F. B. Gummere as 'leaping and lingering'.[54] Action is introduced swiftly and then dallied with, while the listener or reader wonders what will happen next. In the fable about two white swans the sudden illness of the hen-swan is succinctly stated: 'The wife suddenly falls ill', and for three more lines her faltering flight is lingered over. In another fable, which tells of a butterfly snapped up by a nursing swallow (euphemistically described as 'suddenly it meets a swallow'), the action is delayed as the swallow circles slowly round before popping the chewed morsels of butterfly into her chicks' wide-open beaks. Perhaps because the Han songs and ballads are so early in the tradition of narrative art the transitions sometimes tend to be abrupt to the point of senselessness. In 'East Gate' the voice switches so awkwardly that it is difficult in trans-lation to assign dialogue to a specific speaker. In 'Song of Melancholy' the speaker remains the same throughout, but his actions are lurchingly conveyed: first he walks toward the sea, then we are told that he has not got out of bed. In 'A *Yen* Song, A Ballad' the narrative develops elliptically: a girl tells how her brothers are away from home amusing themselves, then she asks, 'Old clothes who must mend?/New clothes who must sew?' Later in the song the mistress's husband is described lurking around the girl's rooms. The girl addresses him with a plea and two proverbs to try and politely make him go away. In this case the abrupt transitions in the narrative are deliberately deployed by the singer who seeks to envelop the girl's predicament in a set of codes, suggesting that his song deals with the social taboo of an unwanted pregnancy of an unmarried girl. The technique of 'leaping and lingering' is also skilfully used in 'Orphan Boy', where the swift change of setting, time, and action underscores the boy's harried life. Other cases of 'leaping' narrative connections have less to do with technique consciously used than with problems of corrupt texts. 'Vermilion Ibis' contains strings of enigmatic phrases and words which are either nonsense like 'hey nonino' or else snatches of song of which the original meaning has been lost or deliberately censored. Clearly, in their original performance the music must have greatly enhanced the sense of the words. What seems meaningless to us was probably clarified by familiar musical refrains and interludes. The tone, tempo, and pitch of the human voice and musical instruments no doubt registered nuances of meaning which remains elusive today.

F. B. Gummere also isolated a device in Western ballads which he termed 'incremental repetition'.[55] Although these Han examples of balladry and song do not reveal such a sophisticated use of this device as in the West, it is present. In 'Two White Swans', the narrative develops through the speech of a male swan explaining to its sick mate why he cannot remain with her. His speech takes the form of a repeated pattern, with slight changes to augment the narrative line: 'I would carry you away in my beak,/ But my beak is sealed and will not open./ I would carry you away on my back,/ But my feathers and tail each day would be crushed.' A more extensive use of the technique occurs in the final passage of 'Mulberry on the Bank', where the pretty mulberry-picker, Lo-fu, describes her dashing husband to a passing official who wants to seduce her: 'At fifteen he was a county clerk,/ At twenty a palace official,/ At thirty a gentleman-in-waiting,/ At forty lord of his own city.'

The dramatic content of the narrative is increased by direct speech, sometimes in the form of dialogue between humans or between animals, sometimes an address by the narrator to the audience, or else a sustained monologue. The patterns of speech are vivid and realistic. In 'We Fought South of the City Wall' a dead soldier cries out to carrion crows: 'In the wilderness we dead clearly lie unburied,/ So how can our rotting flesh flee from you?' In 'Orphan Boy' a cruel brother orders the boy to 'Get the meal ready.' In 'East Gate' a desperate husband leaving home shouts at his wife who is clinging to his clothes, 'Get off! Get away!/ I'm late in leaving./ I can't go on living here when my hair's nearly white.' One of the uses of direct speech is the formula of question and answer: one character says: 'Oh why don't I do it?/ I just have no pole or oar.' Sometimes the formula serves as a means of introducing a set descriptive passage, as in 'They Met' and 'In Ch'angan' where the question is put, 'And your lord's house?' by someone whose carriage has been caught up with another person's vehicle, and the answer constitutes the rest of the ballad describing the house. Occasionally the formula is a kind of riddle: 'Old clothes who must mend?' The formula is employed in a more refined way in ballads which bear a strong resemblance to the European *chanson d'aventure*. For example, in 'Mulberry on the Bank' the formula creates a battle of wits between the sexes. In 'The Lunghsi Ballad' the question, 'What's up there in the sky?' introduces an answering passage which creates a subtly ironic counter-point between the ideal world and the real world.

Balladic art is informed by the regular use of 'remembered phrases', or commonplace phrases within an oral tradition. Han ballads and songs vary between maximal and minimal use of such phrases. Maximal use occurs in ballads like 'Cocks Crow', 'They Met', and 'In Ch'angan' where whole passages appear in all three ballads, differently positioned and worded slightly differently. On the whole, however, the ballads reveal relatively little use of commonplace phrases, in some cases just over 25 per cent.[56] This may have to do with the brevity of the songs and ballads, most of them being no more than 24 lines long, and several being only quatrains. The subject of formulaic expression has generally been discussed on the basis of long epics in the European tradition, in which a composer-narrator's creativity and ability to memorize were extended to their greatest.[57] Implicit in the discussion of formulaic expression is a negative prejudice, exemplified by the judgement of Sir Walter Scott: 'The least acquaintance with the subject will recall a great number of commonplace verses, which each ballad-maker has unceremoniously appropriated to himself, thereby greatly facilitating his own task, and at the same time degrading his art by his slovenly use of over-scutched phrases.'[58] In other words, the use of formulaic expression is evidence of plagiarism, and plagiarism denotes a lack of individual creativity.

Examining the use of commonplace phrases in Han songs and ballads from a more positive standpoint three main artistic aspects may be identified: familiarity, literary quotation, and ironic wit. Familiarity is evident in the repetition of certain tropes, gestures, and names. Gates of yellow gold, going up the hall of the family home, leaving by the east or west gate of the city, tears falling on clothes, cart wheels turning in the guts, epithets such as 'brilliant' or binomes like 'green, green', and stars and planets indicating time are all examples of commonplace phrases used with such frequency that they become familiar to the repertoire. This kind of repetition is posited on the joy of recognition, similar to that aroused by nursery rhymes or a shaggy dog story. It is part of the naive simplicity of the pieces.

Literary quotation involves the use of phrases from the earlier written tradition which have become almost cliché, such as the Taoist allusion in the opening couplet of 'Cocks Crow', or the felicitation closure of 'The White Head Lament' borrowed from songs of ancestral sacrifice in the *Book of Poetry*, or binomes borrowed from the same classic. By the time the Han song-maker used such quotations he was probably no longer citing from the *locus classicus* in Chou literature but was borrowing from a more generalized ragbag of quotation and fancy phrasing. Although literary quotation is not so extensive in the *yüeh-fu* genre as it is in the *shih* lyric in the Han, when it is used as a conscious device it reveals great sophistication, such as the way the girl in 'A Yen Song, A Ballad' quotes allusively to deflect the curious stares of her mistress's husband.

The third use of commonplace phrase displays the song-maker's wit. For example, in 'The Lunghsi Ballad' and 'Walking out of Hsia Gate' virtually the same quatrain describing paradise appears. In 'Hsia Gate' the quatrain ends the piece, presenting a vision of paradise intrinsic to its theme of immortality. In 'Lunghsi' the quatrain opens the piece, positing a vision of an ideal world which the human world fails to attain, thus creating an ironic viewpoint. These and other uses of commonplace phrases and verses, far from demonstrating the makers' lack of originality, seem to me to prove their conscious deployment of familiar material in a variety of ways in order to engage the listeners' interest, to hold their attention, and to amuse them with cunning reversals of expected response.

As one might guess from ballads and songs where narrative and dramatic techniques are dominant, figurative language is sparingly used. This is not to say that lyricism and imagery are almost absent, but that

21

they are subordinated to the demands of storytelling. The clearest illustration of this is in the makers' use of nature imagery, which elsewhere in Chinese poetry forms an imaginative leitmotif. Nature sometimes provides the scenarios of the ballad, such as in the elixir pieces, where mountains belong to the lore of immortality. Nature may serve as an indicator of time or season. It may also create a parallel or contrast between the impassive world and human experience, as in 'Dew on the Shallot'. A vignette based on natural imagery may establish an emotion in the piece, prior to the narrative proper, as in the opening lines of 'Along the Embankment', where luxuriant reeds suggest the beauty and youth of the female speaker, and, through their use in the making of mats, cushions, and beds, also denote the speaker's humble position in relation to the man she is talking about. Nature symbolism features in a number of pieces, either lyrically as white mountain snow in 'The White Head Lament', or ironically as nest-seeking swallows in 'A *Yen* Song, A Ballad'. Symbolism informs the basic structure of some didactic pieces, such as the songs on the poplar and date-tree. In sum, the song-maker does not linger over the imagery in the same way as the *shih* lyricist. Imagery is used to develop the narrative, to set a scene, to suggest a mood or emotion, or to pre-figure the ballad's denouement.

The art of the Han songs and ballads rests firmly on realism. Magic, marvels, the extraordinary, do not generally appear in the narratives. There is little superstition, nothing of ghouls or the grotesque. The supernatural, of course, is present in the elixir pieces, but there the presentation of it is low-key and realistic within the confines of the theme. In general, the stories of Han songs and ballads are tied to everyday situations and the characters' dilemmas arise from these situations. Their dilemmas stem from poverty, ill-treatment by a cruel relative, war, love, imprudent behaviour, and greed. In other words they are problems born of human failing and social ills. The predicaments of the characters are presented through concrete details rather than articulated as abstractions.

In contrast to Western ballads, the Han repertoire appears to exercise a self-imposed censorship on the topics of sex and violence, or perhaps that censorship was imposed by Han officials who simply failed to record lurid songs. The sexual violence of the English ballad, 'Little Musgrave and Lady Barnard' in lines like 'He cut her paps from off her breast;/ Great pitty is was to see/ That some of this ladie's heart's blood/ Ran trickling down her knee', is entirely absent from the Han pieces. Another curious omission is the lack of the heroic. Despite the tradition of chivalry in early Chinese writings, immortalized in the figure of the wandering knight, *yu-hsia*, there is no equivalent in the Han repertoire of the Robin Hood sequence.[59] This lack underscores my earlier point about the avoidance of the extraordinary in most Han pieces, a mark of their

22

realistic mode. In fact, the songs and ballads are anti-heroic. They reveal that the ordinary person does not wish to be a hero or to die for some abstract cause. The will to live, or rather just to survive in a hostile environment is the recurring refrain. The anti-war ballads voice this sentiment most strongly.

Realism is evident in the use of speech. The everyday idiom of ordinary people is reproduced in dialogue and exclamations. Realistic descriptions enhance mundane situations, such as the empty foodbin and bare clothes-hanger in 'East Gate'. Of course, 'realism' is notoriously ambiguous in any literary discussion. It might well be argued that the Han singers' penchant for misery is subjective and runs counter to realistic depiction. Yet in their new focus on other areas of experience than had been explored in the tradition, in their depiction of the unattractive face of common humanity, they sang of the lives they led, the world they knew and understood. Looking beyond the splendour of the imperial court eulogized by Han court poets in near-sycophantic rhapsodies and beyond the glitter of the capital city to the drabness of diurnal reality, the song-makers reminded their listeners of the forgotten and despised, the insulted and the injured, a class of ordinary folk whose otherwise unsung labour had built the empire.

Some Musical Aspects of Han Songs and Ballads

To read only the words of any well-known traditional or modern ballad or blues song prompts the question, why have they become so famous and popular? Once the ballad or song leaves the printed page and rejoins its musical setting the words come alive again. The definition of a ballad proposed by the musicologist B. H. Bronson, 'Question: when is a ballad not a ballad? Answer: when it has no tune', may be modified to suit the context of Han songs and ballads: they may be termed songs and ballads although they have lost their tunes.[60] What little information survives about the Han pieces indicates that they were sung to musical accompaniment. The earliest recorders of the Han repertoire, who were interested in music in relation to poetry, such as Shen Yüeh, classified what we now call popular Han songs and ballads, Han yüeh-fu, under musical headings, such as hsiang-ho, 'Concerted' piece and tsa-ch'ü, 'Miscellaneous Melodic Piece', instead of grouping them under a literary genre or sub-genre.[61] Some songs recorded by Shen Yüeh are listed as 'old songs', ku-tz'u, indicating that music is their underlying system.[62] He also provided information about the sort of musical instruments that were used with these popular songs. This information was expanded by Kuo Mao-ch'ien in his preface to the twelve major categories of his collection, so that there is some indication of what instruments were played in the performance of certain pieces.[63] Yet since Shen Yüeh's information dates from a period two centuries after the end of the Han and Kuo Mao-ch'ien's from about a millennium after the Han, much of this information has to be treated with caution.

The songs and ballads themselves provide firm evidence of their musical background. Many have stanzaic divisions, or *chieh*. Some song-texts are followed by an indication that the stanzas are divided into musical sections. These are a *yen*, or prefatory passage, and a *tsü* or finale passage. The *yen* and *tsü* each required different kinds of musical accompaniment. The *yen* section usually forms the longest part of the whole song. For example, in 'Mulberry on the Bank' the *yen* comprises 35 lines, the *tsü* 18 lines. In 'Two White Swans', long version, the *yen* is 16 lines, the *tsü* 10. On somewhat slender evidence the *yen* is believed to derive from a style of song native to Ch'u state in the late Chou era (a style Emperor Kao-tsu enjoyed), while the *tsü* is believed to have originated in Wu state in the late Chou. This musical designation *yen* may explain why some songs bear cumbrous titles like 'A *Yen* Song, The Whenever Ballad', or 'A *Yen* Song, A Ballad', or 'A *Yen* Song, The Ballad of Lo-fu' (another title for the piece known as 'Mulberry on the Bank'). Such pieces may consist of a medley or suite of passages which originally constituted independent *yen*-style songs. There is only one extant anonymous *yüeh-fu* title bearing the musical designation *tsü*, *Wu tsü hsing*, but it is not clear if this is a Han text.[64] Apart from the *chieh, yen*, or *tsü* some songs contain an envoi, *luan*, usually at the end of the whole piece, or in one rare case in the middle, and consisting of about two or four lines. In fact, this rare use of the envoi in the middle of the piece, 'Ailing Wife', may shed some light on the methods of composition of the Han song. In this instance, the envoi, which normally appears at the end, stands in the middle and divides the narrative into two parts; the second half takes on a new tone which is at odds with the first half, suggesting that two songs have been patched together to form a new piece.

Besides these formal elements of composition, there are other more obvious musical elements common to the songs and ballads of other cultures. These are the repetition of passages, either verbatim, as in 'East Gate', or with a slight modification, as in 'Two White Swans'. Lines are repeated, especially in that most musical of songs, 'South of the River'. Refrains occur throughout the song version of 'Tung Flees!' and in 'A Crow Bore Eight or Nine Chicks'.

The metres generally consist of regular passages and extremely irregular passages, suggesting a relationship between text and music.[65] A melodic line might match or be matched by the metre and at the same time might indicate through the use of irregularity of metre, changes of mood and tone. The metrical irregularity of the 'Orphan Boy' illustrates this bond between metre and emotion, and between metre and episodic structure, which suggests in turn a responsive, evocative musical background. Moreover, the opacity of some song-texts argues for the clarifying presence of music. If, as I have proposed, some Han songs were composed by piecing together previously independent songs, or parts of songs, and by incorporating some echoes of their original music, those listening to the new composition would understand the context of the piece; they would remember the original tunes that went with the original songs and, if only bits were incorporated into the new song, would also remember the context of the original song. It is possible to surmise that just as Han songs and ballads were composed by patching together old and new lines to make a new text, so the music was composed by interweaving remnants of old musical scores into the new idiom. Certainly, the Han song and ballad repertoire, being mostly a popular, oral art form, was designed for lucid communication, especially since a song performance is fugitive and elusive. The listeners would have demanded comprehensibility. That Han music which is now lost must have helped to develop, explain, and emphasize the meaning of the words. But today, without their music, several passages in the song-texts remain opaque.

The Singers of Yüeh-fu in the Han

Hans H. Frankel recently posed the problem of balladic performance in this way: 'An important question, to which there is no easy answer is this: Who were the singers of the *yuèfŭ* ballads?'[66] If the question is focussed more specifically to Who were the singers of Han *yüeh-fu*? the answer becomes even less easy. In the first place, a Han *yüeh-fu* is not amenable to a strict definition. If we accept Kuo Mao-ch'ien's definition, then the impromptu songs sung by early Han emperors, aristocrats, and courtiers, such as Emperor Kao-tsu's 'A Great Wind Rises' and Emperor Wu's 'Autumn Wind', would appear to be the earliest descriptions of Han *yüeh-fu* being sung.[67] Yet these songs are not generally regarded as Han *yüeh-fu* proper, which tend to be anonymous, popular pieces. Secondly, the only recorded description of a trained singer and musician performing at the early Han court, namely Li Yen-nien, does not involve a *yüeh-fu*, but a piece usually classified as a pentasyllabic *ko-shih* lyric (except for its octosyllabic penultimate line).[68] Thirdly, singers in Han China ranked too low in such government organs as the Bureau of Music to merit an official biography. The exceptions, such as Lady Li and Wei Tzu-fu who rose from the humble and anonymous level of entertainer to become a concubine and consort of Emperor Wu, prove the general rule.[69]

Although the question posed by Frankel cannot be answered in definite terms, some clues may be gleaned from various historical, literary, and archaeological sources. J.-P. Diény has pointed a way forward by his brilliant analysis of such Han sources. If we cannot know who sang *yüeh-fu* songs and ballads composed for and arranged by the Han Bureau of Music, we can at least deduce to some extent the taste of the audience for whom the Bureau of Music functioned. Diény presents a list of Han personages—emperor, prince, aristocrat, court lady, and courtier—who performed a song with music and dance, alone or accompanied by a favourite, usually at court. He terms such (court) performances 'l'improvisation pathétique', characterizing them as personal statements, spontaneously composed, and sincere, simply worded expressions of emotion.[70] Clearly, since the Bureau of Music was rejuvenated by early Han emperors, especially by Emperor Wu, its immediate patrons and arbiters of taste were the Han ruler and his favourites at court. They would have imposed their taste in music, song, and dance on performances at banquets and parties, if not necessarily at the more solemn state ceremonies. Since the personal style of musical expression among early Han emperors, aristocrats, and courtiers was simple, direct, and sincere, their taste would have influenced the style of singing and the content of the song at court entertainment.[71]

It is an ironic fact that although as a group entertainers were classless, the dividing line between entertainers and members of the royal family was very narrow in terms of social manner and musical taste. This is especially true of Emperor Wu. His concubine, Lady Li, and his later consort, Wei Tzu-fu, attracted him by their artistic skills far more than the nobler breed of ladies with whom the royal harem was stocked. Li Yen-nien was promoted from kennel lad to Master of Music at court because Emperor Wu enjoyed his musical flair. But in general, entertainers were considered as household slaves, property to be disposed of at will. For example, when Emperor Wu first saw Wei Tzu-fu perform he was so attracted to her that he paid his sister, who owned her, a thousand catties of gold. And later in the Former Han, when Emperor Hsüan responded to a political crisis arising from bad harvests in 70 BC he ordered a reduction in the number of butchers and of musicians in the Bureau of Music (lumping them together), among other measures.[72]

Han entertainers acquired their training through their own family, for generations members of the musical world. Such families tended to come from certain parts of China, such as Han-tan, capital of the old kingdom of Chao in the north and neighbouring Yen, and from Ho-chien. Such places were famous for their glamorous singers with their popular style of performance. By the late Han poets were acknowledging the presence of these regional performers in the Han capital cities of Ch'angan and Loyang. In the course of the Han Dynasty, entertainment became less of a royal privilege than a right of the plutocracy. By the end of the period even eunuchs, such as Ma Jung, held their own musical extravaganzas in luxurious mansions.[73]

Diény has shown that the anonymity of singers as a group was further accentuated by their role in the musical ensemble during a performance. Drawing on archaeological evidence from Han funerary mural art, he presents a revealing picture of a Han singer at a performance: he or she is no more than one of an ensemble of instrumentalists, no one individual stands out from the group. The singer is usually close to a zither-player. Adding to the concept of a performing team is the fact that the singer and instrumentalists were no more important than the dancers. Furthermore, the same archaeological evidence shows that the role of song and dance was no greater than other performances by jugglers, acrobats, buffoons, wrestlers, and so forth.[74] The performance was a series of variety acts, similar to the early European commedia dell' arte, and not far removed in concept from modern Peking Opera. It may be that the style of variety performance popular at Han court entertainment, and entertainment in wealthy mansions, explains the extremely heterogeneous nature of the repertoire I have translated. From this repertoire one might select songs which are maudlin, lyrically refined, humorous, dramatic, meditative, crude, and flippant, to create a programme suitable as a medley to entertain a party of celebrating people, whether in the Han era or two thousand years later in the West.

Criteria of Selection

My criteria for selecting songs and ballads from the large repertoire of the Han are as follows. I have chosen those titles which constitute the generally agreed corpus of anonymous Han pieces, and those titles especially which have been most imitated by later generations of poets.[75] I have added a number of pieces in order to form a collection representative of the traditional categories of Kuo and his predecessors in which Han songs appear. I have also included some titles so as to demonstrate the thematic diversity of the Han repertoire. The resulting total of my selection is 77 songs and ballads, of which seven are different versions of some texts. I have excluded titles from some of Kuo's categories such as Ch'ing-Shang on the grounds that, in his view, Ch'ing-Shang pieces meant certain post-Han popular songs, and that some of his categories do not include Han material. I have also excluded some Han hymns and some Han Songs for the Nao-bell, besides some other anonymous popular Han material, in order to provide a representative selection and to keep this introductory book within reasonable limits of length and scope.

I have also decided to exclude some famous ballads, such as 'A Peacock Southeast Flew', because they are now thought to date from the Southern Dynasties, not from the Han as was traditionally believed. Absent too are some Han pieces attributed to certain authors, such as 'The Imperial Guards Officer' attributed to Hsin Yen-nien, because my selection

27

represents the anonymous Han repertoire of popular songs and ballads. Conversely, I have included some pieces attributed to specific authors in the literary tradition because, on balance, they are to be judged as anonymous Han pieces. For example, 'Watering Horses at a Long Wall Hole', of which traditional critics and anthologists have been equally divided concerning its attribution—either to Ts'ai Yung or to an anonymous Han maker. Those familiar pieces I have excluded, such as those mentioned above, may be found in *New Songs from a Jade Terrace*.[76]

The texts in my selection are not based primarily on Kuo Mao-ch'ien's *Anthology*. I have tried to cite the texts from their earliest sources. My finding is that 54 of the 77 texts appear in one Han source and six post-Han and pre-T'ang sources. This means that two-thirds of the texts are traceable back to pre-T'ang sources. Among them, the primary source is Shen Yüeh's 'Treatise on Music', with 26 pieces. Next, numerically speaking, are Pan Ku's treatises, with 12 pieces. Late Southern Dynasties texts overlap to some extent, but between them, that is, *Anthology of Literature*, *New Songs from a Jade Terrace*, and *Compendium of Literature*, 10 pieces are derived. T'ang sources produce few new texts, but a wealth of fragmentary material. Li Fang of the Northern Sung provides a useful number of fragments, corroborating earlier material. From Kuo's *Anthology* of the late Northern Sung I have drawn 13 pieces not cited in earlier sources, plus three full texts of earlier fragments. Two late Ming sources provide five pieces either cited only in fragments or overlooked in earlier texts. These textual sources number 12 in all. The most important, in descending order, are: Shen Yüeh, Kuo, Pan Ku, Hsü Ling, and Hsiao T'ung and his collaborators. In view of the scattered nature of the material, which only acquired the status of respectable literature in the 5th century AD, the retrieval rate for pre-T'ang texts is very high. The full list of sources and pieces cited appears on pp. 209–10 below.

The principle on which I based my organization of this diverse material is thematic. It seems to me that the original classification system of Kuo Mao-ch'ien does not translate well into Western literature, especially as the musical notation has not survived. Moreover, pieces in a set like the '18 Han Songs for the *Nao*-bell' do not cohere thematically or in terms of content, making them difficult to discuss without their original musical and social context. Although my thematic treatment is arbitrary and my arrangement one of personal choice, I feel that the pieces are well-suited to such a scheme. Naturally, since some songs contain a number of different themes, they might be placed in other thematic groups than mine. On the whole, however, the present arrangement reveals something of their rich diversity in theme, form, and content.

CHAPTER ONE

Hymns

Kuo Mao-ch'ien's one hundred chapter anthology of songs and ballads opens with twelve chapters of hymns.[1] A connection between hymns and ballads might well seem tenuous. Yet in the early years of the Han empire a firm link between the two was forged for reasons of administrative procedure, imperial patronage of the arts, and liturgical reform. In the second century BC, a governmental office was revived to supervize musical arrangements for both religious worship and court entertainment. Its title was the Bureau of Music, *Yüeh-fu*. The director of music was personally appointed by the reigning emperor for his expertise in contemporary, especially foreign forms of music. His official title, Master of Music, *Hsieh-lü tu-wei*, was uniquely devised for him by Emperor Wu and his role was to provide the music for religious and secular ceremonies.[2] The Bureau was in the heart of the capital city of Ch'angan in a palatial compound.[3] In the reign of Emperor Wu (141–87 BC), imperial patronage of the arts was at its zenith; the emperor personally intervened at the policy and administrative levels, imposing his artistic taste on literary, musical, and liturgical developments.

Like previous rulers of the Han, especially the founder Emperor Kao-tsu, Emperor Wu had no inhibitions about class or status, nor was he prejudiced about the social origins or previous occupations of the many gifted people at his court.[4] His was a regal meritocracy of talent. One of his favourite concubines was the younger sister of his Master of Music named Lady Li, who was an entertainer of great beauty. His consort, Empress Wei, was also originally a lower-class singer who had gained employment in the household of the emperor's sister.[5] The emperor's Master of Music, Li Yen-nien, was a talented nobody. Before entering court he had been convicted of a crime and had been castrated and employed in the Imperial Kennels. The emperor had taken a fancy to Li's sister when he visited his own sister's household where she was employed. He brought her back to the palace and at the same time brought her brother, Li Yen-nien, to court.[6]

The poet Ssu-ma Hsiang-ju had a chequered career in his youth; he

29

had eloped with a widowed heiress but lived in poverty when her father disinherited her. At the Han court he became the foremost rhapsodist, eulogizing the splendour of palaces and parks, while ambiguously introducing a critique of imperial extravagance.[7] Among other gifted courtiers and officials who added lustre to the prestige of the emperor was Li Yen-nien's brother, General Li Kuang-li, who after serious setbacks successfully penetrated into Central Asia and captured prized horses from Ta-yüan, or Ferghana. There was also Chang Ch'ien, an intrepid voyager who brought back to the Han court precious exotica from Central Asia and tales of foreign wonders.[8] The court historian, Ssu-ma Ch'ien, who personally witnessed many events of Emperor Wu's reign, chronicled the founding of the Han Dynasty and recorded contemporary affairs, while projecting his historical narrative back into remote antiquity in order to demonstrate that the Han had evolved from a race of gods and super-heroes.[9] In his reign, too, lived the philosopher Tung Chung-shu, the founder of Han Confucianism, a complex syncretic system which ordained a quasi-priestly role for the imperial ruler, mediating between Heaven, Earth, and Man.[10] Also at Emperor Wu's court was the court jester, Tung-fang Shuo, who kept the emperor amused with his parodies of the sages and solemn erudites.[11] This group of artistes, actors, beauties, musicians, poets, clowns, academics, philosophers, historians, and officials which Emperor Wu gathered around him were from varying social backgrounds, but were all chosen for their brilliant talent. In his informal selection procedures, the emperor evinced a plebian, meritocratic trait reminiscent of the humble social aspect of the founder of the dynasty.

The career of Li Yen-nien is a reflection of Emperor Wu's taste for popular forms of music. Some thirty years after he had succeeded to the throne, the emperor became impressed by the eunuch Li's knowledge of contemporary music. Li had become acquainted with Central Asian styles of popular music and was expert in putting songs, old and new, to the new tunes. Once, when discussing music with Li the emperor pointedly addressed his senior ministers with this rhetorical question: 'At the places of worship among the common people, musical instruments and dances are still in use, yet at present no such music is employed at the suburban sacrifice. How can this be right?'[12] When the matter had been duly discussed, the emperor persuaded his ministers to introduce contemporary music in the forthcoming service of thanksgiving for the Han victory over Nan-Yüeh. Hymns were sung by a boys' choir, and non-ceremonial instruments like the harp were played. It is also recorded that Emperor Wu commanded his court poets, among them Ssu-ma Hsiang-ju, to compose the 'Songs for Suburban Sacrifice, in 19 Parts'.[13] In about 114 BC, the emperor reinstituted the Bureau of Music, increasing its permanent personnel from one to three assistant administrators.[14] Li was responsible for arranging music for divine worship which reflected contemporary taste, besides setting music for ancestral memorial services and court entertainment.

Emperor Wu also inaugurated, at about this time, liturgical reforms. In the course of his reign he established numerous cults and ceremonies. His fascination with all aspects of religion was informed with a desire, fanned by his courtiers, philosophers, and the ministers of diverse religious cults, to create an aura of pomp and circumstance compatible with his new imperial stature. He was also extremely credulous and gullible, entertaining superstitious whims and deeply-felt religious conviction side by side. His interest in religion was eclectic. His open-minded tolerance of contradictory cults and beliefs led him to patronize sober court ritualists, mysterious shamanesses, sorcerers, illusionists, alchemists, and mediums. The usual claims of the latter groups were either the ability to transmute cinnabar into gold to gain immortality, or the knowledge of where to find the drug of immortality, or the secret of bringing the dead back to the world of the living.[15] The emperor is reputed to have seen the fleeting image of his deceased favourite concubine, Lady Li, through the illusionist's art and to have composed a poem about the experience.[16] Yet while he could be generous to adepts and cult ministers, his punishment, if they failed to provide proof of their extravagant claims, was severe—summary execution and loss of privilege and title for the entire clan.[17]

The new forms of worship initiated by Emperor Wu were the cult of Hou-t'u, or Empress Earth, in 114 BC, devotion to T'ai-i, Great Unity, in the winter solstice of 113 BC, the honouring of a Spirit Mistress in the imperial park, the commemoration of the Yellow Emperor, the adoration of the Lord on High in the Bright Hall, the veneration of the furnace deity (in connection with alchemy), and the observance of various local sacrificial ceremonies. He also introduced the custom of the ruler performing the suburban sacrifices every three years, and the Feng and Shan sacrifices every five years. He was the first Han emperor to attend worship at these major services on a regular basis.[18]

The visual aspect of religion attracted the emperor as much as its conceptual and doctrinal variety. He concerned himself with the type and colour of vestments, and the design and materials of new altars. At one service, the main celebrant wore purple vestments, while his concelebrants wore black, green, red, white, and yellow. At another the vestments were all yellow, the emblematic colour of earth and of the Yellow Emperor. Yellow became the imperial symbol in 104 BC. The court historian Ssu-ma Ch'ien recorded how the emperor gave orders to K'uan Shu and other officials in charge of sacrifices to fit out an altar to Great Unity, T'ai-i. This was at the new summer palace at Sweet Springs:

'[The altar] had three levels. Surrounding the base of it were the altars of the Five Emperors, each disposed in the direction appropriate to the particular deity. ... Thus the eight roads by which demons might approach were blocked ... the same offerings were used as at the altars of Yung, with the addition of such things as thick wine, jujubes, and dried meat. A yak was also slaughtered and offered with the appropriate dishes and other sacrificial implements. The Five Emperors were given only offerings of rich wine in the appropriate sacrificial vessels. Wine was poured on the ground at the four corners of the altar for the purpose, it was said, of giving sustenance to the lesser spirits. ... When the offerings were completed, the beasts that had been sacrificed were all burned. The ox was white, and inside it was placed a deer, and inside the deer a pig; water was then sprinkled over them while they burned. ... The priest who presented the offerings to the Great Unity wore robes of purple with brocade; those for the Five Emperors wore the color appropriate to the particular deity. The robes of those who performed the sacrifice to the sun were red, and those for the moon white.'[19]

These major liturgical reforms and the establishment of various state cults occurred in the years 114–113 BC. The performance of the new rites marks the fusion of august solemnities with elements drawn from popular entertainment, and the combination of highbrow and lowbrow culture.

At Emperor Wu's insistence, hymns for religious worship were put into the contemporary idiom of music and dance. The words of praise were to be understood by the celebrants and the congregation alike. In the Chou era, hymns had been known as *sung*, an archaic term in the Han which became a generic term for hymns and praise poems. In the late Chou, some hymns were composed in the state of Ch'u, and their texts, which may have been shaped by a literary hand, are known as the 'Nine Songs', *Chiu ko*.[20] Under Emperor Wu, hymns were also called *ko*, or songs, a generic term which embraced the sacred and the secular. Some of the new hymns departed from the impersonal, timeless mould of divine experience in the Han to include contemporary, familiar phenomena, such as marvels and miracles which had been reported in the lifetime of the worshippers. In this sense, Emperor Wu instilled new life into religious worship; he made it more relevant to contemporary needs and more responsive to his own artistic and aesthetic taste.

Fortunately, one set of hymns from this period has survived, and together with an earlier set from the reign of Emperor Kao-tsu, constitutes the earliest extant Han hymn texts. Unhappily, the music has not been transmitted. A comparison of the two sets reveals the radical change in liturgical texts between the founding of the Han and the reign of Emperor Wu, a matter of about a century. The earlier set of 17 hymns, 'Songs to Set the World at Ease, for Private Performance', was said to have been set to music by a consort of Emperor Kao-tsu, Lady T'ang-shan, who was skilled in Ch'u music, a style the emperor enjoyed. The hymns state piously the ethical values of Confucianism, underscoring filial piety and the virtues of the social hierarchy, and extolling the benefits of good government. The hymns were performed both at the worship of imperial ancestors and for entertainment at court banquets.[21] The later set of hymns is more pertinent to the development of Han ballads. Its title is 'Songs for Suburban Sacrifice, in 19 Parts'.[22] Some of its songs and hymns praise the deities associated with the seasonal cycle. Some celebrate contemporary miracles, all duly dated in the Han histories, such as the birth of divine horses from rivers (113 and 101 BC), the capture of a unicorn (122 BC), the capture of six red geese (94 BC), the rediscovery of a lost holy vessel (113 BC), and the appearance of a nine-stemmed plant containing the drug of immortality (109 BC).[23]

Of the 19 hymns, eight have been translated here. The first is a song of welcome to a deity descending to earth. The next five honour the Five Elements, or the Five Emperors (*Wu Ti*) associated with the cosmic elements. The next is a patriotic hymn, couched in terms of the seasonal cycle. Then follows a hymn on a miracle said to have been witnessed in Emperor Wu's reign, the emergence of divine horses in China (two songs). The last two pieces are no longer concerned with prayers for blessings from the gods. They honour local heroes, one a benevolent but stern judge, the others, gifted hydraulic engineers who brought the benefits of irrigation to the land. These are esteemed and venerated as saints who brought material advantages to ordinary people.

We Have Chosen a Timely Day

We have chosen a timely day,
We wait with hope,
Burning fat and artemisia
To welcome the Four Directions.
Ninefold doors open
For the Gods journey forth,
They send down sweet grace,
Bounteous good fortune.
The chariot of the Gods
Is hitched to dark clouds,
Yoked to flying dragons,
Feather pennants amassed.

33

The coming down of the Gods
Is like wind-driven horses;
On the left turquoise dragon,
On the right white tiger.

The coming of the Gods
Is divine! what a drenching!
First bringing rain
Which spreads in sheets.

The arrival of the Gods
Is lucky shade within shade.
All seems confused,
Making hearts tremble.

The Gods are now enthroned,
The Five Tones harmonize.
Happy till the dawn
We offer the Gods pleasure.

Cusps of ritual beasts swelling,
Vessels of millet sweet,
Goblets of cassia wine,
We host the Eight Quarters.

The Gods serenely linger,
We chant 'Green' and 'Yellow'.
All round meditate on this,
Gaze at the green jade hall.
A crowd of beauties gathers,
Refined, perfect loveliness:
Faces like flowering rush,
Rivals in dazzling glamour,
Wearing flowery patterns,
Interwoven misty silks,
With trains of white voile,
Girdles of pearl and jade.
They bear Blissful-night and Flag-orchid,
Iris and orchid perfumed.
Calm and peaceful
We offer up the blessed chalice.

This type of hymn is similar to the liturgy of welcoming a god in the 'Nine Songs' of Ch'u dating from about the fourth century BC. The two closest parallels are 'Lord of the East, The Great One' and 'Thou Amid the Clouds'.[24] In this Han hymn, the worshippers at a seasonal vigil attend the consecrated moment when the gods will come down to the altar and bless the people. To attract the gods they burn fat from sacrificial beasts, which blends with aromatic artemisia and the perfumes of the female dancers. The gods belong to the four points of the cosmos, the Four Directions. Their descent to earth is visualized as a majestic procession of mythical beasts and carriages. It is not clear whether the sky is envisaged as having nine doors, or whether the altar had nine symbolic doors to admit the gods to the presence of humans. Nine was a mystic number.[25] The turquoise dragon was believed to preside over the eastern skies, the white tiger over the western sky as guardian spirits. The gods bring down the blessing of rain which will fructify the earth. The phrase 'shade within shade' is the binome *yin-yin*, which suggests mysterious darkness and the female cosmic principle, complementing the male *yang* principle in a dual system of cyclical renewal.[26] The gods have now descended to earth and are enthroned on the altar. The sacred music of the Five Tones begins.[27] The worshippers offer the gods the fruits of their harvest, grain and wine. The gods are said to preside over the Eight Points of the universe.[28] The choir chants the hymns 'Green' and 'Yellow'; these probably refer to the green colour symbolic of spring and the yellow of the earth.[29] As the chanting ends the worshippers gaze in adoration toward the inner sanctum on the altar, 'the green jade hall', where the gods are enthroned. Then a corps of girl dancers in gorgeous robes and jewels trace delicate patterns in religious dance, wafting perfume on the air. At the hymn's close the worshippers are happy to have received the divine blessing and they offer the libation cup.

If this seasonal rite of the earth's regeneration were enacted at the open-air altar outside the city, it must have been a dramatic and spell-binding ceremony. There is a strong appeal to the senses and to the aesthetic imagination. At the same time the ceremony invokes religious awe and suggests the possibilities of a lavish entertainment.[30]

Lord God Draws Nigh

Lord God draws nigh to the altar of the Centre,
The Four Sides are celebrants.
Careful, careful, our thoughts are unchanged,
Ready to receive what is due.
Pure, harmonious are the Six Points;
They regulate the numbers in fives.
Within the seas there is peace and repose;
Let culture flourish, let warfare disappear.
Empress Earth is the rich Old Woman,
Brilliantly bright are the Three Luminaries.
Sublime, sublime, we are free and easy.
Festive robes honour the Yellow.

35

This and the next four pieces form a set of seasonal hymns which liturgically articulate the Han cosmological theory of the Five Elements and *Yin* and *Yang*. These two concepts had evolved independently in the late Chou era and their origins are not yet known. In the fourth and third centuries BC, a naturalist philosopher named Tsou Yen propounded a cosmological theory which embraced the primitive principles of the Five Elements and *Yin* and *Yang*. The Five Elements (*Wu hsing*) are five stages, phases, or seasons, each dominated by a cosmological power or emperor. After completing their five phases, the sequence recommences in a perpetual cycle of birth, decay, death, and rebirth. The phases are set in motion by the dualistic, symbiotic forces of the universe, *Yin* and *Yang*. *Yin* represents the female principle, all that is dark, cold, passive, water, earth, the moon, nourishment, withdrawal, and the seasonal cycle before spring. *Yang* represents all that is light, hot, active, wood, the sun, and the seasons of spring and summer. Both forces wax and wane, and their movements influence the Five Elements, causing a change in the seasons, the weather, and the growth and decay of the material universe. Each of the Five Elements acquired a system of correspondences, grouped into fives, such as the five colours, the five tones, the five tastes, five bodily organs, and so forth. To fit the four seasons into this system, an extra season, the Medial, was devised between the *Yang* seasons and the *Yin* seasons. Various systems arose, but the following is the most typical:

Season	Date	Colour	Deity	Song	Dance	Element	Direction
Spring	Feb. 5	blue	Kou-mang	Greening Yang	Cloud Plumes	wood	east
Summer	May 6	red	Chu-jung	Scarlet Brilliance	Cloud Plumes	fire	south
Medial	Jul. 22	yellow	Empress Earth	Lord God Draws Nigh	Cloud Plumes and Giving Life	soil	centre
Autumn	Aug. 8	white	Ju-shou	West White-light	Giving Life	metal	west
Winter	Nov. 8	black	Hsüan-ming	Darkness Obscure	Giving Life	water	north

The five hymns have as their titles the same songs as those in the table, and they each contain their own set of correspondences.[31]

'Lord God Draws Nigh' is something of a misfit, because in Kuo's anthology it is placed first, whereas in the Han it was seen as a hymn for the medial season. On the other hand, Pan Ku placed the hymn first in his 'Treatise on Rites and Music'. Its attributes are somewhat artificial but combine well with the other sets of Fives—colours, elements, etc. The 'Four Sides' referred to in 'Lord God Draws Nigh', either means the worshippers and celebrants on each side of the square altar, or the deities presiding over the four sides of the square earth.[32] The Six Points are north, south, east, west, above, and below.

Several concepts in the five hymns derive from early Taoism. In 'Lord God Draws Nigh', earth is called the 'rich Old Woman', an echo of the matriarchal system hinted at in *The Classic of the Way and Its Power*: 'It [the Tao] is capable of being the mother of the world,' and 'The gateway of the mysterious female/ Is called the root of heaven and earth.'[33] Earth has as its colour correspondence yellow—a symbolic link with the Yellow Emperor, a Taoist deity. In 'Darkness Obscure' the ethico-political ideal enshrined in 'The people return to basic old ways' echoes the same Taoist classic: 'Let your wheels move only along old ruts.'[34] The same hymn urges: 'Hug the plain, cherish the simple', which again repeats the conservative values of early philosophical Taoism: 'Exhibit the unadorned and embrace the uncarved block.'[35] While most of the hymns express a vague desire for harmony, some introduce a special concept of moral order which was the hallmark of early Confucianism. That is the idea formulated especially by Mencius, that a ruler's virtue is magnetic and contagious.[36] In 'West White-light' this idea is contained in the line: 'Even the Four Mo, all will obey.' Synthesized in these five hymns, then, are concepts of different ideological lineages: naturalist philosophy, Taoism, ancestor worship, the Confucian moral order, and the agricultural cycle.[37]

Greening *Yang*

Greening *Yang* starts to stir,
Causing root and bulb to obey,
Its rich moisture loving all alike.
Padpaw creatures their own ways come forth,
The sound of thunder brings out flowers' glory,
Lair-dwellers lean to hear.
The barren again give birth,
And so fulfil their destiny.
All the people rejoice, rejoice.
Blessings are on the young and pregnant.
All living things are quickened, quickened.
Such is the good gift of Spring.

Scarlet Brilliance

Scarlet brilliance fullgrown
Makes all creation push forth,
Makes all living things strengthen and be glad.

Nothing is stunted;
It makes all blossoms full bring on their fruit,
So swollen, so large!
It ripens our fields vast.
The hundred ghosts draw near to taste,
Far and wide we set up sacrifice,
Devout, we do not forget.
If, Oh God, you approve and accept it,
We will do it for generations without end.

West White-light

West white-light mists spilling,
Autumn air sternly kills.
Though proud heads of grain hang down,
Continuing from of old, they will not fail.
Wicked evil will not sprout,
Dire sin is laid low and destroyed.
No matter how far off the place
Even the Four Mo, all will obey.
Already we dread such a power,
We only desire pure virtue.
We will submit without arrogance,
We will make good our hearts, devout, devout.

Darkness Obscure

Darkness obscure oppresses with *Yin*,
Dormant insects hide under cover,
Plants and trees shed their leaves.
Here is Winter, sending down frost.
Quelling rebellion, it expels evil,
Reforms alien customs;
The people return to basic old ways,
Hug the plain, cherish the simple.
We regulate faith and justice,
We worship in our vigil the Fifth Holy Hill.
In this season of harvest and gleaning
We store our fine garnered grain.

Lo! Holy Creator

Lo! Holy Creator is adored.
Old Goddess is richly endowed.
Warp and woof of Heaven and Earth

38

Create the four seasons.
Their essense established sun and moon,
Constellations are regulated and ordered.
They cause *Yin, Yang*, and the Five Elements
To revolve and begin anew,
Make clouds, wind, thunder, lightning
Fall as sweet dew and rain.
They let the Hundred Names breed and bear,
All tracing the right line;
Continuing his line he is dutiful,
He conforms to the virtue of the Divine.
Phoenix carriage with dragon, unicorn,
There is nothing not duly designed.
Blessed offertory baskets are ranged in rows
That the festive gifts may be accepted.
Then calamity will be wiped out,
Our exploits will race to the Eight Wilds.
Bell, drum, pipe, reed-organ,
The 'Cloud' dance soaring, soaring.
The Chao-yao Star banner of the Gods!
The Nine Yi tribes will come in surrender.

This hymn opens with acclamations to two deities, Holy Creator, or *T'ai-yüan*, and Old Goddess, or *Wen-shen*, the Earth Goddess, who is elsewhere called the 'rich Old Woman'.[38] *Yüan* means cause or origin. *T'ai-yüan* may be another name for T'ai-i, the deity honoured by Emperor Wu and featured in the first of 'The Horse of Heaven' hymns.

It seems to me that *T'ai-yüan* is a higher deity than Heaven or Earth. This is certainly borne out by an examination of the political philosophy of Tung Chung-shu, the founder of Han Confucianism who lived in the reign of Emperor Wu. Tung Chung-shu (*c.* 179–*c.* 104 BC) articulated a cosmological theory which explained the workings of the universe and gave a rationale to the socio-political order of human society. His theory incorporated Confucian ethics, the concept of natural order, the idea of the political function of portents, and the tenet that the ruler has a sovereign role linked to the divine. In his syncretic system he formulated the idea of a cosmic hierarchy presided over by *Yüan*, the Cause. This vertical structure comprised lower echelons of Heaven, Earth, and Man. The ruler, he proposed, acts as the intermediary of Heaven for Man on Earth. Through his sage and virtuous governance, Earth would yield its blessings and benefit his people. If the ruler erred, this would result in manifestations of misrule on Earth, the aberrations taking the form of omens and portents. The function of the ruler was to maintain harmony between the three levels of the cosmic structure. Tung Chung-shu's concept gave authority to the idea of a centralized state and benign autocracy.[39] In this hymn, therefore, *T'ai-yüan* may be perceived as the Prime Cause of the Universe, setting in motion the cosmic forces of *Yin, Yang,* and the Five Elements. The hymn also introduces the figure of the emperor in the grand design of the cosmos, whose virtue makes the people fulfil the role ordained by the natural order.[40]

The Horse of Heaven

From Great Unity heaven-sent,
The horse of heaven comes down,
Soaked with crimson sweat,
Froth flowing russet.
His courage is superb,
His spirit marvellous.
He prances through floating clouds,
Darkly racing upwards.
His body free and easy
Leaps across a myriad leagues.
Now who is his equal?
Dragons are his friends.

*****

The horse of heaven is come
From the west pole.
He crossed Flowing Sands
When the Nine Yi tribes surrendered.

The horse of heaven is come
Out of Fountain River;
His is the tiger's double spine,
Swift he changes like a sprite.

The horse of heaven is come,
He passed through barren wastes;
Travelling one thousand leagues
He follows the road to the east.

The horse of heaven is come
At Chih-hsü time.
About to rear away
Who would he wait for?

The horse of heaven is come!
Open Distant Gates!
'I stand proud,
For I pass on to K'unlun.'

40

The horse of heaven is come!
Shaman of the dragon,
He roams within heaven's gates,
Looks upon Jade Terrace.

In the reign of Emperor Wu, envoys such as Chang Ch'ien were sent on foreign missions west of China and brought back reports of magnificent horses in Ta-yüan, modern Ferghana.[41] Chang Ch'ien's journey there may have occurred in 115 BC. The emperor consulted the oracular *Book of Change* for a prognostication and read, 'The supernatural horses are due to come from the northwest.' In fact, he received some fine horses from the region of Wu-sun in the northwest, adjacent to Ferghana, and was so pleased with them that he named them the oracular 'horses of heaven'. Later, however, he acquired the Ferghana horses which sweated blood, and he realized they were finer than the Wu-sun horses, so he renamed the latter 'the horses from the extreme west', and gave the name 'the horses of heaven' to the Ferghana horses.[42]

These horses had not been brought to China without violence and political intrigue. In the years 104–101 BC, General Li Kuang-li was ordered to take the famous horses of Ferghana by force. He went at the head of an army of 100,000 soldiers, it is said, and subjected the region to attacks during that time. In the end the people of Ferghana beheaded their own king and replaced him with a ruler receptive to the Chinese emperor's demands. Li's offensive was finally successful and in exchange for gold, 3,000 horses were brought back to China from Ferghana, with an agreement later of an annual supply of two horses.[43] It was the acquisition of these horses which occasioned the composition of two sacrificial hymns on 'the horse of heaven'.[44]

Several theories have been advanced for Emperor Wu's quest for these horses. Arthur Waley suggested that they were linked with the emperor's search for immortality, an idea supported by Edwin G. Pulleyblank. Anthony F. P. Hulsewé rejects this theory as unproven, and puts forward two other suggestions: either the horses were sought for the Chinese imperial stables, or they were prized as a means of improving the Chinese breed of horses.[45]

Whatever the real motive for obtaining the Ferghana horses, one thing is clear: the two hymns refer only to the divine attributes of the animal. They complement each other, the first stating that the super-natural horse was a gift from Great Unity in Heaven and describing its physical appearance and abilities in hyperbolic language.[46] No mention is made of its legendary appearance from a river, rather it is a sky-horse. The second hymn, although it mentions the horse's divine birth from a river, puts less emphasis on the supernatural. At the same time it charts the progress of the horse across the desert from the west to China and up to the palace gates. The description of the horse is brief. Its ability is likened to the tiger's, the emblematic guardian of the western paradise.[47] This hymn has a more musical structure than the first. Its refrain 'The horse of heaven is come' at the beginning of each stanza is an example of incremental repetition, serving to develop the narrative of the divine horse's epic journey from the west.[48] Its progress to China is marked by the miraculous submission of the hostile Yi tribes, and its arrival at the palace gates coincides with the appearance of the Chih-hsü star, symbolic of the east.[49] It is not clear whose voice declaims at the gates. The words may be assigned to the divine horse. It is more likely that they designate the joy of the emperor, perhaps Emperor Wu himself, for he was well known for his fascination with immortality. Both hymns end with the divine horse and the dragon roaming through paradise. It is interesting to note that the dragon and the horse are linked in the *Book of Change*, where they are identified with the first two hexagrams.[50] The two hymns count as the tenth in the set of 19 hymns.[51]

The Song of Cheng-Pai Ditch

Where do we till this land?
By Pondnorth and Valleymouth.
Cheng Kuo's ditch it was first,
Lord Pai's ditch came later.
We lift our spades like clouds,
We cut drains and make it pour:
Water flows beside our kitchen,
Fish leap into our pot!
In a single measure from Ching River
There are several loads of silt.
Let's water! Let's manure!
Make our millet grow.
Lord Pai clothes and feeds the capital,
Ten thousand million mouths!

The title of this hymn praises two men, Cheng Kuo and Lord Pai, whose ditch later bore both their names. Cheng Kuo was an engineer of the Warring States era who, in 246 BC, was sent by Hann state to cut a ditch over a hundred miles long from Shensi, making the Ching River take a double course and debouch into Lo River (of the Latter Han capital city, Loyang). A huge area was made fertile by silt-laden water. The ditch bore the name Cheng Kuo Ditch.[52] His work was continued and developed in the Han by Lord Pai, an engineer in the reign of Emperor Wu. In 95 BC, he successfully constructed a series of drains and ditches to control the flow of water and to reclaim land for local farmers.

The people were so grateful they composed this hymn to him. As with the other hymns, an emphasis is placed on rural prosperity, vividly expressed in the earthy idiom, 'Let's manure!' which is in keeping with the rustic notion of prosperity. The hymn respects the fact that the livelihood of urban centres depended on farms in the country.[53]

The Ballad of the Prefect of Goosegate

In the reign of filial Emperor Ho
The Governor of Loyang was Lord Wang.
He was born a commoner in I-chou, Kuang-han.
As a young circuit official
He had learned by heart the *Five Classics* and *Analects*.

He had a clear understanding of legal governance.
For generations his family wore cap and gown.
From Wen circuit he was promoted to Loyang Governor.
In administration he was most worthy,
Aiding and protecting the common folk,
Nurturing as his own ten thousand souls.

Out of court he practised strict government,
In court he held to kindness and mercy.
His civic and military virtues were perfect.
He expertly managed the people's economic welfare.
He published the names of wrongdoers,
On village gates had bulletins put up.

To mortally wound a man
Resulted in five neighbours equally punished.
He forbade lance and spear eight feet long.
He arrested insolent youths,
Dealt out firm sentences for crimes,
Going to the horsemarket to pronounce sentence.

He did not impose reckless taxes,
But was mindful of controlling costs.
Licensed by imperial mandate, he judged legal cases,
But did not permit litigiousness.
He spent only thirty cash
To purchase land valued by the yardstick.

Worthy man! So worthy was he,
Wang of our district.
An official in cap and gown
He dealt with affairs for the emperor.

43

In the Bureau of Merit or Master of Records
This man was to be found in every case.

When at his department or presiding at his office
He did not presume to show favouritism.
With personal integrity and unstinting toil
He laboured and slaved from dawn till dusk.
In government he had a name for ability,
He was known far and wide.

He did not fulfil his allotted span,
He went prematurely to his deep twilight.
For His Lordship we make sacrifice at his shrine
West of Anyang Pavilion.
We seek to ensure that future generations
Will always and ever commemorate him.

This balladic hymn honours Lord Wang who became Governor of Loyang in AD 103. He held office in the reign of Emperor Ho (r. AD 89–105). After he died in AD 105 the people set up a shrine to him as their saint or local hero. True to the pragmatism of the Chinese, he is revered not for his mysticism, charity, or religious fervour, but for his qualities as a leader, an official lawmaker. He was worshipped by the people because, despite his severity, he was a champion of their common cause.

The title of the hymn does not relate to its contents. It is possible that the original words of the title were lost and that in the Latter Han an anonymous song-maker borrowed the old title, which may have told a similar tale, and composed this eulogy.[54] The diction and point of view indicate that the maker was literate. Yet the hymn seems to constitute an example of the type of composition which, although produced by a literate author (and certainly based on the account of Lord Wang in his official biography) later came into the possession of the people as an oral composition memorized and repeated through the years.[55] Its style is curiously impersonal and cold, reflecting the formality of the official biographical style. It is not a true narrative. It is devoid of drama, direct speech, realism, imagery, and those other features which colour most popular narratives of the Han *yüeh-fu* repertoire.

The hymn introduces another strain of early Chinese philosophy. The theory and practice of Legalism formed the foundation of the Ch'in state and informed the system of government in the Han. The hymn's adulation of a stern but just judge drew its inspiration from philosophical Legalism and found its literary fulfillment in the Judge Pao plays which were popular in the Yüan Dynasty.[56]

CHAPTER TWO

Fables in Verse

The fables in this chapter are songs of varying length in which animals and plants speak and behave like human beings. The intent of their anonymous authors is generally to give instruction to humans, in a diverting and vivid manner, on the lessons of life. The genre of fable in verse does not exist as a recognizable literary form in China; there is no term to define this type of work. Moreover, there is no Chinese Aesop of the sixth century BC, or Phaedrus of the first century AD, or Babrius of the second century AD who formed the Greco-Roman repertory of fables in verse.[1] While no specific genre of fable existed in China, the tradition of fable writing developed comparatively early. It took the form of brief, witty anecdotes interspersed among the writings of philosophers of every school (except the Confucian), in order to illustrate and clarify their intellectual argument. As such, the fable was consciously used as a pedagogic device with the twin aim of instructing through wit and humour. The best examples appear in the writings of Chuang Tzu, Han Fei Tzu, and Lieh Tzu.[2]

The fables have been drawn from a variety of historical and literary sources. In his *Anthology*, Kuo classified what Westerners would term fables in verse under a wide range of categories. The fables of the ibis and the pheasant are in a sub-section of his category three, 'Words for Drumming and Blowing Pieces, Han Songs for the *Nao*-bell'.[3] 'A Crow Bore Eight or Nine Chicks' and 'South of the River' are in his category five, 'Words for Concerted Songs'. The tiger fable comes under the same general category, but in a preface in the sub-section 'Level-mode Pieces', while the poplar fable is in the sub-section 'Clear-mode Pieces', and one version of the white swans fable is in 'Zither-mode Pieces'. The fables of the butterfly, the withered fish, and the date-tree are in Kuo's category nine, 'Song-texts for Miscellaneous Pieces'.[4] So, by the end of the eleventh century AD verse pieces which Westerners would classify as fables in verse had no generic uniformity in China.[5] My own grouping here is therefore based on personal choice rather than on traditional Chinese ways of classifying the material.

The structure of these fables varies from the epigrammatic quatrain (four of the fourteen pieces) to a narrative of 26 lines. Three forms predominate: an encounter between two animals, or between one animal and an unidentified person, presumably the singer; a proverbial statement or a warning introduced by imperatives—Do this! Don't do that!; and a third-person narrative in which a singer tells the story of some animal, bird, or plant. These are based on direct speech, either dialogue, or monologue. While most of the fables employ creatures or plants to make a point, the use of nature itself is limited to carrying the story forward. The setting is invariably outdoors, but there are few lyrical or descriptive passages on nature.

The animals and plants in the fables are of the simplest kind, typical of a farming environment. They do not in themselves suggest a rural rather than a metropolitan ambience. It is the point of view which they project in their proverbial statements, primitive ideas, and traditional wisdom which makes them expressions of folk idiom rather than sophisticated literary artefacts. In the allegory of the white swans it is the mentality of the flock or herd or community which is expressed: the flock must, by definition, cohere in order to survive as an entity, so weak and ill members of it must be discarded. In the fable of the pine tree cut down to make a palace, the idea is conveyed that beauty invites defacement and removal from its natural habitat. In the pheasant fable, showiness leads to the threat of captivity and death. In the withered fish and butterfly parables, imprudence is shown to result in death. In the playful fish song, sexual drive is depicted as a procreative natural instinct. In the fable of the date-tree, fecundity attracts admirers, while barrenness results in neglect. The fable of the ibis suggests that the wrongdoer must be brought to justice. The fable of the high field proves the senselessness of doing things out of context.

These brief plots have a grim quality. They seek to persuade that life is nasty, short, and brutish. Their positive values are linked to conventional wisdom and community mores. There is no reference to ethics or to law, nor to the values expressed in the national hymns. A basic conservatism is promoted as a way of satisfactorily conducting one's life. Negative qualities such as the pessimistic view of prosperity, the tragic implications of beauty and talent, and the failure to merge anonymously with the community are echoes of native Taoist philosophy propounded in *The Classic of the Way and Its Power*, and especially in *Chuang Tzu*.

Unlike philosophical anecdotes, these fables have little humour. Their grim reminder that the wages of folly are death does not lend itself to gaiety. On the other hand, they are not solemn lessons to be earnestly learned. They are rich in entertainment. Vividness of expression, vernacular turns of phrase, dramatic twists in the narrative, and irregular metrical patterns all colour and animate the fables. In their aspirations, their fears, and their grouses they convey something of the narrow realism and rude wit of country people.

Vermilion Ibis

> Vermilion ibis
> A fish spat out:
> Ibis hates the vile.
> Where does ibis feed?
> It feeds under lotus.
> It won't eat this.
> It won't spit it out.
> Let's go and ask the executioner.

The symbol of the vermilion ibis has attracted a great deal of speculation among commentators. Lu K'an-ju, quoting the early T'ang scholar K'ung Ying-ta, noted that in the era of King Wei of Ch'u a flock of vermilion ibis soared and approached dancing, and that this miracle was the occasion for the song's composition.[6] Lu also cites the comment of the late Ming scholar Yang Shen that at the beginning of the Han Dynasty the sighting of a vermilion ibis was taken as an omen; a drum was painted with the likeness of the bird and the 'Vermilion Ibis' piece was composed.[7] Already two traditional explanations of the provenance of the song have emerged. The Ch'ing critic Ch'en Hang, much given to allegorical inter-pretation of the wildest sort, commented that the legendary emperors Yao and Shun had such a drum decorated with an ibis in the act of catching a fish and spitting it out. He suggested that this symbolized an honest minister reporting hidden evil to his lord. Since many of Ch'en's comments on literature suffer from a surfeit of political allegory *à la Songs of Ch'u,* his comment may be discounted.[8] As far as the appearance of the ibis as an omen is concerned, in the Han portents played a signifi-cant part in political life.[9] But to interpret the ibis in this fable as an omen does not get us very far. No matter how many commentators are consulted, the result can only be speculation on the meaning of portents and the significance of allegory.

We are left with the symbols contained in this piece. They appear to be clear enough on the surface. At the literal level they are three components of a natural scene, an ibis, a lotus pond, and a fish. The meaning of the fish and its habitat of the lotus pond may be linked to the sexual symbolism of fish in other poems and songs, especially the marriage songs of the *Book of Poetry*. In another song in this chapter, 'South of the River', I suggest that fish denote a ritualized form of sexual play during spring or summer. The carp, for instance, is often used as a symbol of sexual vigour. By extension, a rotten fish may serve as a euphemism for sexual depravity. The lotus pond is the equivalent of a lovers' lane. In late spring and summer, country people have a respite from work in the fields and this is a time when lovers frequent the lotus pond in boats, hiding under the huge lotus leaves. The fish may represent evil in general terms, rather than sexual depravity, but the combination of features in the fable which hint at sexual punning is perhaps more than coincidental.[10]

The significance of the drum mentioned by several commentators in connection with the vermilion ibis may be clarified by comparing this song with other lampoons dating from the Han, such as 'Short Wheat Green', and 'Crows on City Walls'.[11] In both cases, the last line refers to the beating of a drum and making a complaint to the authorities. In this ibis fable, the drum is absent but the formula of a complaint to an officer is present. To argue on such tenuous connections may be ill-advised, but there is precious little to work from. I would tentatively propose that the same meaning contained in the two lampoons' last lines, 'Please make the drum roll for the gentlemen!' and, 'Under the rafter there is a hanging drum./ I want to strike it, but the minister will be angry,' may be inferred from the fable's opaque last line: the cry of injustice is announced through the roll of the drum.

Apart from the opacity of the imagery and the terse transitions of the fable's brief narrative; a further difficulty lies in the presence of a line which may or may not be nonsense. In line 3 the words may be read as *lu-tzu-yeh*, something like fal-de-lal. Yet if slight amendments are made, the Chinese characters make sense. If the bird radical is added to *lu* we get ibis; if *yeh* is taken as its primary meaning and pronounced *hsieh* we get 'perverse, evil'; if we add the speech radical to *tzu* we get 'revile'. This would result in a line which makes sense in the context of the rest of the song: 'Ibis reviles the vile'. Of course, nonsense words are scattered throughout anonymous Han ballads, and they are a characteristic of ballads in other cultures. If in this instance, however, we give the nonsense sounds their full value, we introduce a criticism of evil, which links up with the complaint against injustice implicit in the last line. A viable interpretation of the song might then be: someone in the community is indulging in sexual depravity, but the people in the community feel powerless to prevent it without recourse to a higher authority.[12]

South of the River

South of the river we can pick lotos,
Lotos leaves so bushy, bushy!
Fish play among lotos leaves,
Fish play east of lotos leaves,

48

Fish play west of lotos leaves,
Fish play south of lotos leaves,
Fish play north of lotos leaves.

The erotic tone of this song is established by its punning and word-play. 'Lotos' (*lien*) is a pun for *lien*, meaning sexual passion, its red colour symbolism enhancing the pun. 'Pick' also suggests enjoy, have pleasure. The binome *t'ien-t'ien*, 'bushy, bushy', suggests the luxuriant growth of the lotos leaves where fish swim. Humans can also hide under the huge leaves for sexual enjoyment. 'Play' develops the idea of sexual frolics hinted at in the pun on lotos and in the hide-and-seek afforded by the leaves. The erotic symbolism of fish playing is universal. The song uninhibitedly rejoices in instinctual love. At the same time, its formal structure might represent the vestige of an old fertility rite: the propagation of the species will ensure the continuity of the rural community. The title 'South of the River' may refer to any river, illustrating the lack of a localized setting in ballads. But the title, in Chinese *Chiang-nan*, also refers to the region south of the Yangtse River, the Ch'ang Chiang.[13]

Young Pheasant Fancy-plume

Young Pheasant,
How fancy-plumed you are!
Going to pheasant-millet
Don't run into the old man and his lads!

Young pheasant,
Know that when pheasants fly they go high and settle,
When brown geese fly they go one thousand leagues—
Such wonderful strength!
Drake comes flying after his hen,
Young Pheasant hurries along the lone pheasant.

Young Pheasant,
The great carriage yoked, the horses racing,
A lively escort goes to the open fields.
Wheel round, fly from royal princes!

This text is probably the most corrupt of all the anonymous Han songs. My translation is therefore only tentative. The gist of the fable seems to be that a young cock-pheasant with brilliant, showy plumage is urged by an older and wiser pheasant, or by a human observer, to keep away from the royal hunt. Yü Kuan-ying believes that the three stanzas describe the three phases of the older bird's address to the younger: first an endearment, with admiration for the young cock's plumage; then an

49

order that it should get out of the way; and finally a lament that the pheasant has been hunted down and killed.[14] This is neat and feasible. Yet the last line seems to contain a warning rather than a lament, and so I have rendered the line differently from Yü's interpretation.

Because the text is so corrupt, different commentators have divided the lines into various lengths, according to their understanding of the meaning of the words. The middle stanza is clearly in a battered shape, even in translation. Its last couplet especially defies interpretation. It might be argued that in the central couplet the cock-pheasant courts a hen pheasant, oblivious of the dangers of being shot at. This garbled couplet may contain musical instructions to the singer, on the other hand, rather than words to be translated as part of the text. The phrase 'Hurried along' renders the word *tsü*, but this may also mean a musical coda, examples of which occur in other Han songs. As such the *tsü*-coda might mean that the final passage of the song, with its accompanying change of music, begins with the last line of stanza two. The last couplet of the song is also open to conjecture. An alternative reading is: 'By royal escort beaters it is hit,' and so the song's final line might mean that the dead pheasant is stowed as game in the back of the hunting carriage.

Despite these textual difficulties, the fable appeals because it possesses a primary feature of Han songs and ballads, realistic presentation. It is full of details about pheasant rearing and shooting which are still true today. The cock's fine plumage makes it clearly visible in the open fields after the harvest of grain crops. The game-keeper, an old man, puts out special feed to lure the game into the open fields away from the safety of trees. After the long months of rearing and the final months of feeding and taming the pheasants, the royal hunt appears on the scene, full of high spirits and keen to get a good bag of game. If we take the middle stanza to mean that the cock-pheasant is chasing after a hen, this is also in keeping with the ballad's realism, for it is stressed throughout that this young cock is too young to have learned the hard facts of the kill.[15]

A Crow Bore Eight or Nine Chicks

A crow bore eight or nine chicks,
She sits up in the Ch'in's cassia tree.
Ah, alas!
The Ch'in clan has a wild, roving boy,
Skilled with his Sui-yang catapult
And Su-ho scented shot.
In his left hand he holds his bow and two pellets,
In and out he goes, east and west of the crow.
Ah, alas!

One pellet fired hits the crow's body.
The crow dies, her soul flies up to Heaven.
When the mother hen bore her crow-chicks
She was in South Mountain's sheer rocks.
Ah, alas!
How do folks know where birds live?
Why do folk pass through narrow, lost paths?
A white hart is in Royal Forest's west garden,
But the master bowman still catches white hart for venison.
Ah, alas!
A brown goose brushes Heaven flying high,
In the rear palace they still get to cook it.
A carp is in Lo River's deep pool,
But the angler still catches the carp by the mouth.
Ah, alas!
In human life each has his allotted years,
So why must we ask in life or death whose turn comes first or last?

This fable exhibits a variety of balladic features. The vague number, 'eight or nine chicks', might suggest an absent-minded mother, but it is clearly a favourite way of describing a family, as other ballads like 'Cocks Crow' and 'They Met' reveal.[16] The surname Ch'in appears to be a specific clan name, but it recurs in 'Mulberry on the Bank' as the name of the heroine, Ch'in Lo-fu, and in 'A Peacock Southeast Flew' in the name of the girl a mother wants for her son.[17] 'Ah, alas!' renders the nonsense words *cha-wo*, which again recurs in other ballads. The epithets describing the Ch'in son, 'wild, roving', are tautological, a feature of almost every ballad. Hyperbole is also evident in the boy's weapons: Sui-yang was a place in old Sung state and denotes the fabulous pearl given to Lord Sui by a snake he rescued; Su-ho was an expensive and rare pot-pourri from Central Asia which has been mixed with clay to form shot. The boy's furtive creeping in the garden to surprise the mother crow is visual drama in the narrative. Comedy, or the mock-heroic, occurs in the description of the mother crow's death. In the Chinese, the crow's *hun* soul and *p'o* soul are said to rise to paradise. The Han concept of the soul has become garbled in this folk piece; it was only the *hun* which was believed to be the spiritual essence of humans and immortal, while the *p'o* was believed to be the animal essence which dissolved with the bodily remains in the earth. The comedy lies in the attribution of a soul to the bird and in the misunderstanding of theology. As with the name Ch'in, South Mountain recurs in some ballads. It is a stereotype for a sacred haven; since the Chou, it was associated with longevity.[18] Its appearance in this song creates a certain irony, for the crow did not live out its allotted span.

The structure of the song seems lopsided; the first section which narrates the fate of the crow reads like an independent piece. The rest of the song, which tells of the fate of other creatures, consists of a series of mini-narratives only a third the length of the first passage. Perhaps the crow narrative was the original ballad, and later it acquired serial passages because the theme proved to be attractive to audiences. The piece deals with the theme of the ultimate meaninglessness of life, the randomness of fate, and the universality of death, no matter how safe and secure one imagined oneself to be.

The story contained in the first passage resembles a narrative in the first century BC anthology of prose tales, *Garden of Anecdotes*.[19] The king of Wu state decided to attack Ching state and announced to his courtiers that if anyone opposed him he would put him to death. One of his retainers thought the king ought to be stopped and so he resolved to advise him indirectly. He spent three dawns in the garden with his catapult and pellets, getting soaked. The king asked him the reason, and the retainer told this parable: 'There is a tree in the garden. On its crown there is a cicada. The cicada stays high up, chirping sadly and drinking dew, unaware that a praying-mantis is behind it. The praying-mantis crouches with bent legs about to seize the cicada, but is unaware that an oriole is beside it. The oriole stretches out its neck to peck the praying-mantis, but is unaware that a catapult and pellet are beneath it. These three creatures all fixed their attention on the prize in front of them, but ignored the disaster behind them.' The king congratulated his retainer on his sound advice and called off his troops. This prose parable deals with several themes: self-interest, greed, imprudence, the brevity of life in a danger-infested world, the savagery of death, and the dispassionate law of nature. The verse fable, while clearly similar to the prose tale, has a different emphasis: no matter how safe one is, no living thing can evade death. South Mountain, the holy mountain of longevity, Royal Forest, the Han emperor's private park for the protection of exotic species, the skies close to Heaven, the depths of Lo River of Loyang may seem to be havens, but in the end they cannot protect one from disaster. The message of the verse fable has a Taoist overtone: humans must not be useful, attractive, or visible if they wish to survive.[20]

If in a High Field

If in a high field you plant dwarf wheat,
It will never ever form ears of grain.
If a man lives in a strange village,
How can he fail to be unhappy?

The proverbial tone of the first couplet, based on rural wisdom, is reminiscent of some poems in the *Book of Poetry*, such as no. 102:

Do not till too large a field,
the weeds will [only] be very high;
Do not long for the far-away person,
your toiling heart will [only] be very grieved.[21]

In the Chou poem and the Han ballad the rural metaphor is juxtaposed with an emotional truth. Both pieces treat the theme of longing for the unobtainable. In the Han ballad the persona feels nostalgic for his home village. This particular facet of nostalgia in Chinese is called *ku-hsiang*, one's old village, and it persists as a theme in Chinese literature, both in the folk idiom and in refined literary modes.[22]

The Fierce Tiger Ballad

Though you starve, don't follow a fierce tiger for food.
Though it's dark, don't follow wild birds to roost.
Wild birds are content to have no nest.
For whom would the traveller feel pride?

In this brief fable the animal world is contrasted with human society. Again, the first line reads like a proverb; the prudent human is advised how to survive in an extremity. The second line is similar, but its meaning is not immediately obvious. The next line amplifies the second and alerts the listener or reader that the import of the fable has to do with social philosophy. It is not just the threat of being eaten by a tiger or spending a sleepless night in the wilds which is being communicated. The message is that beasts are beasts and men are men, and never the twain shall meet. A passage in the *Analects* of Confucius puts the idea more fully. Once when Confucius was passing by two members of the Agronomist Movement on his way to a ford, he sent his disciple to ask where the ford was. They told the disciple to desert Confucius and to join them in their rejection of society. When the disciple told Confucius about them, he said, 'One cannot herd with birds and beasts. If I do not associate with mankind, with whom shall I associate?'[23] In the verse fable the Confucian teaching might also be applied: humans must not sink to the level of wild creatures; man's place is in society, with its rules of decorum and code of behaviour distinguishing him as a civilized being.[24]

An Old Ballad, Two White Swans

Flying this way two white swans
Are from the northwest come,
In ten tens and five fives,
Uneven, straggling formation.

Suddenly one falls ill,
Cannot fly with the other.
Five leagues and one looks back,
Six leagues and one has faltered.
'I would carry you away in my beak,
But my beak is sealed and will not open.
I would carry you away on my back,
But my feathers and tail each day would be crushed.'

How happy they were to fall in love!
Sadness comes with lifetime separation.
Pausing, it looks back on its old flock-mate,
Tears drop trickling criss-cross.
Today let's be happy in our love,
May your years last to ten thousand!

The fable of a pair of white swans belongs to a large repertoire of early Chinese poems featuring birds of different kinds which convey a variety of themes. The peacock in the opening couplet of 'A Peacock Southeast Flew' prefigures the theme of tragic lovers, a husband and wife torn apart by selfish parents, and it foretells the husband's suicide by hanging from a 'southeast branch' in his garden. The second line of the 'Peacock' couplet is almost the same as the eighth of 'Two White Swans': 'After five leagues it faltered.'[25] Numerous early Chinese lyrics also have a felicitation closure in which the persona wishes to be with a lover a pair of flying birds. In this ballad, the hen bird seems to be the speaker in the closure, voicing the lament that a vow made long ago is now broken. In this version of the song the bird expresses the longing and emotion of human lovers, thus maintaining its allegorical framework. The next title, 'A Yen Song, The Whenever Ballad', while following the same allegorical line, interrupts this allegory in order to present a parallel with the human predicament of parted lovers.

Prose fables in pre-Han philosophical texts depict a variety of birds, such as owls, pigeons, and the sparrow, to portray a human foible. The moral of the verse fable here seems not so much related to individual human behaviour as to the behaviour of the individual in so far as he is a member of a group or community. The clue to this interpretation lies in the opening sequence when the two swans, which are mates, arrive on the scene as part of a flock flying in formation. A further clue is the phrase occurring toward the end of the ballad, old 'flock-mate', ch'un-lu. The healthy swan cannot stay with its ill mate, it must rejoin the flock. Without the flock the individual is nothing; survival depends on social cohesion. The strong bird expresses its loyalty to society, a loyalty which is stronger than that owed to its former love. This hard-headed view of human relationships suggests the conventional wisdom of a rural community passed down from generation to generation. The value it places on the demands of society is questioned in the next version of the song.[26]

A *Yen* Song, The Whenever Ballad

Flying this way two white swans
Are from the northwest come,
In ten tens, five fives,
Arranged in even formation.

The wife suddenly falls ill,
Travelling she can't keep up with the other.
Five leagues and one looks back,
Six leagues and one has faltered.

'I would carry you away in my beak,
But my beak is sealed and will not open.
I would carry you away on my back,
But my feathers and tail how crushed they would be!'

So happy with my new love!
Sadness comes with parting in life.
Pausing, it looks back on its old flock-mate,
Tears drop unawares.

I remember parting from you,
My breath catches, I can't speak.
Each one cares for himself,
Counts it hard to come home from the long road.
Your wife will keep an empty bedroom,
Shut the gates, let down the double bolts.
If we live we may meet again,
If we die we'll reunite in Yellow Springs.
Today let's be happy in our love,
May your years last to ten thousand!

In Kuo's *Anthology* this version of the song is divided into four quatrains and one final passage of ten lines, forming a *yen/tsü* structure. It closely resembles the previous version from the first line to line sixteen. The differences are a change of metres in lines 3–5 from pentasyllabic to tetrasyllabic, and some slight modifications in diction, such as 'Sadness comes with parting in life', instead of the first version's 'Sadness comes with lifetime separation', but these changes do not alter the meaning.

The major break in composition occurs in line 17, which introduces the extra passage prior to the closure. This new material completely alters the point of view of the song. The first version maintained the allegorical structure and only implied that the lesson to be learned from the birds' situation was true for humans. This longer version deliberately introduces a passage which breaks the allegory and creates a parallel structure, comparing the animal world with the human. This trend towards eliminating or diminishing the allegory culminated in the lyrical poetry of the late Han and Three Kingdoms era. The Chien-an poets especially focussed on the persona of the abandoned wife while rejecting the allegorical framework of such songs as 'Two White Swans' or 'The Whenever Ballad' on the same theme.[27] Their lyrics took the form of the plaint of a neglected wife in which she narrates the story of her blighted love and affirms her constancy for her fickle husband. The extra passage of the longer version of the white swans song presents a romantic, lyrical point of view that is quite different from the short version which presents in almost equal measure hard-headed realism and a plaintive appeal.

Both versions share a number of commonplace phrases. They are either half-lines such as 'Tears drop unawares', or full lines, 'Each one cares for himself'. Their identical closure recurs in other songs, with some modification. For example, the closure's first line, 'Today let's be happy in our love', is the penultimate line of the long version of 'Along the Embankment', while its second line is the same as that of the long version of 'The White Head Lament'.[28] The description of the swans in formation resembles lines in the passage describing mandarin ducks in 'Cocks Crow' and 'They Met'. The role of the neglected wife, mirrored in the allegory of the female swan, is a stereotype of several songs, such as 'East Gate Ballad', 'The One I Love', 'Along the Embankment', and 'The White Head Lament'.

It is difficult to conjecture which of these two versions of the song is the older. In general, I have accepted Diény's hypothesis that the long version precedes the short.[29] In this case, however, I feel that the short version's straightforward allegory represents the earliest phase in a literary trend which continues with a dual compositional structure of part-allegory, part-parallelism, and culminates in the elimination of the allegory altogether, focussing on the parallel structure in a new way. In this context it is interesting to note that another version of the song exists in a sixth-century AD encyclopedia, *Compendium of Literature*. Since it was the practice of its compiler, Ou-yang Hsün, to present quotations without stating whether they were partial or in full, it is not clear whether the version of the song he quotes is a full text, a brief fragment, or a partial extract. Nor is it possible to date the piece. This version is in six couplets, resembling both previous versions from the first line to the end of the male bird's speech. Its first three couplets are tetrasyllabic, which metre it shares with just lines 3–5 of the long version. Its last three couplets are pentasyllabic, a metre shared by both of the other versions. It is possible to conjecture that Ou-yang's citation of this piece represents just an extract; on the other hand it might constitute the original source on which the other two are based.[30]

The Butterfly

A butterfly flutters in the east garden—
Why now! suddenly it meets a swallow mothering three-month chicks.
She greets me in the rape-seed,
She takes me into the Purple Palace deep,
She goes round close by the cornice,
As sparrows come her swallow-chicks,
Swallow-chicks spy her beak's chewed tidbit,
Heads tremble, wings drum, all so merry and bright!

In this allegory, the victim is a frail, carefree, imprudent butterfly which is enjoying itself in a spring garden oblivious of possible danger. The villain of the piece is a swallow. Its negative, though natural role here is atypical in Chinese verse; usually it figures as the harbinger of spring when it returns to the countryside with the renewal of the calendrical cycle and as the homebuilder caring for its young. In the hard realism of these fables the allegory reminds the listener of the facts of life as seen from the folk-singer's point of view: nature is amoral, it is red in beak and talon. By analogy, the allegory persuades, humans prey on each other and life is a matter of the survival of the fittest. The victim is the unwary and the one who is too noticeable.

The techniques of presentation well illustrate the balladic style. There is a certain realism in the scene of the spring garden where the butterfly idly flits around and in the closing scene of the ravenous chicks being fed a fresh, chewed insect. Counterbalancing the realism is the hyperbolic setting of the royal residence, the 'Purple Palace', with its high cornice selected by the swallow parents for their nest. The technical word 'cornice', *po-lu*, has a comic effect, juxtaposed as it is with the homely scenes of the garden and chicks and with the colloquialism of the singer's dramatic monologue. The narrative has several dramatic devices. The singer makes the listener visualize the butterfly's alarm on suddenly meeting the bird hunting for food, and makes one experience the dizziness of the butterfly as it is flown around the palace ceiling in the bird's beak; and the singer makes one imagine the alarm of the insect as it views in close-up the wide-open beaks of the chicks in their desperate hunger, which is almost as desperate as the butterfly's terror. There is a touch of cruelty in this dramatic presentation. The mocking line of 'A Withered Fish' re-echoes here: 'Too late for remorse now!' The colloquialisms make the drama more vivid. In the first few lines the singer skilfully introduces an exclamation of grief or surprise, *cha-wo*, 'Ah, alas!' or 'Why now!' to describe how the insect and bird come across each other. The pronoun 'me' in the second couplet is introduced to produce a close bond between the singer and the victim. The dramatic monologue contains several shifts of voice and point of view, the singer changing from third to first person, and alternating between the roles of the butterfly, the swallow, the chicks, and the narrator. It is possible to imagine that the confusion in the shifts of role and voice were clarified by the music, which might have had different motifs for each role, and by the singer's modulation of the pitch of his voice.

Like the fable of the pheasant this text is corrupt, especially in its opening lines. The first line might also read, 'Butterfly, ah Butterfly playing in my east garden'. This text has a number of nonsense words. In lines 1, 4, 5, and 8 the sounds *chih* and *nu* appear to have no meaning.[31]

A Withered Fish

> A withered fish by a river wept.
> Too late for remorse now!
> He wrote a letter to carp and bream
> Warning them: Mind how you come and go!

There is something tragi-comical about a dried fish stranded on the shore still able to shed watery tears: 'withered' and 'wept' create an amusing oxymoron. As with the butterfly piece, cruelty informs the humour. There is also a nice ambiguity in the second line; it is left unclear whether the fish is the speaker realizing its mistake too late, or whether the narrator is deriding it. The moral of the fable, like many others in this chapter, is that the imprudent and the unwary will come to a sad end. The comic also fuses with sentiment in the last couplet where the dying fish poignantly tries to warn its brethren by writing them a warning letter. Humour emerges, too, in the juxtaposition of the literary manner of 'He wrote . . .' and the colloquialisms, 'Too late' and 'Mind how you . . .'. The sentiment expressed is harsh: if humans don't watch out they will die the same kind of grisly death. An element of the country-man's prejudice against travelling away from home is faintly perceptible in the fable, suggesting that if one stays at home such a calamity will not occur.[32]

Song of Sighs, The Date-Tree

Under the date-tree what bunches, bunches!
The glorious, the beautiful all have their own season..
At the season when the dates start to redden
People come from all four quarters.
If today its dates were all given away,
Would anyone still admire it?

The allegory of the date-tree admits of several interpretations. Yü Kuan-ying suggests that it serves as a lesson on the fickleness of human nature; humans admire the tree when it is laden with blossom and luscious fruit, but ignore it when the tree is bare.[33] I would carry Yü's line of interpretation further and make the allegory serve as a lesson on the fickleness of a man's love for a childless wife. The grounds for this more specific reading are the punning device employed in the major image and the traditional technique of using a blossoming fruit tree as a metaphor for a young wife. The word for date is *tsao-tzu*, which is a pun for 'Soon bear sons!' The earliest anthology of poetry in China, *Book of Poetry*, contains several poems which draw an analogy between a fruit tree and a nubile girl, such as poem no. 6: 'How delicately beautiful is the peach-tree,/ brilliant are its flowers;/ this young lady goes to her new home,/ she will order well her chamber and house'.[34] In traditional China one of the legal grounds on which a man might divorce his wife was childlessness, meaning her failure to produce a son and heir. The bunches of dates may therefore denote fertility. The brief season of beauty might refer to the tree's lovely spring blossom, a transient beauty like the allure of a young wife. The colour red has conventional associations of eroticism and marriage. The bareness of the date-tree in the penultimate line hints at the barrenness of the wife or her advancing years. She becomes an object of scorn in the community and family. The plaint voiced in the title, 'Song of Sighs', literally 'The Alas! Song', supports this interpretation of the allegory, but it also strangely contrasts with the matter-of-fact tone of the speaker.[35]

A *Yen* Song, A Ballad

On South Mountain's rocks sheer, sheer,
Pine and cypress are so thick, thick.
Top boughs brush blue clouds,
Tree trunks are ten girths round.
When Loyang sends for main beams
The pine tree secretly mourns.

When axe and saw fell this pine,
The pine tree topples east to west.
A specially made four-wheeled cart
Bears it to Loyang palace.
All the onlookers can only sigh,
Asking, 'From what mountain is this timber?'
Who is able to carve this?
Only Master Shu and Pan of Lu state.
To coat it they use cinnabar lacquer,
For incense they use Su-ho scent.
Once it was a pine from South Mountain,
Now it's a beam in a palace hall.

This fable presents an allegory of a perfect tree growing on hallowed ground which is singled out by a carpenter to be used as the main beam of a Loyang palace. It may be compared with an anecdote in *Chuang Tzu*, the classic of Taoist philosophy. Chuang Tzu meets a woodcutter and asks him about his criterion for choosing timber:

'When Chuang Tzu was travelling in the mountains he saw a great tree with luxuriant foliage and branches. A woodcutter stopped at its side but did not choose it. He asked him why, and was told, "There's nothing you can use it for." "This tree," said Chuang Tzu, "by its timber being good for nothing will get to last out Heaven's allotted years, wouldn't you say?" '[36]

The Taoist principle in this parable is that it is best for a person to have no talent and to recede into the background unnoticed, so that one may keep out of harm's way and enjoy one's lifespan to the full. The verse fable is the story of a tree which a woodcutter judged to be useful as timber and so he cut it down. The lyrical opening of the verse fable underscores the ideal state of the pine tree on South Mountain. The symbolism of the pine, which denotes constancy and longevity, and the mountain, which denotes a sacred place and longevity, develops the idealism and at the same time introduces an ironic note which prefigures the dénouement of the story. The tree, which once enjoyed its natural habitat, is destroyed to become an artificial thing, an object of man's pleasure.[37] The fable projects different states of being: freedom and captivity, artificiality and naturalness, and nature and the human world. From these contrasts we may infer that freedom, the natural state of a living thing, and nature itself make for happiness, while the converse makes for unhappiness.[38]

The Yü-chang Ballad

When the white poplar was first born
It was in the hills of Yü-chang.
Its topmost leaves stroked blue clouds,
Its lowest roots reached Yellow Springs.
In cool autumn's eighth and ninth months
Hillsmen take axes and hatchets.
My [?leaves] white, so white,
As they fall [?seem to ?flutter, ?flutter] down.
Roots from boughs are severed for ever
Upside down among cliff tops.
A big sawyer takes axe and rope,
Chops five feet even at both ends;
One heave, four or five leagues,
Boughs and leaves are cast off from each other.
[?   ?   ?   ?   ?   ]
To make a sailing vessel.
My body lives in Loyang palace,
My roots live in Yü-chang's hills.
Many times I said goodbye to boughs and leaves,
When will we be reunited?
I have lived one hundred years [?   ],
Since [?our youth ?we grew up ?   ] together.
Why has the craft of men
Made my boughs part from my roots?

There are many points of similarity between this piece and the previous verse fable. Both are allegories which have as their main symbol a tree. The text of 'Yü-chang' is rather battered, having thirteen words missing and a passage wrongly interpolated. The lacunae in the text are indicated in my translation by [?]. The first line, too, contains a key word which is clearly in need of amendment. I have adopted the sensible amendment of Feng Wei-no in *Notes on Ancient Poetry*, reading poplar for *yang*. In this he was no doubt following the lead of the third-century AD critic Hsün Hsü who referred to an older version of a 'White Poplar' piece but noted that its text had not been preserved.[39] The poplar fits the decription of the tree in the verse fable: the epithet white in the first line and the dazzling white of the (?) leaves that fall when the tree is felled. The type of tree is different in each of the two fables, as is the name of the mountain where it grows—here Yü-chang in the region of modern Kiangsi. A scenic viewpoint called the Yü-chang Kuan, or observatory, was said to have been built in the reign of the Han Emperor Wu on Lake K'un-ming in Ch'angan.[40] In the early Han therefore a relationship existed between the place and the Han palace, a relationship which is developed in the fable. Moreover, the third line of each fable is very similar. But the poplar allegory makes a sophisticated parallelism of colour and place in the second couplet, and introduces a symbolic placename, Yellow Springs, which was the underworld of dead souls, prefiguring the fate of the tree. In both pieces the timber is for a Loyang palace, the capital of Eastern Han. In Yü-chang the hillsmen fell the tree, whereas in the previous fable synecdoche is skilfully used: 'When axe and saw fell this pine.' The text's middle section appears to suffer from a redundant passage, the import of lines 6–10 being repeated in lines 11–16. There is a contradiction between the lines, 'To make a sailing vessel' and 'My body lives in Loyang palace'. The latter line fits in with the numerous points of comparison with the previous 'Yen Song'. The redundant passage and its contradiction of the sense of the piece as a whole suggest that it has been wrongly interpolated, perhaps to serve as an alternative passage rather than as an extra one. The piece reads much better if lines 11–16 were removed.

Although there are numerous resemblances, the point of view of the two fables is quite different. The 'Yen Song' has a strong narrative line, with minimal use of lyricism; it is a story told with detachment, only one comment from those witnessing the event of the pine trunk's removal to Loyang being allowed to intrude. In 'Yü-chang' the lyrical element is extended through the first five lines, continues again in lines 7–10, and reappears in the final passage. The speaker is ambiguously set between third and first person. The tone is plaintive, quite different from the impersonality of the other allegory. The moral of the fable is the same in each case, reiterating that of the pheasant, crow, butterfly, and fish fables.[41]

The Pomelo, An Old Poem

> Where pomelo hangs down lovely fruit
> Is on the deep hill flank.
> I hear you like my sweetness;
> In secret, alone, I make myself lovely.
> I offer my humble self on a jade dish,
> For many years hoping to be eaten.
> My fragrance fair does not please you.
> Green to yellow—swift the colours change.

This piece is an allegory for transient beauty and love. It resembles the 'Date-tree' in its use of a fruit tree as an analogy for a young wife or bride. Rooted in the soil it cannot move from its habitat. It takes nourishment from the rich slope of the hill, an image of male love. The tree looks lovely when its blossom turns to sweet fruit. It is plucked for a wealthy home, resting on a valuable dish. The voice of the tree speaking merges with the voice of a young girl who, through the allegory's deliberate ambiguity, is both the blossom and the fruit which she picks herself and brings into the house. A further refinement of this allegory is that the girl seeks to elliptically convey her wistful message to her beloved lord and master. The muted desire she expresses is that like the tree she will be enjoyed by her lord and she will bear fruit, provide him with a son and heir if he will deign to notice her. He shows no interest and gradually her youth and beauty fade with the years. This allegory is similar in some respects to a piece in *Songs of Ch'u*, 'In Praise of the Orange-tree'.[42] There, however, the allegory contains layers of eroticism, ethics, and politics; the orange-tree addresses a ruler and offers itself to the enlightened service of its young lord, speaking with the voice of a young man rather than as a woman.[43]

CHAPTER THREE

The Elixir of Life

From the third century BC the Chinese began to speculate about the mystery of immortality and embarked on a variety of experiments and ritualistic practices in search of this goal. The cult of immortality took three main forms, some of which were interchangeable among its adepts and practitioners. There was the simple desire to 'nurture one's life', to prolong one's allotted span of years.[1] There was the desire for eternal youth, to stay the ravages of time. Thirdly, there was an aspiration to join the pantheon of the gods, to ride the skies in the company of the host of spirits. At first the pursuit of immortality was élitist, the concern of emperors and princes.[2] The first person in China consciously to try to attain this goal, who can be dated with any certainty, is the founder of the first empire and dynasty, Ch'in Shih Huang-ti.[3] At his court in Hsien-yang he had heard wizards and sorcerers talk of the Isles of the Blessed in the east where the immortals were believed to live.[4] If any man reached these holy isles he would become an immortal. Pragmatic as he was, the emperor sent a group of boys and girls to go in search of them. They returned in failure, blaming adverse winds. A wizard named Han Chung whom the emperor sent to seek the drug of immortality prudently never returned.[5]

It was in the reign of the Han Emperor Wu that the cult of immortality found new inspiration. Under the direction of Li Shao-chün, an adept in the magical arts, the emperor became fascinated by alchemy which promised to transmute cinnabar into gold. If he drank and ate from dishes made of this gold he believed he would prolong the years of his life. Li Shao-chün also assured him that after absorbing the essence from this alchemical gold he would meet the immortals of P'eng-lai, one of the Isles of the Blessed, and he would never die. The magician convinced the emperor that this was just what the Yellow Emperor had done aeons ago.[6] The emperor sent a party of magicians to the eastern seas, but they, too, were unsuccessful in their search. He also began carrying out rites which the legendary Yellow Emperor was supposed to have performed, in the belief that he would be assumed into paradise. In 113 BC, a shaman found a cauldron, said to be one of the nine used by the Yellow Emperor to cook sacrificial offerings for the gods.[7] During a period of tyranny and decadence in high antiquity, however, the nine vessels had disappeared without trace in a river. The single vessel found by the shaman signified to the emperor that he was truly destined for immortality. In the year 110 BC, after sacrificing at the grave of the Yellow Emperor, the Han emperor inquired curiously of his entourage, 'I have been told that the Yellow Emperor did not die. Why is it that we now find his grave here?' Someone explained that after the Yellow Emperor's assumption, his hat and robes were buried in the 'grave'.[8] In the year 109 BC, the fungus of immortality was discovered growing in one of the rooms of his summer palace. The emperor proclaimed a general amnesty and a hymn was composed to commemorate the happy omen.[9]

In the Latter Han, immortality cults, which previously had not been linked to any specific philosophical school, political ideology, or religious system, gradually became assimilated with Taoist philosophy and identified with later Taoist religious practice.[10] The methods used to procure longevity, immortality, or divinity were breathing exercises, certain sexual practices, meditation, trance, diet, the taking of herbs and drugs, alchemy, and the consumption of certain (poisonous in some cases) minerals.[11] There developed a new lore of legendary figures and human beings who had become immortal—the Yellow Emperor, Wang Ch'iao, Ch'ih Sung (Red Pine), and others.[12]

The iconography of these immortals and the paraphernalia of immortality cults of this era are colourful. Sometimes a fairy or immortal is identified as a long-eared man riding a white (the colour of death) deer. Sometimes the divinity was perceived as a pheasant which left huge footprints.[13] Aerial flight and the freedom of the skies are also part of this lore. The usual landscape is a solitary mountain touching the clouds, such as Mount T'ai or Mount Hua. The mountains of the immortals were said to be jewelled, of gold and white jade, the pureness of the minerals denoting the perfect purity of the immortals. Jade in particular was a cult jewel in Taoism. Reclusion and solitude were the hallmarks of the adept. It was an aspect of this lore which so influenced later Chinese literature that it gave rise to a sub-genre of reclusive poetry.[14] The food and drink associated with the cult of immortality were cinnabar (this tone of red, too, had a special symbolic value), hallucinogenic fungi, certain immortality herbs, and pure dew or frost. The avoidance of cereal in the diet was emphasized.[15]

Angus C. Graham notes that when the experts on immortality practices identified with Taoism in the first century AD, and when the Taoist religion was founded in the second century AD by Chang Tso-ling, a new phenomenon emerged: '. . . the Taoist religion . . . extended the promise of immortality from the élite patrons of magicians and alchemists to the common man.'[16] The songs in this chapter are difficult to place in the evolution of the cult of immortality from élitist to generalized practice. Two of them at least, 'Long Song' and 'The King of Huai-nan', have associations with the Han court. Several are written in a liturgical style suggesting that they might have been part of a particular cultist rite. As such they constitute some of the earliest pieces in the repertoire of the occult, of Taoist religion, and reclusion.

Up the Mound

Up the mound so fine fine,
Down to the ford windy and chill.
I ask a traveller, 'Where are you from?'
He says, 'From the river depths.
Of cassia tree is my lord's boat,
Of green silk strands are my lord's moorings,
Of magnolia are my lord's oars
Yellow gold set in them.
Sparrows of the vast seas,
Vermilion wild swans winging,
White geese follow.
Hills, woods may now open, now unfold,
But I have never known the sun or moon bright.
Mine are the waters of nectar springs,
Vivid marshes lush, so lush.
Magic fungus is my chariot,
Dragons are my steeds.
I gaze as I wander
Beyond the four seas.'
Early in Kan-lu's second year
Fungus appeared in Bronze Pool.
Immortals came down to drink.
May you have long life, one thousand myriad years!

The structure of this song is based on the balladic formula of question and answer. An unspecified person has come down from a burial mound and meets a traveller, a stranger. He asks him where he is from and the stranger tells him a fabulous story of his divine master's boat, for his lord is a river god. The formula binds together three themes within this descriptive narrative: the theme of death implicit in the scene of the burial mound and in the felicitation closure; a paeon to a river god; and a eulogy to a reigning emperor of the Han also in the felicitation closure. In his preface to this song, Kuo Mao-ch'ien, quoting Shen Yüeh's 'Treatise', explains that this is one of eight hymns sung at the offertory in ancestral sacrifices performed in the imperial temple in AD 86 when Emperor Chang was on the throne. Kuo also cites the *History of the Latter Han* to the effect that 'Up the Mound' was performed at the rites for the first month of the lunar year after the rites at the altars of the various temples had been concluded.[17] Kuo comments further that in the Former Han there was a Supreme Mound in the capital Ch'angan. Despite this specificity, it is not clear whether the title of this song should be rendered 'Supreme Mound' (*Shang ling*) or 'Up the Mound', because the opening couplet, which repeats the words of the title, is based on a strict parallelism: up/down, mound/ford, fine, fine/windy, chill. The title may therefore allude to the site in Ch'angan and/or it may just be any burial mound. The word *ling* means a burial site in the form of an artificially raised mound where rulers and titled people were buried. As such, the image introduces the theme of death into the song, which the singer seeks to erase at the song's end with a prayer for the ruler's longevity.

The second theme is a paeon to a river god, in which a human encounters the god's acolyte. In some respects this part of the song resembles the song to the river god Ho-po in the 'Nine Songs' of the *Songs of Ch'u*:

> I ride a water chariot with a canopy of lotus;
> Two dragons draw it, between two water-serpents.
> I climb the K'un-lun mountain and look over the four quarters.[18]

The device of replacing the god for his acolyte in the Han song allows the singer to present a long description of the god's magnificent boat and serves to cut the deity down to size. This descriptive passage contains two balladic features: striking colour imagery and commonplace expression. The passage is similar to the description of the lord's mansion and his son's harness in 'They Met', which also shares with this song the formula of question and answer to introduce the florid description. The words 'magic fungus' toward the end of the song (line 16) act as a transition between the two previous themes and the last. The word 'fungus' is repeated in the final quatrain to emphasize this transition. In this closure, time is identified with the reign of Emperor Hsüan of the Former Han, the name of whose sixth reign-period was Kan-lu, Sweet Dew; the date in the song is 52 BC. The two omens referred to in the quatrain, the appearance of a miraculous fungus and of immortals descending to earth to drink are echoes of historical omens of the Chou and a recent miracle in the Han. In the Spring and Autumn era of the Chou, a golden fungus with nine stalks grew in the Bronze Pool at the royal palace. This happened again in 61 BC in the reign of Emperor Hsüan when a nine-stemmed fungus grew in the Bronze Pool of Han-te Hall of the royal palace. Then in 60 BC, a flock of birds of paradise (*luan*) gathered over the capital city as sweet dew fell, yellow dragons descended, withered things flourished and a divine light was seen everywhere.[19] In the Han song the sacerdotal link between these miracles recorded in history and the prayer for the emperor's long life is established by the protagonist of the river sprite.

In making this connection, the anonymous psalmist implies that the emperor is a wise and good ruler; he flatters His Majesty with intimations of immortality, and he delicately suggests that the emperor will join the pantheon of the gods. The song is therefore neither a graveyard meditation, as its opening might have indicated, nor is it merely a paeon to a river god in the manner of the 'Nine Songs' piece. It is a praise-song, a eulogy to a reigning monarch imbued with a courtly, if mildly sacrilegious obsequiousness.[20]

A Long Song Ballad, no. 2

> The fairy riding a white deer
> Has short hair and ears so long.
> As he leads me up Great Mount Hua
> He grasps the mushroom, seizes red-fringe fungus.
> When we reach the Master's gates
> He offers up the drug in a jade casket.
> The Master eats the drug,
> His body in a day grows strong and fit,
> His white hair turns black again,
> His lifespan lengthens, his years are increased.

It is a characteristic of early folk-songs that sometimes passages in them do not cohere. The set of pieces known as 'A Long Song Ballad' is an extreme example of the phenomenon. It is not clear whether the set is comprised of a) one long piece, b) two pieces, or c) three pieces. Following the Sung poetry critic Yen Yü, I have opted for the third possibility on the grounds that the three pieces read perfectly well as three independent songs, whereas they do not seem to cohere as a set, because each has a very different style and content. I have therefore placed the three pieces as separate songs in different chapters under the main themes which I believe they treat: immortality (no. 2), *carpe diem* (no. 1), and nostalgia (no. 3). Because the three have been linked as a set traditionally, one is obliged to speculate what the connection between the parts of the set might be. Perhaps the coordinating links are these: the last line of song no. 1 expresses the idea of growing old; song no. 2 is a short narrative in which longevity cults are mentioned; song no. 3 refers to pining, which conventionally makes a person grow older. I propose that the connection between the three songs or passages is the idea of growing old and that this idea is given three thematic treatments.[21]

This proposal is reinforced by the interpretation of the song title's meaning given by the third-century AD author Ts'ui Pao. He presents his interpretation after his discussion of funeral songs of the Han. He says, ' "Long Song" and "Short Song" tell of the length or brevity of human life', and he links his explanation to the hearse-pullers' songs (wan-ko), 'Dew on the Shallot' and 'Artemisia Village'. He confuses 'long' and 'short' with the human lifespan.[22] In fact, the title of the 'Long Song' set is named for its pentasyllabic metre, not because of the meaning of the title or the length of the song itself. All three parts are pentasyllabic, except for the penultimate line of song no. 2 which is tetrasyllabic. (It is possible that one syllable is missing rather than that the line is intentionally irregular.) The designation long (ch'ang) contrasts with the short (tuan) tetrasyllabic metre of the Book of Poetry of the Chou era and some Han hymns.[23] No examples survive of anonymous Han 'A Short Song Ballad' titles, although some by known poets of the late Han are extant.[24] These pieces reveal that the late Han to post-Han poets interpreted 'short song' both as a meditation on the brevity of life *and* as being in the short tetrasyllabic metre.[25] Consequently, although Ts'ui Pao's post-Han explanation of the meaning of the two song titles, 'Long Song' and 'Short Song', is erroneous and the late to post-Han poets' use of 'Short Song' reflects this error, it is important to bear in mind that they firmly believed in this connection. In conclusion, in the late Han, the idea of long life, which is linked to the fear of growing old, must have been present in the mind of the maker of the 'Long Song' set under discussion.

This section of the set, or independent song, vividly expresses the immortality cult in Han China and contains some features which became associated with later religious Taoism. The fairy riding a white deer is an immortal who is leading an initiate to the gates of the cult Master. White is emblematic of death and of the west where one of the ancient paradises was believed to be. The fairy's long ears were a sign of wisdom.[26] The emblematic white denotes the west, a setting reinforced by Mount Hua, known as the Western Peak, and one of the Five Holy Peaks (modern Shensi). The mushroom and fungus were hallucinogenic and were believed to impart life-giving properties. The vivid colour imagery of the white deer and red fungus enhances the miracle described in the closure, where white hair turns black.[27]

The Ballad Tung Flees!

I long to make a pilgrimage up Mount Ts'ung-kao.
The mountaintop is treacherous, so hard.
I stare far at the Five Peak summits,
Of yellow gold are the turrets,
Jewels of many colours.
Now all I see is the fungus plant,
Leaves fallen in heaps.

One hundred birds flock,
Coming like smoke.
Mountain beasts magnificent:
Unicorn, antelope, chimera,
Jungle birds loudly screeching.
Now all I see are mountain beasts playfully tussling.

I come nearer to Jade Hall,
No more does my heart ache to rove back home.
A command comes from the gates:
'Man beyond the gates, what do you seek?'
What I say is:
'I wish to follow the holy Way, to seek only long life.'

The command comes: 'Mortal, obey my word!
Gather the sacred herb from the tip of Illusion Tree.'
A white hare kneels and pounds the herb, a toad makes a pill.
I offer up to the throne a jade dish:
'Eat this drug, it will make you divine.

Eat this drug divine,
You will all be happy.
May Your Majesty live to a ripe old age.
The Four Corners will bow their heads in awe before you.
A host of heavenly spirits will guard you on left and right.
May Your Majesty be protected as long as Heaven endures!'

This song narrates the initiation of an unknown person connected with the Han court into an immortality cult. As in the preceding song, the initiate ascends a mountain (the site of Ts'ung-kao is not known). The Five Peaks viewed from its summit are the Five Holy Peaks: T'ai in Shantung, Heng in Hunan, Hua in Shensi, Heng (a different character) in Hopei, and Sung in Honan, representing the points east, south, west, north, and central, respectively, in the ancestral heartland of China. The pilgrim admires the jewelled abode of the immortals and sees the magic fungus, which is ripe for gathering. The second stanza pictures a mountain scene imbued with the divine and the marvellous, a scene of magnificence and of harmony where beasts play instead of preying on each other.[28] The pilgrim approaches the gates of the adept and he says the ritual words of the initiation. He is granted his wish to enter the company of those seeking long life, and the symbols of regeneration, the white hare and the toad, prepare the immortality drug for him.[29] At this point the narrative shifts from the account of the pilgrim to an eulogy of the reigning monarch. The emperor is promised longevity, even eternal life, happiness, victory over neighbouring states, and the protection of guardian spirits until the end of time. The dénouement of the song closely resembles that of 'Up the Mound'.

The word 'Flees!' in the title is a misnomer. It came to be applied to the piece in the post-Han era only by association with another song title, which was originally an innocent song adapted by political commentators to serve as a prophecy (see p. 111). The song *Tung t'ao ko* contained in its title a pun on the word *t'ao*, which can mean peach or flee. Peach symbolized immortality in the Han. The Queen Mother of the West was fabled to have peaches which conferred everlasting life and which only formed after several millennia. Peach is connected with the other meaning of flee in the pun on *t'ao*. The link is clarified by reference to the Han text, *Exoteric Commentary on the Han School Text of the Book of Poetry (Han shih wai chuan)*, attributed to Han Ying (*fl.* 150 BC). In a passage from its Chapter 10, it is related that an old man with a peach wand responds to the questions of Duke Huan of Ch'i in the Chou era by explaining that peach is a pun for *wang*, to be destroyed, lost. In his note to this passage the translator, James R. Hightower, comments, 'As the word is a homophone of "to expel" [*t'ao*], peach wood was used to expel [*sic*] noxious influences.'[30]

Because of the elaborate pun, the original song was interpreted as a portent predicting that the Latter Han dictator, Tung Cho, would in the end be defeated and be forced to *flee* the capital city. The song proved particularly attractive because of a second pun on the name Tung Cho, which is written with the same character as Tung in the song's title. The double pun's efficacy is evident in the fact that each line of the song is followed by the refrain *Tung t'ao*, meaning in terms of the political interpretation 'Tung [Cho] flees!' In the third century AD, Ssu-ma Piao wrote a work entitled 'Treatise on the Five Elements' in which he catalogued historical events which had been 'foretold' by the early prophetic songs sung by innocent children. The song *Tung t'ao*, he wrote, refers to the dictator, Tung Cho. Since then the song lost whatever original meaning it had and became what its political interpreter said it was. The character *t'ao* = peach of the original was changed to *t'ao* = flee in the song title.

Another titled existed, *Tung t'ao hsing*, which I translate as the '*Tung t'ao* Ballad'. Its earliest recording is by Shen Yüeh in the fifth century AD in his 'Treatise on Music'. He lists there the title 'Tung Peach *hsing* = ballad', 'I Long to Make a Pilgrimage'. And this is the way Wu Ching (AD 670–749) lists it.[31] But by Kuo Mao-ch'ien's time the inevitable confusion surrounding the correct character for *t'ao* led him to list both the song (*ko*) and ballad (*hsing*) titles with the character *t'ao* = flee, and the practice endured. The correct solution is to reject the compounded error and restore *both* titles to their pristine meaning of 'Tung Peach'. The word 'Tung', in my view, is a surname (by an accident of history the same as the late Han dictator's); significantly, it occurs in connection with literary pieces on the theme of immortality.[32] 'The Ballad' version of the title, 'I Long to Make a Pilgrimage', is clearly based on the theme of immortality.[33] I propose that 'The Song' version, 'Born into a Happy World', shares the same theme. If that song (presented on pp. 111–12) lost its politicized refrain, it would read as a narrative about a man who had every joy life had to offer and yet decided to abandon the world and become an immortal.

The Song of Tung Peach

> He was born into a happy world,
> He roved through the city's four quarters.
> He enjoyed blessings from Heaven,
> Girdled with gold dark red was he.
> He showed his gratitude
> As he prepared carriage and riders.
> Soon to set off
> To the main house he bade farewell.
> As he left West Gate
> He gazed on palace and hall,
> Stared at the capital city.
> The sun was dying at night,
> His heart was broken with sorrow.

The changes in translation reflect the elasticity with which Chinese verse originals may be treated; the changes emphasize the narrative of the 'revised version'. It is of course possible that the refrain existed in the original, reading 'Tung Peach' as a chorus rather than 'Tung flees!'. I present the reconstituted piece only as a hypothesis.

The King of Huai-nan Ballad

The King of Huai-nan
Is himself said to be honoured:
Hundred foot high mansions reach the sky,
In his rear courtyard a carved well, its crib made of silver,
A gold bucket's pure white rope draws up cold frost,
Draws up cold frost
For young boys to drink,
Young boys of tender grace, so worthy,
Lift their voice in sad song, music pierces the skies.
I want to ford the river, river without a bridge.
I long to become two brown swans, return to my old hometown,
Return to my old hometown,
Enter my village;
To wander through my old hometown
Wounds my body endlessly.
Colourful dance, marvellous sounds, they all soothe me.
I wander through mulberry and catalpa trees, drift beyond the skies.

The King of Huai-nan referred to in this ballad was Liu An of the Former Han who died in 122 BC. He was the grandson of the founder of the Han Dynasty. The title, King of Huai-nan, had been created early in the Han in 199 BC, during the fourth year of Emperor Kao-tsu's reign.[34] Liu An was an adept in magic and alchemy. His thoughts and ideas are believed to have been committed to the *Huai-nan Tzu*, an eclectic philosophical work. According to legend the Han Emperor Wu asked Liu An for his secret recipes for immortality but was refused. In a rage he was about to force the king, his relative, to commit suicide, but he heard about it and vanished.[35] The first half of the ballad, in fact, describes some cult practices of the immortality adept.

The structure of the piece seems to consist of two parts. The first sets the scene in the rear courtyard of the king's mansion compound. The 'rear' usually denotes the residence of the ladies of the household and the harem of a wealthy person. The setting therefore introduces into the immortality cult of the king, the sexual aspect with which some cults were associated.[36] The scene is specifically set in that part of the courtyard where the well is sited. Again, in erotic poetry this scene had erotic implications.[37] In the Han ballad, drawing pure frost is a special rite, and the action also serves to set the time of the ballad in autumn or winter. The frost is given to the king's young boys to drink as the drink of immortals, the purest essence of the skies. The youthfulness of the king's choir relates to an important aspect of the Chinese pursuit of immortality: the ideal is never to grow old, but to possess eternal youth. The innocence of the boys is emphasized besides their extreme youth;

they are in a state of almost divine grace. Their song rises to the sky; it is a sad song, perhaps full of regret for being mortal and for not attaining the perfect state.

The lines which begin with 'I want to ford the river' to the end of the piece might be the text of the choir's song. Or they may express the thoughts of the king in his pursuit of immortality. 'Ford the river' is a cliché for reclusion deriving from the encounter between Confucius' disciple and two recluses described in the *Analects*. Confucius asked his disciple to ask the two recluses where the ford was in that part of the district and they replied that he should know where it was, since he was a sage. 'To ask about the ford' became a stock phrase meaning reclusion.[38] On the other hand, the 'river' might also refer to the River of Heaven, or the Milky Way, which according to legend has no bridge. This interpretation of the phrase links up with the last words of the previous line, 'pierces the skies'. Therefore, both reclusion and the celestial abode of immortals might be implicit in 'I want to ford the river'.

If we take the next lines as part of the choir's song, they represent the theme of nostalgia hinted at in the line about the river. The passage is remarkably similar to the central passage of 'Mount Wu is High' in Chapter Nine below. Yet there is one line which points toward a more literary allusion. In the passage, the line 'Wounds my body endlessly' suggests an echo of 'Encountering Sorrow' in *Songs of Ch'u*. In that elegiac poem a courtier seeks to flee a corrupt world and follow the way of immortals. He is permitted to ascend to Heaven, but at the last moment turns to look back at his old home:

> But when I had ascended the splendour of the heavens,
> I suddenly caught a glimpse below of my old home.
> The groom's heart was heavy and the horses for longing
> Arched their heads and refused to go on.[39]

This literary allusion links the theme of immortality cults and the theme of nostalgia in the ballad. It is significantly similar to the closure of my reconstituted version of 'The Song of Tung Peach'. The final couplet of the 'King of Huai-nan' song describes a vision of paradise, which is often alluded to through divine dance and celestial music. It also contains a prayer for immortality which is answered in the aerial flight through the sacred trees of mulberry and catalpa.[40]

The ballad is structured on two main tropes, a cluster of images relating to the sky and the device of repetition. The images include the sky itself, mentioned three times, the colours silver and white, frost, the well, music in the skies, the allusion to the River of Heaven, swans flying, and the trees of paradise. The repetition involves key phrases: sky, cold frost, young boys, river, return to the old home town, and wandering.

The content of the ballad identifies its position in Kuo Mao-ch'ien's anthology among song-texts for dances.[41]

Walking out of Hsia Gate, A Ballad

A by-way leads past an empty hut;
The good man always lives alone.
At death he attains the way of holy immortals,
On high he leans up against the heavens.
After he visits our Royal Father and Mother,
He goes to live in the folds of Mount T'ai.
Going four or five leagues away from heaven
He meets on his way Red Pine for companion.
'Hold the reins, drive for me!
Take me up to Heaven to roam!'
Up in Heaven what is there?
Rows and rows of planted white elm,
Cassia trees lining the way are growing,
Green dragons face to face bow down.

In this piece, the way to immortality is posited on a life of holy seclusion. A hidden path and empty hut are emblematic of the recluse. The word 'empty' indicates that the recluse has died. The material aspects of immortality cults are absent; the emphasis is on holiness. The 'way' of holy immortals is the *Tao*, which gave its name to the philosophy Taoism. His life on earth having been devoted to goodness and purity, the holy man ascends to the heavens when he is perfect, and becomes an immortal beyond the human sphere. The words 'he leans against the heavens' denote a ritual gesture of those who have become immortal, showing through their familiarity with the celestial sphere that they are included as equals among the spirits of the sky.

The first deities the recluse meets are the sovereigns of heaven, Wang Fu Mu, which I have translated as 'Royal Father and Mother'. The phrase may refer jointly to the Royal Lord of the East and Queen Mother of the West, or to some vaguely conceived idea of a celestial matriarch and patriarch.[42] Mount T'ai was one of the Five Holy Peaks. It will become the holy man's new home among the immortals. On his way there he meets a famous immortal, Red Pine, red suggesting the colour cinnabar used in alchemy and the pine denoting constancy and long life. He asks the immortal to show him around the heavens. The description of the paradise in the last quatrain is introduced by a question and answer formula. The names of the trees, white elm and cassia, are also the names of stars. Cassia usually has the connotation of red because of its brilliant foliage. The green dragon is also the name of a star; it is, besides, the emblematic guardian of the eastern sky. The closure of the piece is therefore full of brilliant colour symbolism.

Apart from the balladic formula of question and answer, this piece contains other balladic features. Strong colours in the description is one recurring trait. The use of direct speech is another. The narrative line is also typical. There is, too, use of commonplace expression. This occurs in the last quatrain. Except for a slight change in the last line, this closure is the same as the quatrain which opens 'The Lunghsi Ballad', in Chapter Eleven. Its appearance in 'Hsia Gate' is intrinsic to the narrative move-ment of the ballad on immortality which culminates in a vivid description of the stars in the heavens. In 'Lunghsi' the quatrain has clearly been borrowed to project an ironic viewpoint.

The lack of cohesion between the title and the contents reveals another common feature of some Han songs and ballads. Hsia Gate, the western gate of Loyang city, does not feature in the piece. It is possible that the title originally belonged to another, earlier song, and either its content resembled this narrative, or parts of it were borrowed to make a new composition. The fluctuation of titles in the repertoire is evident from this example, since in some collections 'Walking out of Hsia Gate, A Ballad' is known as 'The Lunghsi Ballad', a confusion which appears in Wu Ching's critical work.[43] The case of 'The Ballad of the Prefect of Goosegate' is similar in this respect. In the confusion between 'Hsia Gate' and 'Lunghsi' we at least know that the identifying link between the two pieces is the quatrain they both share.[44]

An Old *Yen* Song

> Today let's be happy in our love,
> As together we step through cloudy space.
> Lord of the Skies brings out fine wine,
> Earl of the River brings forth carp,
> Green Dragon spreads out mats before us,
> White Tiger holds the wine jug,
> Southern Dipper works the drum and zither,
> Northern Dipper blows the reed-organ.
> Heng O drops down her bright earring,
> Weaver Girl offers her jade girdle gems.
> Through blue-rose mists drift eastern songs,
> On clear winds float western lays.
> Sheeting dew forms curtains,
> Shooting stars escort our rolling carriage.

This song is made up of a variety of themes and components. The first couplet voices a *carpe diem* theme which is sustained by the rest of the narrative. Within this couplet, line 2 and throughout, appears the theme of mystical travel of immortals. In the central passage the pantheon of the gods of the old stellar mythology is presented. Also, the theme of epicureanism, an aspect of the *carpe diem* theme, is put forward. The motif of sexual pleasure is introduced in the second half with the moon goddess Heng O (or Ch'ang O) and Weaver Girl (stars in Vega and Lyra), culminating in the closure which describes two lovers riding in a carriage to their celestial bedroom enclosed with mist and dew. The theme of universal harmony is developed throughout the piece, with the gods preparing a (?marriage) feast, celestial music, and the natural elements responding sympathetically to the lovers or bridal pair. It is not clear who the couple are—the anonymous singer and the moon or star goddess, or the singer and his earthly mistress.

The themes are mostly presented through concrete images of the divine. The Lord of the Skies belongs to Chou mythology, and is particularly associated with the religion of ancient Ch'u. He might be the same deity as 'The Lord within the Clouds' whose praises are sung in the 'Nine Songs'. Earl of the River, Ho-po, is also hymned in that song-cycle.[45] Green Dragon and White Tiger are stars symbolizing east and west respectively. The Dipper is also a star, denoting plenty. Heng O was the wife of the legendary ruler Yi the Archer. She stole the drug of immortality which he obtained from Queen Mother of the West, ate it, and was assumed into the moon. The gesture of dropping one earring is erotic. Weaver Girl's usual role in stellar mythology is the tragic lover parted from her beloved, Herdboy, and meeting him only once a year on the Seventh Night of the Seventh Month. Here she seems to have forgotten him and is paying attention to the singer (or so he flatters himself). Her legend has also been modified to merge with another concerning two water-nymphs who gave their girdle gems to a man named Cheng Chiao-fu as a love-token. Again, the male object of affection, Cheng Chiao-fu, has been omitted from the narrative. What binds these diverse themes and images together is the strict parallelism of the main body of the song.

There is a striking contrast between the point of view of this song and that of the Han hymns. This song is about the gods, not for them. In making the gods of the old mythology play a subservient role toward the human lovers of the song, belief in the gods is weakened. The tone is impertinent and playful. Its irreverence marks the transition of the theme of immortality from ritual to romance.[46]

CHAPTER FOUR

Carpe Diem

Like the imperative of Horace's *'Carpe diem'*, or 'Seize the day!', Chinese verse on this theme is full of injunctions, often repeated to convey a sense of urgency.[1] And as with the Latin word *carpe* the anonymous Chinese song-makers and balladeers rejected moderation: 'Exhaust our hearts with the deepest pleasure!' The Chinese idiom also resembles the Horatian phrase in its use of the word 'day', stressing the immediate present: 'If today I don't make merry,/ How long must I wait?'

Implicit in this urgency is the idea that time is swiftly passing: 'Hasten to make merry!/ Hasten to make merry—/ While there's time'. The theme of *tempus fugit* suggests that it is not momentary time which is slipping away, but life itself. The singers repeatedly remind us: 'Man's life does not last a century', and 'Life is like a spark glimpsed when stone is struck'.

The fear of time passing stems from the singers' awareness of the sadness of the human condition. They exclaim: 'How can I go on in sad despair,/ Must I keep waiting for next year?' Although their melancholy is said to be overwhelming, they do not elaborate on the gloom which palls their life. They suggest that there is a way to 'dispel dull care', through pleasure, through exhausting the senses so as to obliterate the grief engendered by man's mortality. The pleasures they advocate are earthly and aesthetic: intoxicating liquor, rich food, music, song, and dance.

The context of these songs on the *carpe diem* theme is the feast.[2] The inspiration for this probably derives from some passages in the *Book of Poetry*. One such passage connects the theme of the feast with the threat of death:

> death and burial may come any day,
> only a short time can we see each other;
> may we enjoy the wine this evening;
> the lord feasts![3]

Yet, as another passage in this classic makes clear, the Chou *carpe diem* poets do not advocate the extremes of the Han singers; caution is advised in this passage:

> The cricket is in the hall,
> the year draws to a close;
> if we do not now enjoy ourselves,
> the days and months will be passing by;
> but may we not be too joyous,
> may we only think of our positions;
> in our love of pleasure, may we not go to excess;
> the good gentleman is circumspect.[4]

Another aspect of the theme which the Han songs share with the Chou poems is the felicitation formula. In the Chou anthology there are several poems, not on the *carpe diem* theme, in which the head of a household gives a feast in honour of the clan ancestors and is toasted by his guests with felicitations like, 'may the lord have a myriad years', or '(Heaven) rewards him with increased felicity;/ a longevity of a myriad (years) without limit!'[5] The felicitation formula expresses itself in the Han songs in this way: 'If you serenely nourish your bodily vigour,/ Till one hundred years you'll last, to a great old age!' Longevity in the Han was believed to be not a reward from Heaven, but the result of cultist regimens. There is another major difference between the setting of the feast in Chou and Han pieces which share either the *carpe diem* theme or the felicitation formula: with the Chou, the setting is the ancestral feast; with the Han, the feast is unspecified and the singer's preoccupation is not with the clan, but with himself as an individual.

As the Han felicitation formula cited above indicates, there are traces of the cult of immortality in the songs on this theme. In comparison with the songs in the preceding chapter, however, the singer rejects the promise of immortality as a faded dream of a past era. In 'How Wonderful!' the singer passes through the hills of immortality, but does not stop there; and he rejects the elixir offered by a famous immortal. In 'West Gate' the singer admits, 'Since I am not immortal Wang Tzu-ch'iao,/ To count on such a lifespan is hard to expect.' He repeats his admission to emphasize the hard truth. Abandoning the false hope of immortality, the singer of the *carpe diem* songs turns to the solace of earthly, sensual pleasures: 'Playing my lute, wine, song!'

The rejection of immortality does not stop at mere awareness of a bankrupt idea. The *carpe diem* singer rejects the idea that there is a life after death in the religious sense. He abandons the comfort of religion and the consolation of philosophy. Even the Taoist doctrine of resignation in the face of life's troubles finds no adherents here. The singer seeks to annul the past and the future. He refuses to pursue ambition, desiring neither wealth nor fame. The future is dreaded: 'The days to come will be so hard'. He urges his listeners not to shore up for the future, but to spend in the here and now: 'To hoard wealth, to begrudge spending/ Will just make posterity laugh out loud!' This attitude runs counter to traditional socio-ethical values, for it severs the link between himself and his ancestral past, and the bond between himself and his descendants. In one version of a song, the singer seems to be deserting his young family. 'I look back at my yellow-beak babes below'.

Rejecting so much of their tradition, the *carpe diem* singers still have some truths to cling to: the end of human life is extinction through obliterating death; the world exists by chance and not by religious or metaphysical design; life is by its nature a melancholy business; and the way to secure a happy life is through the pleasures of the senses. The pursuit of pleasure is objective, its function is to delete the pain of existence. But because its purpose is so paradoxical, pleasure is tinged with joylessness. Knowing this, the pleasure-seeker is doomed to a feverish pursuit of earthly delight, the efficacy of which can never finally convince. There is a certain courage in the *carpe diem* singers' bleak view of life. At the same time its very bleakness arouses an acute sense of anxiety.

How Wonderful! A Ballad

The days to come will be so hard,
My mouth parched, lips dry.
Today let's delight in our love,
Let's all be merry and gay.

I pass through famous hills,
Fungus whirls, whirls.
The immortal Wang Ch'iao
Offers a pill of the drug.

I pity my sleeves so short—
Though tucked in, my hands feel cold.
I'm ashamed not to have Ling Ch'e
Who repaid Chao Hsüan.

The moon sinks, Orion slants,
Northern Dipper tilts.
Close friends are at my gates;
Though hungry, there's not enough for a meal.

Happy days grow still fewer,
Wretched days grow cruelly more.
With what to forget despair?
Playing my lute, wine, song!

For the eight lords of Huai-nan
The Main Way holds no difficulties:
Driving a carriage of six dragons
They rove and play in cloudy limits.

The song opens with a proverb expressing fear of the future.[6] This fear leads the singer to adopt a hedonist solution to life's problems. The major *carpe diem* theme is stated in the second couplet and is picked up again in stanza five. After the first quatrain stanza, however, the song shifts abruptly to another, contradictory theme, the cult of immortality. The singer describes his visit to the famous hills where the immortals are. He sees the drug of immortality and its motion seems to mesmerize him. He meets Wang Ch'iao, the immortal, who offers him the prepared drug.[7] The song shifts abruptly again with the next stanza to a plaint of poverty and misery. The singer alludes to one Ling Ch'e, an historic figure of the seventh century BC who was rescued from starvation by Chao Hsüan. Later, in 607 BC, when Chao Hsüan's lord, Duke Ling of Chin, tried to kill Chao in an ambush at a state banquet, Ling Ch'e was one of the ambush soldiers and he helped Chao Hsüan to escape. The singer's plaint therefore includes shame as well as misery, for he cannot repay a debt of honour.

Stanza four shifts once again to night. The second couplet of this quatrain is problematic.[8] It is not clear why the meal cannot be taken. I have translated the line to mean that there is not enough food, because the singer-host is impoverished. The line could also mean that there is not enough time for a meal. Or, as Diény translates it, 'Their [good friends'] hunger does not warrant a feast.' In a note he supplements this interpretation: 'Though they are hungry—it is late—their appetite is not up to a feast.' He suggests an alternative reading: 'Though they are starving, they are excluded from the feast.'[9] My translation is intended to refer back to the singer's plaint of poverty in stanza three and to anticipate it in stanza five. Whatever the meaning of this line, it is important for one thing: it introduces the idea of the feast that is central to the *carpe diem* theme, and this theme reasserts itself in the fifth stanza, having lain dormant since the first: 'With what to forget despair?/ Playing my lute, wine, song!'

The end of the song reverts to the immortality theme of the second stanza. The singer refers to the early Han adept, the King of Huai-nan, Liu An, who, according to legend, disappeared with eight lords among his retainers and became immortal.[10] The 'Main Way' is Taoist philosophy which at this point in its evolution is becoming tinged with cultism. It is possible that this song has a somewhat different ending, in which the singer voices the wish to become a bird to join the immortals in the sky, or to have freedom as birds have in flight: 'Like those winged birds / That sometimes fly across the sky.'[11]

In his discussion of this song Diény notes that its anarchic design is counterbalanced by a perfect regularity of rhyme, stanzaic length, and metre. The metre is tetrasyllabic. Each stanza contains meaning that is sufficient to itself. The 'anarchy' Diény speaks of lies in the lack of apparent connecting tissue between the stanzas. He suggests that a melodic line using musical schemes and formulas would no doubt, in performance, have imposed logic and coherence on the song as a whole.[12]

Yü Kuan-ying, on the other hand, classifies this as a feasting song, and attempts to order the random statements by treating the stanzas as conventions of the form. Stanza one in his view is a host's exhortation to his guests to be happy; stanza two is the host's hymn to long life; stanza three is the guests' statement of their penury and shame at being unable to repay their host's generous hospitality; stanza four is the host's observation that the festive night is ending and his invitation to the guests to stay with him; it is also his statement that he is so happy that he forgets to eat or sleep; stanza five is the guests' response as they compare their host with the King of Huai-nan and wish him long life. Yü reads the piece as a feasting song with conventions of compliments and responses between host and guests. Certainly this genre of poem was current in the late Han era.[13]

What is clear is that the two themes of immortality and *carpe diem* coincide in this song, as they do in other songs in this chapter, and both themes are given an extra dimension of meaning by the setting of the feast. The two themes are present without one dominating. They are intellectually incompatible, for if one truly believes in the possibility of immortality one does not then simultaneously, without risk of contradiction, admit the impossibility of the afterlife. I would suggest that the singer is attracted to both ideas, and cannot resolve the incompatibility. He cannot forsake one without the other. I would conclude that as such this song stands midway between the two intellectual trends of the belief in immortality and hedonism. The singer's adherence to both ideas results in the song's ambiguities and artistic tension.[14]

A Long Song Ballad, no. 1

Green, green mallow in the garden,
Morning dew awaits the sun to dry.
Sunny spring spreads kind moisture,
All nature grows shining bright.
I always fear when autumn's season comes:
Burned yellow blooms and leaves will fade.
'One hundred rivers moving east to sea,'
When will they ever westward turn again?
If while we're young and strong we don't strive hard,
When we're grown old, no use whining then!

This song forms part of the set already discussed in Chapter Three, of which parts two and three appear in that chapter and Chapter Nine. I have included the first part of the song title here not so much because it elaborates the *carpe diem* theme, but because it contains concepts intrinsic to the theme and in its closure it echoes 'A *Yen* Song, The Whenever Ballad' later in this chapter.

The structure of the song rests on the analogy drawn between the seasonal cycle and the life of man. A series of natural images stresses the concept of the beauty of young growing plants which inevitably wither and decay. The first quatrain is almost a hymn to spring. The green mallow in a spring garden is soaked with nourishing dew. Yet within this lyrical passage two images anticipate a sombre view of nature and life. The image of the mallow denotes vulnerability and susceptibility to change, for it depends on the sun for its existence, yet that same sun will kill. The image of dew is also ambiguous and denotes vulnerability for it nourishes plants yet will evaporate in the sun. Numerous songs and poems of this period use the trope of evaporating dew. One of the most famous is a burial song opening with the image: 'On the shallot the dew—/ How easily it dries!'[15] The third couplet develops the sensory image of dryness leading to decay. Autumn's frosts and searing winds scorch and discolour plants which had seemed everlasting in spring.

The next couplet continues the dewy image with a proverb about the flow of rivers.[16] The ideas implicit in it are that the flow follows a destined course and serves as a metaphor for passing time. It acts as a transition between the sustained nature imagery of the first passage and the comment on human life of the final passage. The song's analogy between nature and man is posited on a linear progression through the seasons, spring and autumn serving for the course of the calendrical year and, by extension, the four ages of man: youth, manhood, old age, and death. The closure contains an exhortation to the young generation, based on the meditation on the meaning of existence lyrically presented through the earlier analogy. The singer urges the young to achieve something worthwhile while they are young. He contemptuously dismisses the bleatings of those who have failed to be wise. The theme of *tempus fugit* predominates throughout the song; it colours the analogy and underscores the final exhortation. While the pursuit of pleasure is not advocated, the temporal aspect and the tone of anxiety which inform other hedonistic songs are clearly articulated.[17]

Song of Melancholy

Hardly had I known brief happiness,
When I fell into the world's ambush;
I have met with these hundred troubles,
Alone in bitter venom,
In sad grief hard to bear.
I stare far at polar Ch'en star;
Skies brighten, the moon travels on.
Melancholy comes crowding my heart.
Who of those facing me would know?

Sad, sad my many pensive cares,
Grieved, grieved I am restless.
Fortune, misfortune are not defined.
I just remember the men of old
Who gave up their rank to farm for themselves.
If I follow my own desire,
That way I would calm myself.
Since finding refuge in these rustic hills
I have guarded this one glory.

Twilight autumn's fierce winds rise.
Westward I plod to the huge sea,
But my heart will not rest.
I hold my robe, rise, stare into night:
Northern Dipper aslant,
Starry Han shining on me,
Then it goes, goes, leaving myself to me.
I support my two kin,
I could tell of my burdens.

Failure, success are acts of Heaven.
Wise men do not despair,
So most bring few troubles on themselves.
Calm in poverty, happy in the right Way,
They imitate yon Chuang Chou.

84

Those who leave behind a name are honoured,
With Tzu-hsi they roam together;
Two sages of the past,
Their names bequeathed one thousand autumns.

Drink wine! Sing! Dance!
Not be merry—why wait longer?
How wonderful! Radiant I gaze on sun and moon,
Sun and moon galloping forward.
Luckless we stumble in this world.
To have, to have not,
To covet wealth, begrudge spending—
How foolish this all is!
Life is like a spark glimpsed from flint-stone,
Our dwelling in the world, in the end, how long can it last?
We must be happy, just be merry, amuse ourselves!
Exhaust our hearts with the deepest pleasure!
If you nourish serenely your bodily vigour,
Till one hundred years you'll last, to a great old age!

This is not an easy song to follow, because so many themes and sentiments are expressed in a haphazard and repetitive manner. If we take each component as it occurs, we may come closer to understanding the song's random structure. The first line states the *carpe diem* theme, which is resumed in the final passage. The rest of stanza one and stanza two express the speaker's deep anxiety and unhappiness in language reminiscent of the pessimistic elegies of *Songs of Ch'u*. The indeterminate nature of his agony of mind is a convention of the Ch'u elegy. Implicit in the genre are these motifs: the persona is a man in political exile; he has been slandered at court; he is obsessed with the evanescence of his youth; and he is convinced of the purity of his ideals in an evil world. It is possible that the same motifs are to be understood in this Han song. The next couplet takes up the theme of time passing with the image of the moon's swift journey through the sky. The moon might also serve as a symbol of pure idealism. The celestial imagery of the polar Ch'en star suggests the remoteness of an impersonal world, silent and impassive, contrasting with the seething emotions of the speaker. The first stanza closes with a repetition of his melancholy mood and solitary suffering.

The second stanza opens with another statement of his melancholy. The third line states the law of chance. The speaker recalls idealists of the past, recluses like Hsü Yu, Ch'ang Chü and Chieh Ni who rejected political life and devoted themselves to farming. Political idealism and reclusion merge in the last couplet. The speaker says that he has become a recluse and is nurturing his ideals, metaphorically termed 'this one glory', a floral metaphor in the manner of the Ch'u elegy.[18]

The third stanza opens with a panorama of blazing skies, stormy winds, and a vast sea, providing a majestic background for the moral heroism of the persona. The gloomy image, 'Twilight autumn', central to the elegiac tone of the Ch'u pieces, develops the theme of time passing. In his despair he contemplates the sky again, searching for guidance and comfort. A brief moment of accord with the tranquil motion of the heavens soon passes. The persona introduces for the first time a small detail about his personal life, in contrast with the earlier generalities. He announces abruptly that he is maintaining his family (it is not clear whether this means his parents or his wife and children).[19]

In the next stanza the persona repeats the idea that fate is blind. He acknowledges that wisdom brings a measure of peace. He recalls exemplars of the past, men of noble ideals who were content to live in poverty, rather than sacrifice their principles. One famous example was Yen Hui, a favourite disciple of Confucius.[20] He is not named, however; instead, surprisingly, the song refers to Chuang Chou, or Chuang Tzu, one of the founders of Taoism, the philosophical system antagonistic to Confucianism. The other example is Tzu-hsi whose identity is not known.[21] In this merging of Confucian principles with Taoist exemplars one discerns the incipient elements of the system of thought known as Neo-Taoism which developed in the post-Han era.[22]

The final section of the song reverts to the *carpe diem* theme voiced in line 1. The persona again ponders the mystery of the heavenly bodies and meditates on the passage of time. He expresses his pessimistic view of life dominated by random chance. He says that the only response is to seek pleasure and spend money on earthly enjoyment. The temporal aspect implicit in his contemplation of the heavens is pronounced more dramatically with a simile of a spark of light. The pleasure principle is also stated more urgently, with the advice to dismiss moderation and to obliterate pain. The song closes with a felicitation formula in which the singer wishes himself and his audience longevity.

The contradictions in this song's themes and moods may be judged as an indication of compositional flaws. Yet I would suggest a more sympathetic reading which interprets the ambiguities as a mirror of the singer's anxiety and as a reflection of the fusion of disconnected belief systems taking place in the Han. The Taoist ideal of reclusion, the Confucian concept of moral example and rectitude, the Yangist idea of 'Nurture of Life', the nihilism of the concept that life is governed by random chance, the pessimism of the view that life is but a brief moment signifying nothing, the *carpe diem* concept, and the longevity cult all constitute philosophical ideas floating around in Han society. If there is a logic to the song, it would appear that the singer turns these alternative ideas over in his mind, and while not entirely rejecting them decides to devote himself to one, the pursuit of pleasure. In this song the grief which impels the singer to 'the deepest pleasure' is amplified more than in any other in this selection. In 'West Gate' this effusion of grief has become eclipsed to 'it': 'I pace and think of it.'

There is another version of this song. I have not reproduced it here in translation because it does not differ fundamentally from the other, compared with some title versions I have included. Both versions are fifty lines long and arranged into four stanzas of nine lines each, with a finale (?tsü) of fourteen lines. The metres of both are predominantly tetrasyllabic, but where the syllabic line changes, the two versions diverge. In the version I have translated, the last hexasyllabic six lines are replaced in the other version by tetrasyllabic lines. The diction of the two versions varies; there are 21 variants. There are also extra phrases in each, the translated version being more expanded than the other. The substance of the two remains very similar.[23]

A *Yen* Song, The Whenever Ballad

Whenever will I be quite happy
Without any worries?
All I must do is drink strong wine,
Roast the fat ox.

The eldest brother has two-thousand-bushel rank,
The middle brother is robed in sable furs.

The youngest brother, though without a post,
Saddles his horse and gallops, gallops,
Having fun in company with prince, lord, high official.

All I must do is stay in halls of prince and lord,
Be quite happy with dice and toss-pot,
Seated at the gameboard.

For young men living in this world
Each must try hard;
Hurried on toward his twilight,
No one lingers long.

Youngsters clash with each other,
Coldness and bitterness always ensue.
Is violent rage worth the fight?
Midway I am parted from you.
I will curb myself, offer service to my lord,
I must not be remiss in rites and decorum.
I am shamed before blue-wave Heaven above,

I look back at my yellow-beak babes below.
What to do with my troubled, troubled heart?
Who can know of my lonely grief?

This song has the same title as the swan fable in Chapter Two, but its theme and structure are very different. In common with other *carpe diem* songs, its emotional mainspring is grief tinged with an awareness of time passing. The song appears to provide more background to the persona and more reasons for his intense grief than is usual in such pieces. After stating the *carpe diem* theme, one which is typically imbued with anxiety, the singer proceeds to describe three brothers in a family. We are not told whether they are his brothers, or the young masters of the household where he is employed, or an idealized family the singer dreams of belonging to. We learn that the family enjoys wealth, status, and happiness.[24] In the fourth stanza, the repetition of 'prince' and 'lord' appears to link the life of the youngest brother with the singer's own life. It is not specified whether the two young men are the same person. Or perhaps the youngest brother is the master, the singer the servant who must keep him company in his revels. Thus far, however, the motif of personal failure begins to emerge. The singer does not have a high official post, he does not wear furs, he does not ride with high society.

The fifth stanza develops this motif and introduces the theme of *tempus fugit*. The singer stresses that one must achieve something while one is young, and he makes his appeal to the young generation as if his own chance has eluded him. This passage is similar to the closure of 'A Long Song Ballad, no. 1'. The final passage continues the account of young men in society first mentioned in stanzas two, three, and five. The youths of this passage seem to represent a more generalized concept than before. The first mention indicated young brothers in a family; the second mention referred to young men starting out in life in a generalized statement about a career and achievement; the third seems to continue the generalized statement, but leads into a personal, highly emotional passage about the singer's own life. We may take the link between these references as follows: the three brothers may be intended to serve as a model for a happy family free from strife and financial problems, a paradigm against which the singer's own circumstances may be measured. In this *tsü*-finale the singer implies that he has had a violent argument (?with his older brother), which has led to a permanent estrangement. There is a separation; the singer has to leave home. He decides to serve a lord with honour. Yet in making this decision he has to leave his young family of infants behind, causing him deep shame. He has no alternative because he is penniless. His misery is compounded by the awareness that no one can share his troubles.

This interpretation of the narrative line of the song is supported by references to commonplace phrases and similar passages in other Han songs.[25] The same *carpe diem* refrains recur in other songs in this chapter. The passage describing three brothers of a wealthy and successful family occurs in three other Han songs, 'They Met', 'In Ch'angan There is a Narrow Lane', and 'Cocks Crow', with the difference that the number of brothers is vague in all but the second song. The passage stating that the young must strive for success appears in 'A Long Song Ballad, no. 1', and the *tempus fugit* theme appears in all *carpe diem* songs. In the *tsü*-finale the phrase 'offer service to' occurs in 'Song of Melancholy'. The couplet, 'I am shamed . . . babes below,' occurs in both versions of 'East Gate', with some alterations in phraseology. The theme of quarrelling brothers in the final passsage of 'Cocks Crow' might be the same as this song's theme of quarrelling youths.

There is another perspective from which this song may be viewed. It is so similar to two versions of another Han song, 'West Gate', that it might even constitute a third version, with a different title. Accordingly, I have placed the three together. 'West Gate' develops the theme of *carpe diem* more fully. It lacks the passage about brothers in a wealthy family. The long version of 'West Gate' elaborates the *tempus fugit* theme more than the other two songs. The theme of poverty which is significant in 'A *Yen* Song' is reduced to a brief reference in the last line of the short version of 'West Gate'. The long version of 'West Gate' cynically refers to immortality, a reference lacking in the other two pieces. This recurrence of commonplace expression and similarities in theme and structure show how the Han song was constructed and perhaps will provide clues about the approximate dating of each of the three pieces.[26]

West Gate Ballad

long version

Leaving by West Gate
I pace and think of it:
If today I don't make merry,
How long must I wait?

So make merry!
Make merry we must while there's time!
Can I let cares overwhelm me?
Must I keep waiting for next year?

Drink strong wine!
Roast the fat ox!
Call for my heart's delight,
May be to dispel dull care.

Man's life does not last a century,
He ever nurses worries of one thousand years.
Morning is short and night is long,
Why not hold a candle and have fun?

Since I am not immortal Wang Tzu-ch'iao,
To count on such a lifespan is hard to expect.
Since I am not immortal Wang Tzu-ch'iao,
To count on such a lifespan is hard to expect.

Man's lifetime is not of metal or rock,
His destined years—what can he expect?
To hoard wealth, to begrudge spending
Will just make posterity laugh out loud!

This *carpe diem* song focusses on different aspects of time. The source of hedonism, personal grief and a vague effusion of sorrow, is eclipsed to the words 'think of it' and 'dull care' in stanzas one and three. The elision contrasts markedly with 'Song of Melancholy' which is dominated by the grief motif, as its title suggests. The temporal motif in 'West Gate' begins with the conventional *carpe diem* refrain linking pleasure with the immediate present, 'today'. As with other songs on this theme, the structure is based on a paradox: how to transmute grief into joy. Here the paradox is obliquely presented through the sombre connotations of the West Gate. Graveyard poetry of the Han often opens with the symbol of a gate, creating a boundary between the living world left behind at the city gate and the land of the dead beyond the city gate. Poem no. 13 of the 'Nineteen Old Poems' opens with this symbol: 'I drove my carriage from the upper East Gate,/ Stared far away at tombs north of the wall.' The symbol may derive from poem no. 141 of the *Book of Poetry*: 'By the gate of the graveyard there are plum trees;/ there are yao birds collecting on them.' Bernhard Karlgren glosses yao birds as 'birds of evil omen'.[27] The trope also appears in 'East Gate Ballad' with a similar connotation of profound despair. The paradox of the opening couplet in 'West Gate' develops through the song and is accompanied by a sense of urgency born of anxiety. The temporal motif expresses this disquiet: 'How long must I wait?' '. . . while there's time!' 'Must I keep waiting for next year?' The anxiety becomes meditative in the final stanzas. Human mortality is bleakly stated, 'Man's life does not last a century', and it is linked to the hyperbolic measure of human concerns, 'worries of one thousand years'. The singer refuses to accept that a century is in fact a long time to live. In his pessimism he eclipses the century to one day, repeating how short a time it is. Because daylight is so brief he urges his audience to extend time by lighting the darkness artificially. The extra time may then be enjoyed.

The singer attaches no other value to existence than the pursuit of pleasure. He rejects religion, philosophy, and social ethics. This rejection is emphasized in stanza five with the expression of doubt concerning the concept of immortality. Human mortality is underscored with the repetition of the idea expressed in stanza four; this time the idea is expressed through the metaphor 'Metal or rock', a symbol of permanence, and it is understood that humans will not last as long as insentient nature. The metaphor has an ironic ring, for it is often used in expressions of fame and achievement, such as a name that will endure like metal or rock. The singer dismisses the concept of achievement. Reminding himself and his audience of the brevity of life he urges them to spend not save, to enjoy the present, not shore up for the future. The song ends with a harsh warning, reflecting the singer's bleak view of life. He says anyone who has stinted himself will be ridiculed after his death by the relatives who will be the beneficiaries.

The structure of the song is remarkably free from the multiplicity of themes present in other songs in this chapter. Its logic is enhanced by the concentration on one major motif within the dominant *carpe diem* theme. This structural control is further emphasized by extensive use of repetition of key phrases: 'make merry', 'wait', 'time', 'dull care', followed by 'worries', 'life', 'lifespan', 'year', and 'lifetime'. These repetitions link the motifs of transience, anxiety, and sorrow. The commonplace expressions also link the song with others in the repertoire, enriching its significance. The first line echoes that of 'East Gate', intimating perhaps that poverty is one of the singer's 'worries of one thousand years'. The *carpe diem* expressions recur in other songs in this chapter. So do the gloomy meditations on the brevity of life. The final couplet closely resembles the couplet in the middle of the final passage of 'Song of Melancholy'. Against the enhancing familiarity of expression is set the courageous rejection of a dearly-held belief in immortality through drugs, and a belief in the afterlife: 'Since I am not immortal Wang Tzu-ch'iao'. This song deals with the *carpe diem* theme in a sophisticated manner. While it is firmly based on thematic conventions and it is full of commonplace expression, its innovative creativity is evinced by the firm control of theme and structure and by the hard courage of its anxiously expressed conviction.[28]

West Gate Ballad

short version

Leaving by West Gate
I pace and think of it:
If today I don't make merry,
How long must I wait?

Hasten to make merry!
Hasten to make merry—
While there's time!
Can sad despair overwhelm me?
Must I keep waiting for next year?
Brew fine wine!
Roast the fat ox!
Call for my heart's delight,
May be to dispel dull care.
Man's life does not last a century,
He ever nurses worries of one thousand years.
Morning is short alas! night is long,
Why not hold a candle and have fun?
Let's go and have fun, away! away! as clouds pass on.
But a worn cart, a lean nag, that's my lot!

This version is very close to the preceding one, yet its points of divergence, slight as they appear, reveal a quite different artistic intention. The first quatrain is the same. The second adds to the urgency that is present in the preceding version. The third quatrain repeats the other version's lines (I count from short version 'Brew fine wine!', acknowledging that the preceding passage has nine lines, one repeated). But one detail, 'Brew fine wine!' contrasts with the other version: it suggests epicureanism, against the hearty desire for oblivion implicit in 'Drink strong wine!'. The former relishes refinement, the latter seeks swift euphoria. The fourth quatrain again seems to be a verbatim repetition, except that the exclamation 'alas!' is inserted. This small detail is again significant: it accords with the epicureanism of 'Brew fine wine!' and reveals that the persona is a man of refined sentiment who perceives the tragedy of human mortality. The absence of the repeated refrain about Wang Tzu-ch'iao (in stanza five of the long version) suggests that by the time this song was being performed the audience no longer believed in the concept of immortality. All that is left of the concept in this short version is the brief allusion to immortals in the sky expressed in the words 'as clouds pass on'. This allusion may be no more than a nod in the direction of convention: hitherto *carpe diem* songs contained some reference to immortality.

The last line differs markedly from the long version. There the singer spoke of wealth, and urged his audience to squander it in a frenzy of pleasure. Here the singer ruefully admits to poverty; he is unable to pay for the fun he has been advocating. This closure completely reverses the expectations aroused by the song's earlier lines: 'Brew fine wine!/ Roast the fat ox!' and in so doing presents an ironic anticlimax.[29]

It is interesting to compare the treatment of the subject matter of these two versions of 'West Gate' with that of a poem in the formal style, the *ku-shih* no. 15 of the 'Nineteen Old Poems'. In its ten pentasyllabic lines the old poem compresses the substance of the two songs. As Diény points out in his analysis of the old poem and song versions, the formal elegance of the old poem is achieved at the expense of the song's vivacity, rhythmic variation, rhetoric, exclamations, repetition, and dramatic imperatives.[30]

'Nineteen Old Poems'

ku-shih no. 15

Life's years do not last a century,
Man ever nurses worries of one thousand years.
Morning is short alas! night is long,
Why not hold a candle and have fun?
Make merry we must while there's time!
Can I wait for next year?
The fool who begrudges spending
Will just make posterity laugh out loud!
The immortal Wang Tzu-ch'iao,
It's hard to expect to equal him.

CHAPTER FIVE

Burial Songs

Graveyard verse dominates the Han in a manner not experienced in the earlier tradition. One of its major themes, the melancholy awareness of mortality, also informs *carpe diem* verse. The difference between Han songs on this theme and earlier poems featuring death is that in the Han death was made the subject of the song, whereas in the Chou death was alluded to obliquely. In the Chou anthology, death seems to be almost a taboo topic. Even in war poems the poets turn away from those who fell in battle, focussing instead on the homesick survivors: 'When in the East we spoke of returning home,/ our hearts yearned for the West'.[1] Another important group of Chou poems dealing with the theme of death is devoted to ancestor worship. Yet in these the anonymous Chou poets emphasize the living descendants who pray for blessings from the seemingly living dead, their ancestors. The dead ones of the clan are treated with great respect; if they are feasted and entertained with due decorum they will bless their descendants. This positive relationship between the living and the dead is expressed in this passage from a Chou poem:

> The wild ducks are on the sands;
> the representative of the (dead) princes comes and feasts and finds it good;
> your wine is plentiful,
> your viands are fine;
> the representative feasts and drinks;
> felicity and blessings come and favour you.[2]

Apart from these two groups of poems on war and ancestor worship, death is absent from the Chou anthology.[3]

Death is also treated obliquely in the anthology of the late Chou, the *Songs of Ch'u*. Much critical discussion has been generated by the enigmatic ending of that anthology's pivotal poem, 'Encountering Sorrow' (*Li sao*).[4] A Ch'u courtier who has fallen from political grace and lives in exile declares at the end of the long narrative: 'I will go and join P'eng Hsien in the place where he abides'. P'eng Hsien was thought to be a shaman ancestor who lived in the Shang Dynasty prior to the Chou and committed suicide by drowning.[5] Some commentators have construed the words 'join P'eng Hsien' to mean that the courtier has followed him in suicide. On the other hand, the words may also mean that the courtier has decided to join the shaman as an initiate into the way of immortality, abandoning the world. Whatever the true meaning of the poem's ending, and if one takes it to refer to the suicide of the protagonist, the declaration cannot be said to form the poem's main subject. In the 'Nine Songs' of *Songs of Ch'u* appears a hymn to the fallen which sings the praises of patriots who died in battle, 'Heroes among the shades their valiant souls will be'.[6] Closer to the Han attitude to death are two shamanistic poems in the same anthology, in which a shaman summons the soul of a dying king back to the land of the living. His summons takes the form of a catalogue of the horrors the soul will meet in the land of the dead, followed by an enticing litany of the charms of life. The land of the dead is described as a wasteland full of monsters and ghouls:

O soul, come back! In the south you cannot stay.
There the people have tattooed faces and blackened teeth;
They sacrifice flesh of men, and pound their bones to paste.
There are coiling snakes there, and the great fox that can run a hundred
    leagues,
And the great Nine-headed Serpent who darts swiftly this way and that,
And swallows men as a sweet relish.
O soul, come back! In the south you may not linger.[7]

The closure of the poem seeks to persuade that earthly pleasures outweigh dark mortality.

While poets of the early Chou avoided the topic of death in its negative aspects, and poets of the late Chou presented death as a grim world to be evaded, Han poets and singers paused to reflect on its reality. Chia I of the early Han, for example, composed a poem reflecting on his own impending death in 'Prose Poem on the Owl', an elegy charged with the philosophical lyricism of Taoism.[8] Some poems in the 'Nineteen Old Poems' may be truly termed graveyard poetry of the Han, in which a person leaves the city gate and drives out to contemplate the distant burial mounds. These short poems ponder the enigma of death in lines of poignant grandeur.[9] The meditative strain in graveyard verse, then, is a phenomenon of the Han.

The few songs included in this chapter include the earliest surviving examples of anonymous funeral songs. Two are said to have been sung by those who pulled the hearse along the road to the cemetery. As such they may be seen as work-songs of undertakers in Han China.[10] They have some artistic merit. The anonymous singer no longer bothers to pose the questions of life and death which preoccupied the *carpe diem* singers. Death is now a fact of life. Its grimness is not mitigated by a promise of paradise. Yet the hearse-puller has a less grim view of life after death than the *carpe diem* singer, for he at least appears to believe in the hereafter.

The first song stresses the brevity of life and the finality of death—no one will 'come back'. The concept of immortality through elixirs and the like is clearly bankrupt. Ideas of transience and extinction are underscored by the ironic comparison of nature with man: nature enjoys an eternal cycle of return, man lives his allotted span and returns no more. The second song perhaps forms a sequel to the first, providing a stark view of the afterlife. The next world is seen as a village of the dead where no differentiation is made between those who had once been wise men or fools. Superimposed on this concept of equality is the idea of authority in the person of a King of Ghosts who rules the dead relentlessly, giving souls no respite from their travail.

The last song clearly belongs to a literary style with its historical references, its focus on political ethics, and its elaboration of the nature of personal honour. Here again the song presents a bleak view of life after death. For three heroes who have died for the sake of honour there is no reward in paradise. The immortality they have gained is through this song.

Funerary literature flourished in the centuries from the late Han onwards. By the sixth century AD the imperial anthology, *Anthology of Literature*, which was arranged on generic principles, identified no fewer than nine funerary genres out of 37 literary genres: the *lei* (dirge), *tiao* (condolence), *chi* (requiem), *pei* (threnody), *ai* (lament), *pei* (epitaph), *chieh* (columnar inscription), *chih* (necrology), and *chuang* (obituary).[11] Hearse-pullers' songs (*wan-ko*) do not themselves appear under any of these funerary genres, but are subsumed under the category of *yüeh-fu* songs and ballads, and then only in literary imitations. The humble form of the anonymous Han hearse-pullers' song was imitated in theme, if not in content, by the greatest poets of the late Han and post-Han era, men like Lu Chi, Ts'ao Ts'ao, Ts'ao P'ei, Ts'ao Chih, and T'ao Ch'ien.[12]

Dew on the Shallot

On the shallot the dew—
How easily it dries!
The dew dried at bright dawn once more will drop.
Man dies—once he's gone when will he come back?

There are a number of different traditional explanations about the circumstances of the composition of this funeral song. The earliest mention of the title occurs in a literary piece attributed to the third century BC Ch'u courtier, Sung Yü: 'There was a man who sang "Nether Village" and several thousand people joined in. But when he sang "Dew on the Shallot" only several hundred people joined in.'[13] Of course, there is no evidence that this title in the quotation refers to the same text as the song translated here. On the other hand, since the other title in the quotation, 'Nether Village', closely resembles the next song title, 'Artemisia Village', and since 'Dew on the Shallot' and 'Artemisia Village' have traditionally been associated together, the quotation's two titles might well refer to these two songs. This speculation is not fortified by the fact that a number of literary works have been dubiously attributed to Sung Yü which may well belong to a later date.

Two authors of the third century AD provide elaborate anecdotal background to the composition of the song, 'Dew on the Shallot'. Ch'iao Chou dates it from about 200 BC when T'ien Heng continued to reign as King of Ch'i in defiance of Emperor Kao-tsu, who had just established the Han Dynasty. The emperor invited T'ien Heng to court, but the latter committed suicide in his hometown before reaching the capital. His retainers did not dare to mourn him openly, so they composed this funeral song to express their grief.[14] Ts'ui Pao expands this story, adding that T'ien Heng's suicide was due to shame and that his retainers committed joint suicide at the grave of their lord. Ts'ui Pao also explains that Li Yen-nien, Master of Music to Emperor Wu of the Han, created a social distinction between 'Dew on the Shallot' and 'Artemisia Village', claiming that the first was to be sung when escorting the hearse of a king, duke, or aristocrat, the second when escorting the hearse of officials and commoners.[15]

Another commentator of the third century, Tu Yü, suggested an earlier origin of the genre of funeral song. The *Tso Commentary* narrates how Kung-sun Hsia, commander-in-chief of Ch'i state, when about to engage in battle in 484 BC against Lu and Wu states, ordered his soldiers to sing 'Sacrifice for the Dead' (*Yü-pin*). In his commentary on this classical text, Tu Yü notes that this title was 'a song for escorting a hearse to the graveyard; this meant that [the troops] were certain to die.'[16]

The metaphorical associations of the image of dew are transience and vulnerability. The image derives from poem no. 172 of the *Book of Poetry*, of which the opening lines are almost echoed by the Han song: 'Soaking is the dew, / without the sun it will not dry.'[17] The significance of the shallot image has not often been questioned in discussions of this Han song. (The word *hsieh* has also been translated as garlic or onion.) The character for *hsieh* consists of a plant signifier and a compound which includes the signifier for death or dying. The whiteness of the shallot may serve as a symbol of death. An interesting cultural aspect of

97

the image is that in the late Han, shallots or garlic were hung on red cords on gates and doors as part of the Midsummer Festivals, in order to repel destructive insects.[18] The primary reason for the choice of vegetable as a repellant must have been its strong smell.[19]

Artemisia Village

Artemisia Village—whose is this land?
It's for teeming souls and spirits, none wise, none fool.
The King of Ghosts, how he hurries them along!
Man is fated never to linger long.

The title of this song derives from an old legend that when a person died his two souls, *hun* and *p'o*, went back to live in Artemisia Village. This place was also known as Burial Village.[20] The generally accepted belief in the Han held that the *hun*-soul eventually went to the Supreme God, while the *p'o*-soul remained with the corpse for some time and then dissolved into the earth, descending to Yellow Springs beneath the ground.[21]

The Lament of Liang-fu

I walked from Ch'i city gates
And gazed far off to Tang-yin village.
In the village there were three burial mounds,
Piled up, one just like the others.
I ask, 'Whose family graves are they?'
'T'ien Chiang, Ku Yeh-tzu.
Their strength could topple South Mountain,
And could sever the Ropes of Earth.
One morning they were defamed.
Two peaches slew three knights.'
'Who could have hatched such a plot?'
'Prime Minister of Ch'i, Master Yen!'

Liang-fu of the song title is a sacred mountain near Mount T'ai (in modern Shantung). People were buried at Mount Liang-fu and it was said that there their souls were laid to rest. If a man was buried there, legend went, his song was buried with him. The song opens with the familiar symbolic movement of leaving the city gates to meditate on distant tombs. The setting is historical: the events in the narrative occurred in the sixth century BC.

The first quatrain is a prosaic narrative, which establishes the scene and the theme. Line five introduces the prosaic formula of question and answer. A stranger sees the three identical tombs and asks a local person about them. Neither person is identified, but it is possible to infer from the local man's explanation that he knows his history and admires heroism, and, from the stranger's questions, that he is sympathetic to the noble cause for which the three men died. T'ien Chiang, alias T'ien K'ai-chiang, Ku Yeh-tzu, and Kung-sun Chieh were famous knights who served Duke Ching of Ch'i in the sixth century BC. Their physical prowess is described in hyperbolic language in the fourth couplet: South Mountain was also known as Ox Mountain and was situated in Ch'i state; the Ropes of Earth were the legendary connections between Heaven and Earth.[22] The duke's prime minister was named Yen Ying, or Master Yen, who was determined to rid the state of the three heroes. He devised a cunning plot: he sent the three knights two peaches, telling them that the two who had the greatest claim to meritorious service to the duke might eat them.

The first to take one was Kung-sun Chieh who claimed that he had grappled with a tiger for the duke's sake. Then T'ien K'ai-chiang took a peach, saying that he had killed an enemy of the duke. Finally, Ku Yeh-tzu recalled that once he had forded the Yellow River with the duke when a river monster dragged the duke's horse away. Ku plunged into the river and resurfaced more than three miles away, holding the horse and the monster, which people on the river bank said was the river god. Perhaps, Ku suggested, he might deserve to eat a peach for this exploit? The other two apologized to him and then committed suicide from shame. Ku deeply regretted their death and he committed suicide too, not wishing to be sole survivor of the grisly plot. Hence the saying, 'Two peaches slew three knights'.[23]

This song is a narrative based on the double use of the question and answer formula. It employs hyperbole in description. It also brings into play that familiar device of the folk tale, repetition of significant numbers. Although the local man who narrates the story of the heroes fails to fill in the details of their brave deeds, they are certainly to be understood by anyone hearing just their names. So there are three tombs, three heroes, and three tales of bravery or trials of the hero implicit in the narrative. In the penultimate couplet the device of numbering is developed with 'One morning' and 'Two peaches' which makes a sequence of one-two-three in the same couplet. The effect is concisely dramatic.[24]

CHAPTER SIX

Political Broadsides

Vox populi is a primary concept in classical Chinese political theory and practice. Numerous early texts emphasize the idea that a ruler will achieve good government if he is attuned to what his people are thinking and saying. Criticism of his policies might not reach him at court, because it might be blocked by corrupt officials, or because the people might be afraid to voice open dissent. The good ruler, ancient political theory persuades, seeks out the grumbles and grouses of the mean streets and alleys, and he ensures that satirical songs and poems of social protest are collected and brought to court for careful consideration. The classical Chinese equivalent of the idiom *vox populi* is a more concrete metaphor. The political theorists refer to public opinion as the mouth of the people (*min chih k'ou*). For example, when a tyrant in the Chou era boasted that he had silenced his critics, he was told by his minister:

> 'You have erected barriers against them, but it is more difficult to stop up the mouth of the people than to stop up a river. When a dammed river breaks through the barrier, the number of victims killed is great. It is the same with the people. That is why when you control a river you allow an escape route. When you govern the people, you allow them freedom of speech.'[1]

Later in his forceful and eloquent persuasion, the tyrant's minister declared:

> 'The people have a mouth, just as the earth has mountains and rivers and in these are to be found the source of wealth. . . . It is because it utters words that the mouth gives rise to good and evil. To activate the good and be forearmed against evil is the way to amass wealth, clothing, and food.'[2]

A later classic dating from the first century BC, which contains some texts from the Chou era, gives an account of the ruler, or Son of Heaven, conducting a state visit to the eastern region of his realm. After sacrificing to holy Mount T'ai, he enquired about the local views and opinions expressed in verse ditties in order to ascertain the efficacy of governmental policies at the district level:

'The Son of Heaven went every five years to visit his feudal states. . . . He ordered the senior Masters of Music to present the poems in order that he might consider popular mores. He ordered the Market Supervisors to observe what the likes and dislikes of the people were, what extremist leanings they had, or penchant for vice.'[3]

This account in the *Record of Ritual* is not based on fact. It represents a political persuasion. The ruler's policy of attending to public opinion was a potent political myth in the Han.

In the same period as the *Record of Ritual*, a Han court writer of the Confucian school, Liu Hsiang, developed a theory of 'poetic omens'. As James J. Y. Liu explains it:

'According to this theory, when the ruler is tyrannical and the subjects are too frightened to air their grievances, then popular songs and ballads will appear to portend evil, and these are called "poetic omens". The belief in omens was of course not confined to China; but it seems a peculiarly Chinese belief that omens (as distinct from satires) can take the form of anonymous folk songs (as distinct from divine oracles), and Chinese historical works are full of examples of "poetic omens" that augured ill and reflected the abnormality of the times.'[4]

A generation after Liu Hsiang, the historian Pan Ku expanded the theory and incorporated it into his concept of history, showing how the practical application of 'poetic omens' worked in the explanation of dynastic events.[5] As the historian explained it in his 'Treatise on the Five Elements', the phenomenon of prophetic songs dates from the Chou era and works on the principle that an arcane pronouncement will 'come true' and reveal its mystery long after its first utterance.[6]

Prophecy had a long tradition in China before the theory of 'poetic omens' took hold in the Han. The oracle bones of the Shang Dynasty are incised with the question of a ruler to a diviner, and the diviner's answer. One of the classics, the *Book of Change*, contains much divination material dating from the early Chou.[7] The early Chinese fascination with prophecy is illustrated in the late Chou historical classic, the *Tso Commentary*. In its narrative, dreams, hallucinations, and apparitions all portend future events in the lives of the characters. Many of its prophecies are based on the chronicler's observations of human behaviour. The manner of a person's death was determined by that person's behaviour and was foretold in a prophecy.[8]

By the Han, the influence of strange portents on political life reached its highest point. Comets, eclipses, earthquakes, landslides, and other phenomena were duly noted and heeded as warnings of impending doom. The birth of freaks, sudden accidents, a plague of locusts, and poor harvests were interpreted as criticisms of imperial policy by Heaven and Earth. Similarly, miracles like a swarm of dancing rats, snow in summer, a rain of white hair and so forth were given a specific interpretation.[9]

Although portents, omens, prodigies and prophecies were rife in the Han, no oracular tradition as such existed. Instead there was the prophetic song sung by ordinary children in the 'streets and lanes', usually in the capital city. The link with the Western oracular tradition lies in the innocence of the children singing the songs, perhaps at an age when they were too young to rationally discern events of the day.[10]

The prophetic songs translated in this chapter constitute public criticism of political realities and social mores. Although most were innocent songs, in their politicized interpretations they came to be seen as satire directed against the ruling class by the ruled. The imperial consort Chao Fei-yen and the usurper of the Han, Wang Mang, both attracted particular venom. Other popular targets were greedy officials, avaricious members of the royal family, and conscription officers in the countryside. The ditties, or prophetic songs, are essentially metropolitan in outlook and reflect the values of the Confucian hierarchy. They are often colourful in their use of language and some are scurrilous. Although they lack the polish and finesse of the written court remonstrance, they convey the same moral outrage.

Well-water Overflows

> Well-water overflows
> Extinguishing the hearth,
> Pouring into jade halls,
> Flowing through golden gates.

The Han historian Pan Ku presents this ditty in his 'Treatise on the Five Elements', prefacing it with this explanation of its political symbolism:

'This is a children's ditty from the reign of the Han Emperor Yüan. In the reign of Emperor Ch'eng, on the day mou-tzu of the third month of the year 31 BC, the well-springs in the north palace gradually rose and overflowed, streaming in a southerly direction. "Well-water" is the power of *Yin*; "the hearth" is the power of *Yang*; "jade halls" and

102

"golden gates" refer to the residences of royalty. This symbolizes the flourishing of *Yin* and the extinction of *Yang*, and corresponds to the usurpation of the throne. Wang Mang was born in the fourth year of the reign-period ch'u-yüan [46 BC] of Emperor Yüan. In Emperor Ch'eng's reign he was ennobled; he became assistant-in-government to the Three Ministers and then he usurped power.'[11]

Pan Ku's explanation of the portent of the flooding of a Han palace well-spring refers to the ancient theory of the Five Elements and *Yin* and *Yang*, which was elaborated into a system of cosmic correspondences in the early Han (see p. 36 above). Each dynasty acquired its own 'Power' within this system and an appropriate set of correspondences. Various systems circulated and there was no fixed orthodoxy in the Former Han. Thus, the Han Dynasty was originally believed to be governed by the Power of Water, but this was changed to the Power of Earth when Emperor Wu became obsessed by the idea of emulating the Yellow Emperor. Clearly, the Power had changed yet again by the end of the Former Han, for Wang Mang himself, and Pan Ku too, believed that the Han was governed by the Power of Fire. Wang Mang was convinced that his New (Hsin) Dynasty would be governed by the Power of Earth, but, as his interpretation makes clear, Pan Ku believed that Wang Mang was governed by the Power of Water.[12]

So the historian viewed the flood of 31 BC as an evil omen of the rise to power of Wang, the usurper of the Han. Water is an element controlled by *Yin*, of which the attributes are the female, submission, the north, and so forth. According to the theory, water could not, or rather should not extinguish fire. For the flood in the palace to have extinguished the hearth was a manifestation of cosmic disturbance: Heaven was manifesting disapproval of Earth and Man. It is particularly ironic that a flood should have been chosen as an omen of Wang's evil, for the floods of 31 BC caused panic in Ch'angan.[13] It is evident that the principles of interpreting portents were elastic. It is equally evident that the principles were based on a necessary time-lapse between omen and event. Pan Ku implies in his explanation that this time-lapse was in operation: Wang was born in 46 BC, the song circulated in Emperor Yüan's reign (49–33 BC), and the flood occurred in 31 BC; Wang proclaimed himself emperor in AD 9, reigning until AD 23. Thus the innocent song was made to 'come true' several decades later.[14]

Crooked Paths

*A Ditty from the Time of
the Han Emperor Ch'eng*

Crooked paths ruin fine fields,
Twisted words confuse good folk.
Cassia blooms, but bears no fruit.
A yellow sparrow nests in its crown.
Once the envy of others,
Now pitied by all.

This song is an interesting example of the protean nature of the interpretation of prophetic songs. In his 'Treatise on the Five Elements' Pan Ku gives this interpretation of it:

'This is a ditty from the period of Emperor Ch'eng, which also says [text of the song]. The "cassia" tree is red in colour, which is the symbol of the Han house; "blooms, but bears no fruit" means to be without offspring. Wang Mang assumed the symbolic colour yellow, which is indicated by the "yellow sparrow" which "nests" on the "crown" of the tree.'[15]

Emperor Ch'eng reigned during 32–7 BC. Wang Mang usurped the Han throne and set himself up as emperor in AD 9. So, according to Pan Ku's interpretation, the song circulated for at least thirteen years before the prophesied events occurred. According to the Five Elements theory in this interpretation, Wang Mang is said to be governed by the Power of Earth, yellow, in contrast to Pan Ku's previous interpretation in which the Power was Water. Pan Ku makes 'Crooked Paths' serve as another critique of usurpation.

A quite different interpretation was attached to the song in *New Songs from a Jade Terrace* in the sixth century AD. The text was altered, the song being shorn of its first couplet and placed after a scurrilous song lampooning Emperor Ch'eng's favourite, Lord Chang, and his favourite consort, Chao Fei-yen. A preface precedes both pieces which interprets them in the light of Chao Fei-yen's scandalous activities at court. I present it here, retaining only the relevant sections:

'Fei-yen [Flying Swallow] was insanely jealous; she had not borne a son to the emperor. That is why in the ditty there are the lines ... and "blooms, but bears no fruit". . . . In the end Fei-yen was demoted from the rank of empress and died. That is why there is the line "Now pitied by all".'[16]

This preface interprets the ditty as a critique of the empress who was infertile and forced to commit suicide for her crimes, which included royal infanticide.[17]

Swallow, Swallow

A Children's Ditty from the
Reign of the Han Emperor Ch'eng

Swallow, swallow,
Sleek, sleek is your tail!
Lord Chang
Is always having audience
At timbered gates with green bronze rings.
Swallow flies in,
Pecks at princes;
The princes die,
Swallow pecks their dung!

As the repetition of the word 'Swallow' suggests, this ditty was taken to be a lampoon of Flying Swallow, [Chao] Fei-yen. Pan Ku placed the ditty at the end of his official biography of her and also in the 'Treatise on the Five Elements', together with his interpretation:

'This is a children's ditty from the period of Emperor Ch'eng. Later, when the emperor left the palace incognito on pleasure outings, he was always accompanied by the Marquis of Fu-p'ing, Chang Fang, and pretended he was one of the marquis's household. He once called on Princess Yang-a who used to hold musical performances, and there he saw Chao Fei-yen the dancer and favoured her sexually. That is why the ditty says, "Swallow, swallow,/ Sleek, sleek is your tail!" as she was lovely in appearance. "Lord Chang" refers to the Marquis of Fu-p'ing. "Timbered gates with green bronze rings" refers to the bronze metal rings on the palace gates, which indicates that Lord Chang had been elevated to the peerage. Later on when Chao Fei-yen was promoted to the rank of empress, she brought criminal harm to the imperial heirs. She conceded her guilt, which is alluded to in the lines, "Swallow flies in,/ Pecks at princes:/ The princes die,/ Swallow pecks their dung!" '[18]

The interpretation explains that the prophetic song had circulated in the early period of Emperor Ch'eng's reign, before he met his future consort, Chao Fei-yen. Pan Ku carefully introduces the time sequence, 'Later', which was so important for the functioning of political interpretations of omens and prophecies. The interpretation then narrates the story of Chao Fei-yen, emphasizing how the emperor came to meet her at his sister's mansion, and how this was made possible through the wiles of his favourite, Chang Fang, who disguised the emperor as a servant. Chang Fang was ennobled for these services.

The full biography of Chao Fei-yen, on which Pan Ku's interpretation is based, gives an account of her behaviour at court when she had become empress but was unable to produce a male heir. She forced the imperial concubine, Ts'ao Kung, to surrender her son, the heir to the throne, and to commit suicide by poisoning. Pan Ku records: 'No one knows what became of [the prince].'[19] It is also thought that she was responsible for disposing of the royal son of Lady Hsü. He was ignominiously buried near the jail tower wall where earlier Ts'ao Kung has been forced to swallow poison. The biography also explains that after Emperor Ch'eng's death Chao Fei-yen was demoted and then impeached by the inspector of prisons, Chieh Kuang. In the end she was made a commoner and exiled to her hometown, but committed suicide on the same day as the verdict was announced.[20]

In *New Songs from a Jade Terrace*, 'Swallow, Swallow' is followed by a second song, consisting of the last four lines of 'Crooked Paths'. Both pieces are preceded by a preface which is worth quoting in full because it provides more details about the empress as well as giving a completely different interpretation of the 'Crooked Paths' song minus its first couplet:

'Emperor Ch'eng's consort, Chao, named Fei-yen, had enjoyed his sexual favours in the harem and was with the emperor when he came to and fro from the imperial palace. At that time there was a man, the Marquis of Fu-p'ing, Chang Fang, who was a clever talker and was graciously permitted to ride with the emperor to Ch'i Gate. That is why, in the ditty, it says, "Lord Chang/ Is always having audience." Fei-yen was insanely jealous; she had not borne a son to the emperor. That is why in the ditty there are the lines, "Pecks at princes", and "blooms, but bears no fruit". Wang Mang himself said that the man who supplanted the Han Dynasty would have the Power of the Earth Element and would honour the colour yellow. That is why there are the words "yellow sparrow". In the end, Fei-yen was demoted from the rank of empress and died. That is why there is the line, "Now pitied by all".'[21]

The ditty contains several targets of abuse. It lampoons the evil of illicit sexual activity, especially between royalty and members of the entertain-ment world.[22] It condemns the elevation to high rank of mere commoners whose sole achievement was to cater to the emperor's particular proclivities. It also lampoons the depraved world of harem politics. Its most scurrilous attack is directed against the crime of regal infanticide.[23]

East of Flat Mound

East of Flat Mound
Are pine, cypress, catalpa.
I don't know who seized the Good Duke,
Seized the Good Duke,
Near the high hall,
Ransomed him for a million cash and two racehorses,
Two racehorses.
And it is truly hard
When I look back at the officers, my heart sickens inside me,
My heart sickens inside me,
My blood drains away.
I go home and tell my family to sell the brown bullock.

Two early commentators provide an historical context for this song. Ts'ui Pao of the late third century AD specifies that it was composed by the retainers of Chai I at the end of the Former Han. Wu Ching of the early T'ang explains that Chai I was the younger son of the prime minister. When Wang Mang was poised to usurp the Han throne, Chai I raised troops to cut him down. His attempt failed and he was killed. His retainers composed this song to mourn him.[24]

There are two arguments against this historical specificity. The first is that the details in the biography of the prime minister, where Chai I is mentioned, do not correspond with the details presented in the song.[25] The second is the fact that no clan names of historical personages appear in the song. It is, no doubt, purely coincidental that the *i* of *i-kung*, 'the Good Duke', is the same character as the I of Chai I. It is upon this kind of punning coincidence that the politicized interpretation is based in this type of song. The song equally well tells the story of any good nobleman who is wrongfully kidnapped and ransomed.[26] The villains of the piece are 'officers', not the ubiquitous Wang Mang. I prefer to read the original song as ahistorical, but with an overlay of politicized interpretation.

The setting is a graveyard, Flat Mound (*P'ing-ling*), a few miles north-west of Ch'angan, where the Han Emperor Chao was buried in the early first century BC. 'Pine, cypress, catalpa' enhance the idea of a hallowed ground at the royal graveyard, for pine and cypress denote constancy and eternity beyond the grave, while catalpa denotes the sacred tree of paradise. Someone at the graveyard narrates the story of the Good Duke, whose grave might also be there. He relates how he was powerless to intervene when the officials kidnapped the duke and put a price on his head, a fortune which must have ruined his family. It is not clear whether the narrator is one of many local people who jointly contributed to the ransom: 'to sell the brown bullock' suggests that the local people felt obliged, each in his own way, to meet the exorbitant sum of 'a million cash', line 6. The narrative is well sustained by the strong rhythms and the device of incremental repetition. The repetitions, 'Seized the Good Duke' and 'My heart sickens inside me', not only drive the narrative forward but also highlight the emotional drama. The structure is based on the question and answer formula, 'I don't know who . . .', followed by the story. Incidentally, line 9 reveals that the narrator does 'know who seized the Good Duke'.[27]

Straight as a Bowstring

*A Children's Ditty from the Capital City
at the End of the Reign of Emperor Shun*

> Straight as a bowstring
> You'll die by the wayside!
> Crooked as a hook
> You'll be dubbed a duke!

The title indicates that this ditty originated in the streets of the capital city Loyang in the Latter Han during the years AD 142–144. Emperor Shun reigned for almost two decades, from AD 126 to 144. Two separate historical episodes are represented by the two epigrams of this song. The usual formula is used of citing an early song which portended later events. Commander-in-Chief Liang Chi (d. AD 159) was promoted to office through the influence of his sister who entered the harem of Emperor Shun. When the emperor died, Liang Chi was invited to act as Regent for the infant emperor. The infant died and Liang put a boy-emperor on the throne. When the boy, Emperor Chih, proved to be too astute for the commander, he had him poisoned and put Emperor Huan on the throne (r. AD 147–167). Liang continued to abuse his powers. A loyal officer, Li Ku, was imprisoned and assassinated in AD 147. His corpse was later found on the wayside. In the end, Emperor Huan's palace guard surrounded Liang Chi's house and he and his wife were forced to commit suicide.

The second political event 'foretold' in the second epigram involves Commander Hu Kuang (d. AD 172), who in the reign of Emperor An (r. AD 107–125) swiftly rose to high rank and office from humble social origins.[25]

Short Wheat

*A Children's Ditty from the Early Years
of the Reign of the Latter Han Emperor Huan*

Short wheat green, green, tall wheat shrivelled.
Who must be the reapers? Wife and mother-in-law.
And where is the husband? Out west fighting Huns.
Officials bought the horses,
Gentlemen provided the carriages.
Please make the drum roll for the gentlemen!

The space of time between the song's alleged origin around AD 147–150 and the events it foretold, between AD 151–153, is very narrow. The author of the historical treatises attached to *The History of the Latter Han*, Ssu-ma Piao (AD 240–306), included this song in his 'Treatise on the Five Elements' and presented this interpretation of it:[29]

'In the early years of the reign of Emperor Huan of the Han this was a children's ditty which circulated throughout the empire. In the yüan-chia reign-period [151–153] the Ch'iang tribes of the Liang-chou area all rose up in revolt, and moving south invaded the Three Metropolitan areas of Shu, Han, and Eastern Ch'ao, extending as far as Ping and Chi, causing great hardship among the people. Specially commissioned generals proceeded with large forces, but each time they met in battle they were defeated. Throughout the country, men were increasingly inducted as conscripts, so that the wheat harvest was ruined, there being only the womenfolk to harvest it. "Officials bought the horses,/ Gentlemen provided the carriages" means that the levy was rigorous, extending down to officials of minor rank. "Please make the drum roll for the gentlemen!" means that these subjects did not dare to speak out publicly, but muttered about it privately.'

The first line of the song describes the promising crop of wheat in spring which was ruined in late summer because of the revolt of the Ch'iang, disparagingly referred to as *hu*, barbarians. Liang-chou was in north-west China (modern Kansu). The song was popular throughout China, its political and social significance apparent to all classes of people. The kind of situation described in the song and its interpretation frequently occurred in the Han. Even as early as 61 BC, the same tribe rebelled and the ensuing conscription of Chinese resulted in a shortage of food because harvests were neglected.

The song does not merely side with the local countrymen whose farms were adversely affected by this endemic problem, but it includes all the minor local officials and lower ranks of the gentry in rural areas. The song ends with a plea for justice for this rural gentry; the drum roll expresses the private grievance of this group who, unusually, had to bear the brunt of a particularly harsh levy.[30] No doubt the song's truer purpose was a more generalized, less specifically historic criticism of the perennial government practice of removing men from the land for various campaigns.[31]

Crows on City Walls

A Children's Ditty from the Early Years
of the Reign of the Latter Han Emperor Huan

Crows on city walls,
Tails down in retreat.
Father became an officer,
Son became a conscript.
One soldier dies,
One hundred chariots.
Chariots clatter, clatter
As they enter Ho-chien.
At Ho-chien a pretty girl is skilled at counting cash,
With her cash she makes a mansion, with gold she makes a hall.
On the stone-mill, greedy, greedy, she pounds yellow millet.
Under the rafter there is a hanging drum.
I want to strike it, but the minister will be angry.

Ssu-ma Piao also included this song in his 'Treatise on the Five Elements'. He dated the origin of the ditty at around AD 150 and the events it 'foretold' at around AD 167. He attached this interpretation to it:

'This is a children's ditty circulating in the capital in the early part of Emperor Huan's reign. It refers to government greed. "Crows on city walls,/ Tails down in retreat" means to occupy a position of great advantage and eat on one's own, refusing to share with those beneath one, which refers to those in authority who amass a great fortune. "Father became an officer,/ Son became a conscript" says that when the Man and Yi tribes rebelled, a father had to become an officer in the army, while his son became a conscript and went out to attack them. "One soldier dies,/ One hundred chariots" says that when one man dies in the punitive expedition against the Huns, behind him are another hundred war chariots. "Chariots clatter, clatter/ As they enter Ho-chien" says that when Emperor Huan was about to die, chariots clattered into Ho-chien to welcome Emperor Ling. "At Ho-chien a pretty girl is skilled at counting cash,/ With her cash she makes a mansion, with gold she makes a hall" means that when Emperor Ling ascended the throne his mother, the Yung-lo Dowager Empress, loved to amass gold to make a hall. "On the stone-mill, greedy, greedy, she pounds yellow millet" says that although the Yung-lo Dowager Empress piled up gold and cash, she was so greedy she never had enough and she made the people pound yellow millet for her own use. "Under the rafter there is a hanging drum. / I want to strike it, but the minister will be angry" says that the Yung-lo Dowager Empress ordered Emperor Ling to sell offices as a source of cash, and that those who received official emoluments were not the right people. It says that we are loyal and sincere; we are men of honour who look on all this with resentment and want to strike the hanging drum in order to seek an audience. But the chief minister is the one who controls the drum and he for his part is a flatterer and toady. He is angry and stops me from striking the drum in protest.'[32]

The place-name Ho-chien is the only detail which permits a link between the song and historical events. Ssu-ma Piao's interpretation focusses on two targets in the late Latter Han: social upheaval caused by war and the greed of the emperor's mother. The song originated, according to Ssu-ma Piao, in the early years of Emperor Huan's reign, c. AD 150, and described the events surrounding the emperor's death and Emperor Ling's accession, c. AD 167. His interpretation also makes the point that the loyal subject who contributes to the war effort with his property and his life feels embittered by the injustice of a prominent member of the royal family making a fortune in a time of national peril. The song reads just as well, however, if it is taken as a general criticism of graft and corruption in officialdom and in high places. Of officials in the Latter Han, Hans H. Bielenstein notes that apart from the lowest paid officials, 'The rest of Han officialdom was not forced into corruption by insufficient salaries. Where venality occurred, it was motivated more by greed than economic necessity.'[33] As with the other songs, this may be read both as an innocent, ahistorical song of the Han and as a politicized broadside.[34]

The Song Tung Flees!

Born into a happy world
Tung flees!
Roving through the city's four quarters
Tung flees!
Enjoying blessings from Heaven
Tung flees!

Girdled with gold dark red
Tung flees!
Showing his gratitude
Tung flees!
Preparing carriage and riders
Tung flees!
Soon to set off
Tung flees!
To the main house bids farewell
Tung flees!
Leaving West Gate
Tung flees!
Staring at the capital city
Tung flees!
The sun dying at night
Tung flees!
Heart broken with sorrow
Tung flees!

Ssu-ma Piao includes this text in his treatise, explaining that it was a song which originated in the capital city Loyang in the reign-period AD 184–189 of Emperor Ling (r. AD 168–189). Ts'ui Pao, his contemporary, adds that the song was made by children at play at the end of the Latter Han, when Tung Cho fomented revolt but was killed in his flight from the capital.[35] Tung Cho was a regional commander in Ho-tung, north of Loyang, who was called to the capital in AD 189 to deal with unrest and intrigue in the palace. In the mêlée, the Commander-in-Chief Ho Chin was murdered and Tung Cho emerged as the successful leader of a palace coup. He had the emperor deposed and a year later assassinated. He sacked the capital and moved the new emperor in AD 190 from Loyang to Ch'angan. His success was short-lived. In AD 192 he was killed when attempting to flee his pursuers and his mutilated corpse was exposed in the market-place. Three years later the emperor was safely restored and reigned with Loyang as his capital until AD 220, during years of increasing civil unrest. The name of Tung Cho is reviled as a traitor who caused the downfall of the Han Dynasty.

The contents of the song do not tally with the historical events in which Tung Cho participated. The last part especially is at odds with the image of the dictator who had devastated Loyang and had caused mayhem in numerous towns and villages. The song and its title have been discussed at some length in Chapter Three, where an hypothetical 'original' form of the song was proposed. The origins of the song are not known, nor is it clear whether the lines are in their original order. The refrain has probably been adapted, on the basis of a pun on Tung Cho's name, to provide a satirical chorus mocking the dictator.[36]

112

The Ballad of Breaking Willow

Though darkly, darkly we do wrong,
The penalty will always follow the deed.
Mei Hsi slew Lung-feng;
Chieh was exiled to Ming-t'iao.

Tsu I's advice was not taken;
Chou's head was hung from a white standard.
When he pointed to a deer, taking it for a horse,
That is how Hu Hai lost his life.

Fu Ch'ai was nearing life's end
When he said, 'I betrayed Tzu Hsü'.
The Jung king accepted girl musicians as a gift,
That is how he lost his Yu Yü.
When the jade tablet and horse disaster befell K'uei,
Two states together became burial mounds.

Three men resulted in the market tiger.
A kind mother threw down her shuttle and ran.
Pien Ho's feet were amputated.
Chieh Yü returned to his grass hermitage.

This song is a literary piece, like 'The Ballad of the Prefect of Goosegate'. It is full of historical allusions and classical references which are so well-known that they have acquired the status of proverbs and household names. There is no narrative. Almost every line represents an allusion to an historical event. Since they cannot be understood without explanations, I will provide a brief commentary to the litany of encapsulated anecdotes, stanza by stanza.

In stanza one, Mei Hsi (or Mo Hsi) was the concubine of the last ruler of the mythological Hsia Dynasty whose name was Chieh, dubbed 'The Tyrant' by the chroniclers. She was accused of causing the downfall of the Hsia, first by goading Chieh to extreme folly, and later, when Chieh discarded her, by plotting with Yi Yin, counsellor of the Shang ruler, Ch'eng T'ang. Kuan Lung-feng was a worthy minister of Chieh who protested against the tyrant's excesses. Eventually, Chieh was exiled to Ming-t'iao (Chirping Branches, in modern Shensi). It is thought that Chieh was defeated by the Shang and died in exile there.

In stanza two, Tsu I was the worthy minister of King Chou, the last ruler of the Shang and also branded as an evil man. Tsu I warned King Chou that the Shang was no longer favoured by the Mandate of Heaven, nor did it represent the will of the people. When the Chou invaded Shang territory King Chou burned himself to death. King Wu of the

Chou cut off his head and hung it from the top of a standard. Emperor Hu Hai of the Ch'in Dynasty favoured Chao Kao with high office, but the latter abused his powers. He tried the ministers' loyalty to himself by daring them to contradict him when he said a deer was a horse. Those who told the truth were executed. In the end he assassinated Emperor Hu Hai. Chao Kao, who was a eunuch, was killed by the grandson of the founder of the Ch'in Dynasty to avenge his father in 207 BC.

In stanza three, Tzu Hsü, also known as Wu Yüan, was an old minister of Wu state in the sixth and fifth centuries BC. He helped Wu to resist its aggressive neighbour, Yüeh state. When King Fu Ch'ai acceded to the throne in Wu, the king's favourite denounced Tzu Hsü and the king ceased to heed his minister's counsel. The king sent him a handsomely carved sword to indicate that he had permission to commit suicide, which his loyal servant did. His corpse was wrapped in a leather sack and thrown into a river. Later, the king realized his error when he was defeated by Yüeh and was nearing his end. On his deathbed he declared that he would never be able to face his minister for shame. The episode of the Jung king dates from the Spring and Autumn era of the Chou. The Jung people had Ch'in state as their neighbour. Duke Mu of Ch'in tried to stir discontent in Jung by sending the king two sets of (28 or 16) female musicians to distract him from the affairs of state. The Jung minister was a worthy man named Yu Yü. He realized what the plot was, but to no avail, and so he removed himself from Jung. The last episode in this stanza concerns Duke Hsien of Chin state who wished to attack Kuo state, but needed permission to pass through Yü state to do so. Duke Hsien made his request, offering Yü state gifts of fine horses and a valuable jade tablet. The ruler of Yü was delighted with the gifts and allowed the Chin army to pass through his territory. After Chin had destroyed Kuo, it proceeded to destroy Yü.

In the last stanza, the first line refers to P'ang Ts'ung's warning to the King of Wei that if three people in succession say there is a tiger in the marketplace, everyone will believe them, whether it is true or false. The next line alludes to Tseng Ts'an, or Tseng Tzu, a disciple of Confucius. His mother was told by three separate people that he had killed someone. The truth was that someone with the same name as Tseng Ts'an had committed the murder. The mother refused to believe the report the first and second times, but the third time she dropped her weaving and fled, fearing the penalty that accrued to a felon's family. In the next anecdote Pien Ho of Ch'u state found a rare uncut jade and offered it to the throne as the law required. King Li had the stone examined by his experts, but they rejected it as a rock. The king punished Pien Ho by having his left foot cut off. King Wu succeeded to the throne and Pien Ho offered his jade to the throne again, but it was again rejected. The king had Pien Ho's right foot cut off as punishment. King

114

Wen succeeded to the throne, and once more Pien Ho offered his jade. He wept tears of blood, not because of his amputated feet, but because his integrity had been questioned. The king realized that, in fact, the stone was the finest piece of jade. He wished to ennoble Pien Ho, but he refused the honour. The final allusion concerns Lu Chieh Yü of Ch'u state, who was called the Madman of Ch'u. He refused a lucrative government post offered by the king and became a recluse in the countryside.

The opening couplet threatens those who think their crimes will never be discovered with the sort of punishment meted out to miscreants in history. Then follows a litany of famous and infamous cases of political crime. Its message is based on a simple notion of cause and effect. Its lesson is twofold: that politics is a dangerous business which should be avoided or one will come to a grisly end; and that people should not blind themselves to life's dangerous realities, for tragic results will follow errors of judgement. The didacticism of the song, bolstered with historical allusions, is unusual among the Han repertoire of *yüeh-fu*. It contrasts markedly with fables in verse which teach through indirection.

The title does not accord with the content. The symbolism of 'breaking willow' is of leave-taking, deriving from a custom in the early Han of giving a willow branch to a traveller whom one is seeing off. One reason for the custom was probably the pun on the word for willow, *liu*, which is a homophone of *liu*, detain, written with a different character.[37] On the other hand, the meaning of the title may involve a quite different pun on *liu*-willow and *liu*-execute, which accords better with the grim theme of the song. A third possibility is that, as in the case of 'The Ballad of the Prefect of Goosegate', the title 'The Ballad of Breaking Willow' may belong to another song-text, no longer extant, on a theme appropriate to its title.[38]

CHAPTER SEVEN

Anti-war Ballads and Songs

Popular songs and ballads of the Han do not glorify war, nor do they celebrate national victories. It is ironic that they sprang from the great age of Chinese imperialism, when Han armies pushed the frontiers eastwards far into Korea, north into the steppes, west to Central Asia, and south into Vietnam. The songs of the people do not commemorate this conquest and expansion. The anonymous singers seem not to belong to the great enterprise of the state. They even sound unpatriotic. There is no concept of military honour, nor of the immortality to be gained through acts of bravery on the battlefield. The dramatic evocation of exciting battles and the glorification of the heroic are absent from the songs of war. It is as if the people contributed their labour and their life to imperial foreign policy, but expected no reward. Their contribution was not voluntary. Most armies were mustered by conscription. Often men were taken from their fields at harvest time to fight far from home. To them—the ordinary folk of the land—wars of conquest were an abstraction, not a living reality like the spasmodic raids of tribesmen into their northern homesteads. The idea of loyal service owed by a vassal to his lord was no longer dominant in the Han as it had been in the Chou. Rather, the Han dynasts continued the policy of the dissolution of the old Chou aristocratic orders which had been introduced by the Ch'in rulers. The private armies of Chou feudal states were disbanded and the old bond of loyalty between lord and people disappeared.[1] Under the Han, the fighting man was an anonymous soldier who often did not comprehend the impersonal cause for which the ultimate sacrifice was demanded of him. In general, Han war songs and ballads reflect this anonymity and incomprehension. They are songs of protest, not hymns of praise and thanksgiving.

The tradition of protest did not originate in the Han. The Chou *Book of Poetry* contains numerous anti-war pieces, in which the anonymous poets often voice the same complaints as the Han song-makers.[2] Yet the classic also features marching songs and victory songs expressing the soldiers' pride in their lord's achievements and joy in their own acts of valour. The two types of song, praise and plaint, coexisted. In the later anthology of the Chou, *Songs of Ch'u*, the only war poem is a battle hymn glorifying war and commemorating the dead as heroes whose names will live for ever.[3]

Han war songs and ballads continue the plaintive strain of similar poems in the *Book of Poetry*, but reflect the changes in the social and political life of the Han. The resemblances between the two periods can sometimes be very close. The expedition described in the Han song, 'Light in the East', echoes these Chou lines:

> We were led by Sun Tzu-chung
> To subdue Ch'en and Sung.
> He does not bring us home;
> My heart is sad within.[4]

Both pieces end with a plaint, both express nostalgia. But the Chou passage reveals an important cultural difference: the soldiers' leader is personalized, he is a lord whom they know by name and to whom they are attached by a bond of service. Also, they know where they are fighting The Han soldier did not know his leader, and is vague about the place and object of war. The army of the Han song consists of rabble rounded up because war was unpopular at harvest time. Both traditions, however, share a pervading sense of war-weariness and a mood of nostalgia. Again and again the soldier's thoughts turn homewards to his farm and family. He feels powerless to avert his own fate and his family's, and he rails against the injustice of it all. Though he voices his plaint, he does not take action.

Apart from the cultural differences between the Chou and Han war plaint, a new element of realism colours the Han songs and ballads. Bodies lying dead on the battlefield were not a fit subject for the poems of the Chou classic. In *Songs of Ch'u* they are hymned as immortal heroes in a idealizing manner: 'Their bodies may have died, but their souls are living:/ Heroes among the shades their valiant souls will be.'[5] The Han singer does not treat death as a taboo topic, nor is he interested in idealizing death in hymns. He cynically refers to the dead on the battlefield as 'fodder for crows'. A soldier returning home after a lifetime in the army finds his home has become a wasteland: 'Pheasants flying through rafter tops;/ The inner garden grown wild with corn.'

The anonymity of Han war songs and ballads accentuates their timeless quality and their universal appeal. It is interesting that despite their insistence on the futility of war and their non-militaristic spirit, two of the titles translated here were included traditionally in categories of military music. It is probable that officials responsible for arranging military music sensed that these songs struck a chord deep in the hearts of fighting men.

Light in the East

Is there light in the east?
Then why not yet in Ts'ang-wu?
In Ts'ang-wu so much rotting grain,
No good as provisions for troops.
The troops are all vagrants.
On early march so much aching grief.

This short song may be read at several different levels. In general it is a song about war. Whether is is construed as a plaint against war or as a more militaristic song depends on which textual variants one accepts. My own translation is based on the text in the compilation of Shen Yüeh in AD 488, 'Treatise on Music', which text is reproduced by Kuo in his anthology. The variants occur in the first couplet. The Yüan commentator, Tso K'o-ming (14th century AD) amends the reading 'Light in the east?' (*Tung kuang hu*), to 'Tung-kuang (place-name) at peace' (*Tung-kuang p'ing*, *hu > p'ing*). In fact, the two characters, *hu* and *p'ing*, are fairly similar. Tso makes the same amendment in the second line: 'Ts'ang-wu why not yet?' (*Ts'ang-wu ho pu hu*), becomes 'Ts'ang-wu why not at peace' (*Ts'ang-wu ho pu p'ing*). Tso's reading makes the song's opening more pugnacious than the fifth-century text. His version reads: 'Tung-kuang is at peace,/ Then why is Ts'ang-wu not at peace?' The soldiers want to get on with the war, and then return home. Militarism tinged with nostalgia informs the Tso version.[6] War-weariness dominated by nostalgia and despair informs the text of the Shen Yüeh and of Kuo Mao-ch'ien. I prefer to reject Tso's suggested amendment and retain the earliest text's reading.

The song has been taken as the expression of an historical episode of the year 112 BC when Emperor Wu of the Han sent a military expedition against Nan-Yüeh kingdom, in the south-east of the empire. The war was unpopular, and officers found it difficult to muster an army, so they pressed convicts released by a general amnesty into military service. One contingent was ordered to enter Ts'ang-wu. Eventually, the expedition was successful and Nan-Yüeh was conquered.[7] It is recorded that prayers for the success of the campaign were offered to the deity Great Unity and '. . . prayers for the soldiers were offered' prior to this campaign, the Han historian, Ssu-ma Ch'ien himself taking the spirit banner and pointing '. . . it at the country that was about to be attacked.' In 111 BC, '. . . prayers of thanksgiving for the success of the expedition to Southern Yüeh [Nan-Yüeh] were offered to the Great Unity and the Earth Lord.'[8] One flaw in this attempt at historical reconstruction of the song is that the word 'vagrants' (*yu-tang-tzu*), does not necessarily mean criminals; in Ssu-ma Ch'ien's history the soldiers are explicitly described as ex-convicts. By the same process of arbitrary inference the song might also be read on a mythological level. If the character for *Ts'ang* in Ts'ang-wu is emended to *Ts'ang* with Radical 140 (an amendment suggested by the Chung-hua editors of Kuo's *Anthology*), we arrive at the mountain named Ts'ang-wu where the legendary Emperor Shun, the virtuous and sage ruler, died. The song might then be construed as an overt complaint to the sage's spirit. The Chinese written language lends itself to this sort of reconstruction, based on loan-words and puns, an impulse which must be held severely in check! I prefer to read the song as an ahistorical war plaint.

If the early version of the song-text is accepted, the piece becomes an impersonal plaint of a soldier weary of war. The song's movement is based on an almost imperceptible image of light. The title and the first line announce the dawn, signalling another day of misery for the reluctant soldier and suggesting a glimmer of hope that the expedition might soon be over. Faint though this image of light is, it is negated by the song's closure. In Ts'ang-wu all is darkness and gloom; the army is hungry, bewildered, and homesick. The song is also based on realism. It is introduced through an ironic pun on the name Ts'ang-wu; *ts'ang* is a granary. But instead of a well-stocked granary, the soldiers on the march see rotting grain. This realistic detail recalls other Han songs, especially those taken as political prophecies, such as 'Short Wheat', which complain of ruined harvests when men are taken from the land. The Western dictum, 'An army marches on its stomach', acquires a deeper significance in the Chinese context because in numerous songs and ballads the characters often urge each other 'Try and eat' at a time of emotional crisis.[9] The realistic mode springs from an innate pragmatism. At the end of the song the soldier voices the grief felt by one and all, echoing the Chou soldier of long ago, 'My heart is sad within'. The anonymous Han singer seeks to win sympathy from his audience and to make them identify with the soldiers' fate. It is mainly for this reason that I find the historical interpretation so forced. If, as the Han historian stated, the army was made up of criminals, then this sympathy for the soldiers would not be so prompt. The song is best read, therefore, as the plaint of the ordinary foot-soldier anywhere and at any time against the hardships of a forced march, inadequate provisions, and against war itself.[10]

We Fought South of the City Wall

We fought south of the city wall.
We died north of the ramparts.
In the wilderness we dead lie unburied, fodder for crows.

Tell the crows for us:
'We've always been brave men!
In the wilderness we dead clearly lie unburied,
So how can our rotting flesh flee from you?'
Waters deep, rushing, rushing,
Reeds and rushes, darkening, darkening.
Heroic horsemen fought and died fighting,
Flagging horses whinnied in panic.
Raftered houses we built,
And south, alas! and north;
If grain and millet aren't reaped, what will you eat, Lord?
We longed to be loyal vassals, but how can that be?
I remember you, good vassals,
Good vassals I truly remember:
In the dawn you went out to glory,
At nightfall you did not return.

The opening lines establish a contrast between the city and the wilderness. The dividing line between the two is the city wall and ramparts. We have seen elsewhere how the city gate functions as a symbolic boundary between the security of daily life and the world of the dead or some catastrophe beyond. Here the city, for which men died fighting, represents safety and civilization. The wilderness where the battle took place represents danger and barbarism. The semantic contrast is heightened by the parallelism of 'south' and 'north', and 'fought' and 'died' in the first couplet. The neatness of the couplet's structure contrasts with its content and with the ragged, untidy structure of the following passages which recount the horror of death and the confusion of the battle. The third line of the song fulfils the soldiers' horror of the wilderness with the taboo image of dead bodies; for a body to be exposed without burial was considered to be the worst fate that could befall a man. The revulsion is expressed through the stark realism of 'fodder for crows'. No metaphor so savage had appeared in earlier poetic diction, nor did it find an echo in the later literary tradition. War imagery in the late and post-Han era tended to become muted and abstract, often stylized, and sometimes decorative. 'Their white bones lay and bleached in the wilderness' was the favourite image of the aftermath of war, rather than the realistic, but brutal image of carrion.[11]

The starkness of the narrative continues with the voice of the dead defiantly addressing the carrion crows. Unfortunately, the text becomes garbled at this point. Line 4 has a variant which reads: 'We address the crows'. Line 5 has a variant making 'brave' into the verb 'wail'. Yü Kuan-ying prefers this reading, rendering the line, 'Wail, please, for our men!' He interprets this as a request to perform the old custom of 'summoning the soul' of the dead and wailing for them before the crows eat their flesh.[12] This is ingenious. In principle, however, I would oppose any amendment by a modern author when the line reads perfectly well as it stands. If the original text is retained, the words of the soldier are addressed to the crows; they are not a plea, but a defiant challenge.[13]

A brief lyrical passage follows the realism. It serves to relieve the harshness of the first part of the narrative by suggesting a scene of refreshing respite from the savagery of battle. This couplet, 'Waters deep . . . darkening', also acts as a transition to a passage which shifts the time from the present back to the scene of the battle before the men died and even further back to their homes before the war began. The description of the battle is terse; although it praises the soldiers for their heroism to the last, it does not constitute a glorification of war. Rather it conveys the desperation and confusion of defeat. This brief flash-back to the battle is effective and eloquent.

The second flash-back to the soldiers' homes is again, unfortunately, beset with textual problems. One problem involves a word which may be taken as a nonsense word, or as a word with meaning in the narrative, in lines 12 and 13. Yü Kuan-ying takes the word *liang* to be a nonsense word in line 12. *Liang* may also be read as 'bridge', giving '(sentry) huts built on the bridge' for line 12, which is how Burton Watson and Peking University's editors read it. *Liang* also means the 'ridge-pole' of a house, which is how I read it: 'Raftered houses we built'. Line 13 also contains the same *liang* character. Yü and Watson both read it as a nonsense word, and so do I in this instance, rendering it as 'alas!'.[14] In the early text of Shen Yüeh's 'Treatise', line 14 reads 'Grain, millet, reaped, Lord what eat?' in which the particle *erh* after 'millet' is amended by most commentators to *pu*, 'not' giving: 'If grain and millet aren't reaped, what will you eat, Lord?' I have adopted this sensible amendment. I interpret this passage as a flash-back to the time when the men were on their farms in the service of their lord. They express their loyalty to him even while they are dead, and regret that their farms are abandoned and the crop will not be harvested. The same topos of war occurs in 'Short Wheat'. The dead also regret that they can no longer serve their lord: '. . . what will you eat, Lord?' and 'We longed to be loyal vassals, but how can that be?'

The last section of the song, lines 14 to 17, contains the vocabulary of the quasi-feudal system prevailing during the Chou: *chün* (lord), *chung ch'en* (loyal vassals), *liang ch'en* (good vassals). It is possible that the song dates from the early Han when the remnants of the system were still evident, if not in socio-political reality, then certainly in speech patterns and cultural attitudes. The song closes with resonant echoes. The Chou soldier had complained: 'we marched away but do not come back', and the Ch'u hymn sang: 'They went out never more to return'.[15] The Han song ends in an elegiac mood.

There are several features of song and ballad in this piece. The song rushes into a crisis; the battle is over, but the dead scornfully challenge their cruel avian companions. They bitterly recall their defeat, they remember their homes and farms, and they shamefully apologise to their lord. Speech punctuates the narrative, the indeterminate nature of the song making it hard to decide who the speaker is at times. Questions are asked, which hang in the air unanswered. The narrative reveals abrupt shifts in setting, speaker, and tone. Parallelism in the opening and closing couplets, and the central passage seem to bring order to the chaos of the narrative, but perhaps in the end only heighten the sense of confusion. The confusion of the song is deliberate; war has ruined the lives of honest, brave men—the singer is not concerned with themes of peace and harmony. The agitation of the song is mainly conveyed through the shift in speaker. It is hard to tell if the speaker of the whole narrative is the same, or if there are different speakers. Is the omniscient, omnipresent narrator of the first couplets, who surveys the grisly scene of defeat, the same as the survivor of the bitter fight who voices the final lament? Is the speaker of the first part the spokesman for a group of local men, while the speaker of the final part their lord speaking for the dead from their local district? Certainly, the speaker of the final quatrain who voices quiet thanks for the sacrifice of human life is different in tone and diction from the rest of the narrative. In fact, almost every translation of this song offers a different story with different spoken parts assigned to the characters. My own version is far from secure, but it tries to reconstruct a reasonable narrative. Despite its difficulties of inter-pretation, and fraught as it is with textual problems, this song retains its age-old power to inspire admiration and sympathy.[16]

Watering Horses at a Long Wall Hole

Green, green river bank grass.
Skeins, skeins of longing for the far road.
The far road I cannot bear to long for.
In bed at night I see him in dreams,
Dream I see him by my side.
Suddenly I wake in another town,
Another town, each in different parts.
I toss and turn, see him no more.
Withered mulberry knows wind from the skies.
Ocean waters know chill from the skies.
I go indoors, everyone self-absorbed,
Who wants to speak for me?
A traveller came from far away,

He brought me a double-carp.
I call my boy to 'cook the carp'.
Inside there is a white silk letter.
I kneel down and read the white silk letter.
What sort of letter is it then?
Above it says, 'Try and eat'.
Below it says, 'I'll always love you'.

The title of this song provides its narrative background. The Long Wall was a series of fortifications along the borders of the northernmost states of the Chou era which were constructed to keep out marauding tribesmen of the steppes. In the Ch'in Dynasty much work was done by conscript labour to link this series of disconnected fortifications, and by the Han the defense line stretched from the east as far as Tun-huang in the west. The cost in human life was enormous. Apart from the output of labour in constructing the wall, this part of China required a huge defense army since it was the most vulnerable border. Military outposts became Han colonies. In his preface to this song Kuo Mao-ch'ien cites a popular song, *min-ko*, which evokes the waste of human life in building and guarding this fortified wall:

If a son is born, mind you don't raise him!
If a girl is born, feed her on dried meat.
Don't you see below the Long Wall
Corpses and skeletons prop each other up?[17]

(The term, 'dried meat', far from being derogatory, implies that the girl in the family will be cherished and fed well because she will not be torn from the family to serve the nation.) The narrative of 'Watering Horses at a Long Wall Hole' may be inferred in this way: a woman looks out from her home beside a river in spring and watches the road leading out of the village. She longs for her lover, or husband, who has left for corvée work on the Long Wall. She has not heard from him for some time. Her only contact with him is through memories and dreams. She has no one to confide in and no one who can help her. One day a traveller from the far north brings her a letter from her lover or husband. She reads it in a submissive pose. There is no news of his return, but he tries to cheer her up and vows eternal love. The implication is that they will never meet again.

The song is rich in balladic features. Repetition is the key device in the first eight lines: the binome 'Green, green' denoting spring and youthful beauty parallels 'Skeins, skeins' which suggests an endless thread of silk (*ssu*, a pun for love). The image of the 'far road' along which the lover, or husband, travelled is repeated, and the word for love or longing,

'Dreams', and 'another town' conclude the pattern of repeated echoes. The device continues in the last section of the song with the new image of the letter, bringing both hope and despair; the word 'letter' is repeated three times, 'white silk letter' twice, and 'carp' twice.

The next couplet is a brief lyrical interlude marking a transition from the song's opening lyricism and its more prosaic closure. This interlude ends the soft lyrical imagery of spring in the first passage. The absence of love makes the world seem a colder place to the woman who is left behind. Mulberry has an association with a woman's work; its leaves are picked in spring to feed silkworms, and their cocoons are washed before their silk thread is spun and woven. The mulberry image therefore resumes the semantic pun of 'Skeins' and 'longing', but now serves as a negative image of neglect. The use of tree imagery also suggests the fixed place of a woman at home who cannot travel; she is rooted in domesticity. The letter must come from a traveller to her. The image of water in this transitional couplet also denotes the feminine psyche, from its association with passivity in philosophical Taoism and its significance in the Five Elements Theory.[18] This unobtrusive couplet also contains a classical allusion. Poem no. 58 of the *Book of Poetry* uses the mulberry image to narrate the story of a wife who has been abandoned by her husband; the seasons of the mulberry mark the stages of her marriage up to her present discontent:

> When the mulberry tree sheds it leaves,
> they are yellow and drop;
> since I went to you,
> for three years I have eaten poverty;
> (and now) the waters of the K'i are voluminous,
> they wet the curtains of my carriage.[19]

The phrases in the Chou poem, 'went to you' and 'curtains of my carriage', mean marriage and divorce. While the quotation or allusion in the Han song does not mirror the same narrative as the classic, it acts as a mood indicator and links the desolate woman of the Han song with the grieving wife of the Chou classic.

The last section of the song moves away from the pattern of memory and echo. It becomes a prosaic narrative. A letter comes to the woman from the man at the Long Wall telling her there is no hope of a reunion, and so fulfilling the premonition of tragedy in the central lyrical couplet. A 'double-carp' is a euphemism for a letter; it is a wooden container shaped like two carp with a silk letter inside; opening the container is euphemistically called 'cook the carp'. The carp symbolizes fertility, a reference which suggests that the woman in the song is still young and fertile. The symbolism is ironic, since she will never meet her lover or husband again, and she appears not to have started a family before he left.[20] The prosaic tone continues with quotations from the letter, its neat parallelism contrasting with the emotional confusion conveyed in the opening passage of the whole song. In its formal neatness the technique suggests that the woman will bear her grief with quiet dignity. The dramatic technique of the question and answer formula are rightly reserved for the song's closure. The direct speech is restrained and dignified. The last passage contains several commonplace expressions. 'A traveller came from far away' is the same as line 7 of no. 17 of the 'Nineteen Old Poems', and both texts share the same letter, the same message of undying love, and the same female persona.[21] Poem no. 1 of the same Han series resembles the last couplet of the Han song's closure.[22] The first line of the Han song is almost the same as that of no. 2 of the same series, which narrates the story of a deserted entertainer.[23]

In some anthologies this song is attributed to the Latter Han poet, Ts'ai Yung; for example, *New Songs from a Jade Terrace* compiled in the mid-sixth century AD.[24] But one slightly earlier anthology, *Anthology of Literature*, and the later *Compendium of Literature* both list the song as an anonymous old *yüeh-fu* poem, and Kuo Mao-ch'ien follows them.[25] The song's cogent use of the techniques of popular song and ballad, its literary reference, and its key trope of the letter with its refined epithets, suggest the confident hand of a literate composer.[26]

At Fifteen I Joined the Army

At fifteen I joined the army,
At eighty I first came home.
On the road I met a villager,
'At my home what kin are there?'
'Look over there—that's your home!'
Pine, cypress, burial mounds piled, piled high,
Hares going in through dog-holes,
Pheasants flying in through rafter tops;
The inner garden grown wild with corn,
Over the well wild mallow growing.
I pound grain to serve for a meal,
I pick mallow to serve for broth.
Once broth and meal are cooked
I'm at a loss to know whom to feed.
I leave by the gates, look east.
Tears fall and soak my clothes.

The narrative is constructed throughout in lines of formal parallelism. The tidiness of the narrative line serves to underscore the confusion of the old soldier coming home after a lifetime in the army. He does not remember where his home is, nor does he know who might be his relatives after his absence of some generations. He finds his home has been destroyed by some unexplained disaster. Everything has reverted to wilderness: his home has become a graveyard inhabited by wild creatures; his kitchen garden has gone to seed. The sub-text of the song suggests that the old man must have been looking forward to his family reunion as he walked along the road to the village; home (chia) is his first word to his fellow villager, a stranger to him. Yet despite his eagerness at coming home his words to the villager are restrained and formal, and this restraint foreshadows the quiet dignity with which he surveys the scene of desolation of his former home. No loud lament, but diligent calm is his response to the crisis. His gesture of preparing food might be seen as a topos of realism in these songs of war and its aftermath. The gesture tells us something of the character of the veteran. Sixty-five years of army drill have trained him to be busy and to survive. At the end, however, his emotions spill over his restraint, because he must now, and for ever, go through the communal act of eating in isolation. He faces east, source of light and hope, and silently weeps. All his life the soldier believed that the chaos of war was related to his army job, not to his house and home. He finds at the end of his hard life that the chaos of some unknown event has engulfed his family and friends. The disparity between his expectation and the reality he encounters creates an ironic conflict between time past and time present. The formal parallelism of the piece reinforces the formal character of the long-trained veteran, but at the same time runs counter to the song's emotional confusion, generating a second layer of irony.

The anti-war sentiment of this piece is focussed on the character of the simple, frail old man, creating a mood of pathos. His confusion, moderated by formality and restraint, begs the question, 'Why?'. In terms of poetic rhetoric the question remains unanswered. Yet a response arises from the ironic refrain of the temporal conflict and the formal parallelism. In a sense, a response also arises from the anonymous singer's decision to cast the main character in the mould of an unknown veteran, a low-ranking soldier, who stands against the forces of barbarism, venerable and alone. The singer persuades the audience to believe that despite the venerable age and feeble body of the veteran, he will survive and build a new future. This will be possible because of his stoicism, rooted in rural values, and his sense of duty, instilled by army service. Such courage, tempered by humane courtesy, becomes the soul of rural China.

Kuo prefaces this narrative with a passage of eight lines:

Burning fires set wild fields ablaze,
Wild ducks fly up to skies.

A young lad marries a widow,
A buxom lass laughs fit to kill.
Tall, tall, hilltop tree;
When the wind blows, leaves fall and are gone,
Once gone many thousand miles,
How will they come back to their old home?

While it is customary for songs and ballads of the Han to have a prelude, which is often enigmatic in its imagery and sometimes seemingly unrelated to the narrative theme, this prelude is usually only one couplet long. Here the eight-line passage preceding the narrative proper about the soldier seems too long to serve as a prelude in the ordinary sense. It constitutes a separate poem, a regular, pentasyllabic, eight-line piece on the theme of lifelong separation from home. The first image of fires in the plain suggests the turmoil of war in the countryside. The next image of ducks flying high continues this idea, denoting the flight of all living creatures from their homes. The second couplet seems to express the idea that when menfolk go off to war and get killed, the usual behaviour of the local people becomes erratic: a war widow will marry a young man instead of remaining chaste. The final image of the tree might represent the village community; when disaster hits the village, the villagers flee and sometimes never return. It is easy to see why such a passage might have become attached to the narrative beginning 'At fifteen I joined the army', for it describes the sort of events which might have occurred in the veteran's own village before he returned home. Most anthologies present the piece as I have, without the prelude Kuo provided for it.

The characterization and general mode of expression of the song contrast markedly with Han songs more recognizably popular in expression, such as 'We Fought South of the City Wall', 'The Ailing Wife', and 'East Gate'. Its sophisticated techniques indicate that it is more likely to be the composition of a lettered poet who adapted the theme from a popular song for the more formal *ku-shih* genre. In fact, it is often classified as a *ku-shih*, old poem, as is the 'The Pomelo'.[27] Despite these reservations, I include it among the Han songs and ballads because it is a borderline case and because it may be viewed as a transitional piece between the popular song style and the formal literary style.[28]

CHAPTER EIGHT

Domestic Drama

The pieces in this chapter are more nearly recognizable as the Western genre of narrative ballad. Their setting is the home. Their situations are grim. The titles inform us of the domestic story to be unfolded; for example, 'Orphan Boy' and 'Ailing Wife'. The characters of the orphan boy and the wretched wife are recurring types.

Domestic drama was treated as a theme for the first time in the Han. In the earlier poetry of the Chou, attention focussed on personal, rather than family problems. Poetic settings were outdoors rather than in the home. Home was projected as a vision of peace and comfort in Chou poems portraying nostalgic soldiers on campaign.[1] The home was also the setting for ancestral sacrifice. Among the characters of girls and women in the Chou classic, brides rather than wives were portrayed, and then it was often a royal bride. Children were not mentioned, except in abstract terms, such as grandsons prayed for in formal felicitations at ancestral sacrifice.

One reason for this difference in depicting the domestic theme is the new mood of realism in the Han.[2] Elements of realism are perceptible in the Han rhapsody, but it is only fleetingly present as a novel trope.[3] In the formal *shih* ode or lyric of the Han period, realism is often presented in a stylized, even decorative manner.[4] It is in Han songs and ballads that the realistic mode is most evident, and nowhere more evident than in the mundane setting of the home. Singers often preferred to depict sordid and ugly aspects of life. There are no songs or ballads describing a happy wife with her children or a father at home with his family. It is as if the Han singers deliberately turned away from the overly lush brilliance of the rhapsody which extravagantly praised Han palaces, exotic royal parks, and magnificent capital cities. Perhaps from boredom, or from a growing sense of unease the balladeers rejected traditional themes and the subjects of the rhapsody and looked for material for their songs in the ordinary stuff of everyday life. They certainly belonged to a different social circle from the rhapsodist, who was a court poet and official like Chia I, Pan Ku, Chang Heng, and Ssu-ma Hsiang-ju, the rhapsodist *par excellence.*

One interest of this group of songs and ballads lies in the moral questions they provoke in their narrative. These moral issues arise from human relationships as much as from social ills, such as poverty. In 'The Orphan Boy', an older brother's ill-treatment of his younger brother creates the domestic drama. In 'East Gate', a man is torn between deserting his impoverished family and making his own way in life. The moral issues are projected through opposing characters whose actions and dialogue display noble and ignoble facets of human nature—fortitude and integrity, bullying and rudeness. The conflict is usually between the strong and the weak in the family, the weak falling victim to the rapacity and obstinacy of the strong.

The Ballad of the Orphan Boy

The life of an orphan boy—
An orphan boy's encounter with life:
Fated to be wretched and alone.
When Father and Mother were alive
We rode in a strong carriage,
Drove a team of four horses.
Now Father and Mother are gone,
My older brother and his wife make me trade:
South to Chiu-chiang,
East to Ch'i and Lu.
In the La month I come home,
But daren't speak of my misery.
My hair is full of nits,
My face and eyes full of dust.
My big brother says, 'Get the meal ready.'
My big sister says, 'Look after the horses.'
Up I go to the high hall,
Then hurry down to the lower hall.
The orphan boy's tears fall like rain.
They make me go and draw water at dawn,
At dusk I must fetch water again.
My hands have become chapped,
My feet go without straw sandals.
Aching, aching I tread on frost,
Among many prickly root crops I walk.
I pull up and break the thorns,
My calves hurt so I want to scream.
Tears fall spurting, spurting,
Clear tears flooding, flooding.
In winter I have no lined coat,
In summer no unlined robe.

129

To live unhappily
Is not as good as an early death,
Following on down to Yellow Springs.
Spring air quickens,
Grass shoots sprout.
In the third month silkworm mulberry,
In the sixth month I harvest melons.
Pushing the melon cart
I come back home again.
When my melon cart overturns
A few help me,
But many devour my melons.
I want people to give back the vines—
Brother and his wife are strict.
Empty-handed, I'd better hurry home
To face their reckoning.

Envoi
'In the village what shouting, shouting!
I want to send a foot-long letter
To the underworld to Father and Mother:
With Brother and his wife I can't live much longer.'

This narrative is one of the most lucid in the Han repertoire. Although it shares several features with ballads of other cultures, there is one which is distinctly Chinese. This is the character of the villain. When Western ballads or fairy tales deal with the theme of ill-treated children, the villain is often a stepmother. In Han songs and ballads this role is played by the older brother. The characterization of the evil older brother has its roots in traditional society. As an adult the older brother occupied a position of power and authority in the family, even overriding the authority of the father, according to literary evidence at least. The social aspect of this system is reflected in some poems of the *Book of Poetry*.[5] In the Han collection of anonymous songs the problems ensuing from the system are highlighted, as here in the story of the orphan boy, in one of the love songs, and, not so prominently, in 'A *Yen* Song, The Whenever Ballad' on the *carpe diem* theme, and in 'Cocks Crow'.[6]

Hans H. Frankel has made a special study of this ballad, and has singled out a number of sophisticated narrative techniques. He notes that different time sequences punctuate the long narrative: the recent time prior to the action of the ballad when the orphan boy was born and his parents died; the present phase of the narrative action; and sometime in the near future when it is anticipated that the ill-treated boy will die. The unifying element in the temporal scheme is the orphan boy's memory of his parents' death at the beginning of the story and his own

130

death-wish at the end. Various kinds of time markers are worked into this 'chronological frame': seasonal time (winter, summer, spring), festival time (the La month), and other unspecified periods. They show how the young boy's life is a series of busy jobs and they reveal indirectly the cruelty of the boy's guardians, his older brother and his wife. Festival time underscores the pathos of the story. La was the twelfth month of the lunar calendar, the time when families held a reunion to celebrate the New Year.[7] Instead of a joyful reunion he is made to run around like a slave at home. This pattern is repeated at the end of the ballad when he brings home an empty cart and gets a scolding. The pathos is deepened by the pun contained in the word *kuei*, return home, which also means to die.

The narrative is also marked by three typical journeys the orphan boy makes, prefiguring his eventual journey to the underworld to rejoin his parents. He peddles goods between Chiu-chiang (Kiukiang), Ch'i, and Lu; he fetches water for the house; and he collects food, either roots or melons.[8] Each journey is beset with troubles. Water imagery in the narrative, Frankel observes, is linked to the inevitable movement towards death: spilling tears, rain, drawing water, and Yellow Springs or the next world.

Frankel also comments on the device of paired images in the narrative. The carriage the boy rode in with his parents was a strong vehicle drawn by four horses. After their death he is made to work like a pack-horse pulling the cart of melons, which is so rickety that it overturns. The team of four horses drawing the family carriage become beasts the orphan has to look after as if he were just a stable lad. The contrast between these and other pairs of images is bathetic. They serve to emphasize the downward movement of the young master to young slave, from a high point of prosperity and happiness to a low level of destitution and misery.[9]

The narrative employs a dramatic change in point of view. The singer's voice moves from the boy speaking in the first person, to the narrator, to the brother and wife, and back to the orphan. The singer's tone ranges from pathos to impersonality, bringing the audience closer to the little human drama, then distancing it to provoke reflection. The narrative also becomes linked to other ballads through its use of commonplace expression. The closest link is with 'The Ailing Wife'; its central pathetic couplet, 'In winter I have no lined coat,/ In summer no unlined robe', re-echoes in the central envoi of the other narrative ballad. The last line of 'The Orphan Boy' is similar to the last line of the short version of 'East Gate', 'I can't go on living here . . .' These narrative techniques of shifts in time, place and speaker, the blend of pathos and bathos, and sparing but significant use of imagery, make this ballad one of the best in the Han repertoire.[10]

The Ballad of the Ailing Wife

A wife was ailing, year in, year out.
She called for her husband to come for a word.
About to speak, before she could yet speak,
Unawares her tears fell, such a spilling stream!
'I entrust to you the burden of two or three orphans.
Don't let my infants hunger or go cold.
Though they do wrong, take care not to thrash them.
I am going to die very young.
Think it over and remember.'

Envoi
As nurslings they have no coat,
Nor are their tunics lined.

He shut the gates, blocked the windows,
Settled the orphans, went to market.
On the way he met a good friend.
He sat down in tears and could not get up.
Then he begged him to buy some cakes for the orphans.
Facing his friend he wept tears and couldn't stop:
'I don't want to grieve, but I can't help it.'
He reached inside his breast and handed him the money.
The friend entered the gates.
He paced through the empty hut:
'Soon they are going to follow their mother.
Stop that—say no more!'

From small details in the narrative we may infer some background to the story. The poverty-stricken family portrayed is a recently married couple with 'two or three' very young infants. They live in an isolated spot, some way from neighbours and the market. This setting creates the dramatic crisis of the story. It is because the market and help are so far away that the father has to leave his infants untended in their home. The remote setting heightens the pathos of the family and provides a tragic cause in the story. The two focal points of the home and the market, which is mentioned but never reached, interact in ironic play. The one person who might have averted the tragedy is a friend who happens to be passing by on the road to the market, but he is too late.

The time sequence helps to unify the story, but less tautly than in 'The Orphan Boy'. It begins with the past, some years back when the wife began to be chronically ill, from poverty it is presumed. The second line plunges the audience into the dramatic crisis, when the wife talks to her husband on her deathbed. She utters a prophetic statement about her infants: 'Or they're going to die very young'. It is echoed later in the story,

'Soon they are going to follow their mother.' The wife's death is not mentioned. After her deathbed scene the narrative continues with the husband's story. His downward spiral into failure is as predictable as that of the orphan boy. He is shown begging on the road in tears. The narrative is ambiguous, it turns out, concerning the husband's reason for locking the infants in the house and leaving for the market. The last line says, 'Speak no more of deserting them.' It seems that the father had told his friend that he had contemplated abandoning them to their fate, but the audience is not aware of this possibility until the end of the story.

This ambiguity may be intentional, or it may indicate a flaw in the song's narrative structure. The text of the first half is clear and straight-forward. From the end of the envoi to the last line of the whole piece the text becomes muddled. It is unclear whether the father takes any children with him. Nor is it clear whether the friend buys food for the children or whether the father does. This creates a confusion in the last passage, for we are not sure if the friend or the father, or both, return to the house, and if it is the friend or the father who is the speaker in the last couplet. My translation gives the story more cohesion than is present in the text, and the second half might be translated quite differently. It is possible that the stylistic differences in the two halves of the ballad, and the curious placing of the envoi in the middle instead of the end of the song may signify that the original ballad stopped at the end of the envoi, and later acquired an extra passage.

Taken as a whole, the presentation is in the pathetic mode. From the first line which tells of the wife's long-term illness to the last line the story is marked by pathetic statements and description. The wife utters a gentle, helpless dying wish. She prophesies her infants' early death. They are described as inadequately clothed. They are left without a mother, and then locked up without any parent or friend. The father is forced to beg. The children cry for their dead mother. The mother's prophecy is repeated. It is typical of the Han ballad, however, that this pathos is handled without undue sentiment. The tearfulness of the mother, father, and infants is not overly emphasized, but follows from the narrative line. The singer does not intrude with additional asides or comment. He does not apportion blame for this tragedy and does not point to social injustice as its cause. The audience is left to consider if the tragedy is due to individual human error or to some wider social problem, or a combination of both factors.[11]

East Gate Ballad

long version

Leaving by East Gate
I did not look back home.
Coming inside my gates
I despaired and wanted to lament:
In the bin not a peck of grain was stored,
Then I saw on the rack no clothes hanging.

I drew my sword, left the gates,
Babes and woman clung to my robe weeping:
'Other families just long for wealth and honour,
Your poor wife will share her meal of gruel with you.

'Share her meal of gruel.
Follow the will of blue-wave Heaven above,
Look after your yellow-beak babes here below!
Today you have clear integrity,
You can't transgress the moral code!
If you only have self-regard,
Won't that be wrong?

'Today you have clear integrity,
You can't transgress the moral code!
If you only have self-regard,
Won't that be wrong?'
'Get away! I'm late leaving!'
'Mind how you go.'
'Watch for my return!'

The setting is a poor home and the characters are again a young family of a wife, a husband, and infants. In contrast with 'The Ailing Wife', pathos is now a sub-theme. The major theme is the conflict between family morality and individual freedom. The conflict is precipitated by poverty in the home. It is dramatically presented through well-defined characters. The wife, no longer portrayed pathetically on her deathbed, is a strong, principled woman who has a more positive role here as the custodian of family values. She opposes her husband who tries to deny his family responsibilities and make his own way in life. The ballad consists of eight lines of narrative spoken by the husband and thirteen lines spoken by the wife in direct address to him, the final quatrain consisting of dialogue between the two. The structure is mainly based on the dramatic conflict between the two characters and between their two opposing, irreconcilable points of view.

The story is at first told by the husband. He confesses his emotional turmoil as he views his family life in ruins. The symbolism of the gate emphasizes the enormity of the decision he has to make: within the gate he has the security of his home, despite its poverty, and the inner comfort of knowing that by staying at home he is doing what is right. Beyond the gate lies the unknown, a decline into inhumanity, even crime. The first quatrain is ambiguous. I have rendered it to suggest that the husband is torn by anxiety and indecision. It might also be rendered to suggest that the husband has once left home and now returns to find the terrible tragedy at home.[12] The gate symbolism of the title and song-text has additional meaning through a literary echo from the *Book of Poetry*:

> I leave from the north gates,
> My despairing heart in distress.
> I am straightened and poor.
> No one knows my hardship.[13]

The unknown man in the Chou classic is leaving the city in an attempt to shed his problems. He is poor and feels utterly alone with no hope of help. In the Han ballad the husband's world is not the city but his family within his own gates. He wishes to leave that world behind. The image of his sword is linked to the symbolism of the gates. It reveals him as a man of action, perhaps a fighting man who will offer his services to a lord or join some outlawed band of men in a life of crime. The fact that his wife warns him against transgressing the moral code indicates that she fears he will become a criminal.[14] The image of his physical strength is dramatically contrasted with the image of her weakness and vulnerability as she and the infants cling to his robes. The image of weakness, however, masks an inner strength, just as the sword's power hides an inner weakness.

In her feminine pose of weakness, the wife begins her plea to her husband to stay with her and share the crisis. She insists that she is not a seeker after wealth and status, whatever the cost. She values her family. She shows her maternal instinct in offering to share her meagre plate of food with her husband to try to coax him to stay. She reminds him of their infants, a Heaven-sent gift. In looking after them, she argues, he is doing what is right. If he is selfish and goes in pursuit of his own career, he will be morally wrong. He rejects her pleas and arguments with a rude curtness, born of anguish and despair. She bids him farewell with the same tender generosity of spirit as before: 'Mind how you go.'[15]

The ballad has several typical features which are skilfully integrated into the narrative. Dialogue is a mixture of colloquial speech and formalities. Two-thirds of the piece is given to speech, allowing the characters to reveal themselves. Some of the dialogue is repeated, especially the pathetic line, 'Share her meal of gruel', and the central moral argument of the wife. There is repetition in the parallel structure of the first quatrain, which focusses on the symbolism of the gates. There are commonplace expressions, such as 'Leaving by East Gate', the image of weeping infants and wife, and the couplet, 'Through the will of blue-wave Heaven above/ Are your yellow-beak babes here below.' This couplet is almost the same as the penultimate couplet of the *carpe diem* song, 'A *Yen* Song, The Whenever Ballad', which echoes this ballad's moral dilemma, despair, and poverty. As I suggested in my discussion of that less clear-cut, sometimes enigmatic piece, it is through the relationship between certain passges in the Han repertoire that some of the enigmas may be resolved. It is probable that the dramatic conflict of 'East Gate' informs to some extent the elliptical finale of 'A *Yen* Song', suggesting its possible social context.

Realism is a characteristic of 'East Gate'. The borrowed phrase, 'yellow-beak', denotes the desperate hunger of children like hatchlings clamouring with beaks upstretched for their parents to bring food. The picture of poverty is realistically conveyed in the first passage: an empty foodbin and an empty clothes-line graphically illustrate the family's poverty. The ballad is important in the Han repertoire for its portrayal of the wife's courage. This portrait is somewhat idealized, the idealism nicely accentuated by the touches of realism in the descriptive vignettes. As a heroine she is stronger than other wives in tragic balladic narratives, such as Lan-chih who drowns herself in 'A Peacock Southeast Flew', and the wife of Ch'iu Hu in 'Harmonizing with Mr. Pan's Poem', who also drowns herself.[16] She is not so entertaining or independent as Ch'in Lo-fu, who jauntily flirts with an importunate official and then rebuffs him. She is more credible than the good wife in 'The Lunghsi Ballad' who is idealized for the purposes of irony and satire. The wife of 'East Gate' may perhaps be seen as the prototype of heroines in the later literary tradition, such as Tou O or Li Wa in drama and fiction.[17]

East Gate Ballad

short version

Leaving by East Gate
I did not look back home.
Coming inside my gates
I despaired and wanted to lament:
In the bin not a peck of rice was stored,
Then I saw on the rack no clothes hanging.
I drew my sword, from East Gate I went,
In the hut my babes and their mother clung to my robe weeping:
'Other families just long for wealth and honour,

Your poor wife will share her meal of gruel with you.
Through the will of blue-wave Heaven above
We now enjoy these yellow-beak babes here below.
Today you are doing wrong.'
'Get off! Get away!
I'm late in leaving.
I can't go on living here when my hair's nearly white.'

The first section of narrative is almost the same as that of the long version. In the second section the short version deletes the speech on morality and its repetition, reducing the long passage's eight lines to just one. The repetition of line 11 in the long version is also deleted. Line 21 of the long version is expanded to two lines in the short. The closures of both versions are different. In the long version the harshness of the marital quarrel is softened by the wistful farewell. In the short version the husband's angry frustration is developed into a final explosion of anger about his wasted life at home. Its diction is a half echo of 'The Orphan Boy'. The singer of the short version clearly felt that the long passage of moral censure was not only tedious in its repetition but unattractive in content to his audience. This short version brings the song closer to the pathetic mode than the other's dramatic clash of personalities and points of view. The techniques of song, such as repetition of lines or words or phrases, are subordinated in the short version to the narrative line.[18]

The Ballad of Shang-liu-t'ien

In the village is a weeping boy
Just like my own father's son.
As I turn my carriage to question the boy
I cannot check my heartfelt sorrow.

The indeterminacy of character, setting, and situation of this song has attracted several specific interpretations. The third century AD commentator, Ts'ui Pao, explains that Shang-liu-t'ien is the name of a place where a certain family lived. The parents died, and the eldest brother refused to care for his orphaned younger brothers. His neighbours composed this sad song on behalf of the younger brothers to satirize the elder brother.[19]

Yü Kuan-ying offers a different interpretation. He cites a song entitled 'The Old Ballad of Shang-liu-t'ien', which clearly expresses the theme of fraternal cruelty:

137

As I leave by this West Gate of Shang-tu
Three thorn trees are growing from the same single root.
One thorn is broken off, not fully grown.
Brothers there were two or three,
The younger brothers were thrown out, alone and poor.[20]

The title of this old song relates to that of the Han quatrain. On the other hand, the two verses have in common only the theme of a luckless boy. Hu K'e-chia (AD 1809 ed.) amends the text of the old song so that Shang-tu becomes Shang-liu, which forces a comparison between the two stories and texts. But it would be imprudent to make that amendment and that comparison serve as evidence that the old song constitutes the background story of the Han song. While it is true that several Han ballads deal with the theme or sub-theme of the cruelty of an older brother to his younger brother, the theme is not necessarily present in the Han quatrain.

The unexplained individualized emotion here contrasts with the social specificity of the emotion expressed in other Han domestic ballads. The vagueness itself provides a clue to the interpretation of the piece. The stranger who happens to be driving in his carriage through the boy's village sees the weeping child and responds to him as an older brother, 'Just like my own father's son'. The curious turn of phrase may denote that the stranger's father had a son by a different mother than the stranger's, and that this son is perhaps a generation younger than the stranger. The brief narrative merely relates that he turns back to talk to the child; no dialogue expands the story line. But this quatrain is not really concerned with the boy's story. It focusses on the stranger's emotional response to the sight of the child. That the mere sight of him in tears provokes such a strong reaction from the stranger points toward the cult of sentiment and the rejection of the stronger narrative of Han songs featuring children. The effect of the quatrain is an appealingly sentimental scene which depicts the persona's fine sensibilities. It is notable for the absence of that stoicism which is the hallmark of the typical Han repertoire. This quatrain marks a transition between domestic narratives and those sentimental lyrics of the late and post-Han which explored not so much the reality of everyday life as the inner workings of the human psyche.[21]

CHAPTER NINE

Homeward Thoughts

The theme of nostalgia developed in the Han and later became an important sub-genre of Chinese poetry. Like many other literary themes it has its origin in the *Book of Poetry*. In certain Chou war poems, anonymous soldiers expressed a simple longing to return home from the battlefield: 'Oh to go home!'[1] Nostalgia also formed a leitmotif of some pieces in the *Songs of Ch'u*. It took its inspiration from the first long poem, which talks of political exile. When the unhappy courtier of 'Encountering Sorrow' is about to flee from the turmoil of the world he hesitates and says, 'I suddenly caught a glimpse below of my old home.'[2] This yearning for the cherished dream of former happiness in the familiar surroundings of home is the major theme of this next group of Han songs.

The reasons for absence from the home are not always given in the songs. Some form of official work is vaguely mentioned or referred to in a small detail. A 'capstring' indicates that the character is a male official. A 'feast' suggests that the character is some sort of a male functionary. The 'land of the Huns' reveals that the setting is border warfare or border guard duty and that the character is a military officer. Some songs lack these clues; their setting and characters are more indeterminate than is typical of popular Han songs. The clues sometimes imply that the characters belong to the upper classes of society. Moreover, diction and tone remove them from the impoverished, desperate families and from the ranks of the ordinary soldier encountered in anti-war and domestic songs. Brutal dialogue and desperate behaviour are absent. The songs are coloured by refinement of diction and a genteel sensibility. Absent too are the qualities of toughness, stoicism, and courage which characterized the soldiers of the anti-war songs. The theme of nostalgia, when it is the dominant theme, in itself suggests a tender sentiment, and this group of songs is more than a little awash with the fruits of sorrow. Apart from the elliptical references to the identity of the characters and the refined diction which separate them from ordinary folk, the fact of travel itself suggests that this group of songs has to do with the upper echelons of society. Except for conscription or corvée labour the ordinary man would not normally leave the land to travel long distances for long periods. It was not part of his way of life. Travel in the ancient world was essentially part of the business of the metropolitan, educated class of men undertaken for the purpose of administering the empire and ensuring social and political control. It was also, of course, the occupation of the merchant class, but they do not feature in these songs, partly because of a deep-seated cultural prejudice against merchants from the late Chou era on.[3] In general, songs and ballads which have as their main theme a longing to go home have less to do with humble folk than the class of high-ranking official who ruled and administered the provincial regions of the empire. This kind of song reflects a man's world. The man travels and longs for home, the woman stays at home, longing for her absent man.

Much of the language and imagery of later nostalgic verse was crystalized in these anonymous Han songs. The travel topos developed a cluster of motifs and images. The far road, *yüan tao*, is travelled by a man called a wanderer, *yu-tzu*, who often seems to be on a futile mission. The typical pose of the wanderer is gazing far back (*yüan wang*) towards his old village (*ku-hsiang*), or birthplace (*so sheng*). He voices his longing to return home (*kuei*). The images are of the long road, wheels turning back along the track home, tumbleweed whirled about torn from its roots, the season of autumn, coldness, blustery winds, plaintive sounds in nature, natural barriers which forbid return, and the wasted appearance of the wanderer. Such songs usually end with an expression of helplessness tinged with rage, despair, and tearful grief.

The theme of nostalgia inhibits any sense of the excitement of travel, or desire for adventure, or even curiosity about distant regions and foreign parts. Leaving home means unending misery and a blighted existence. Despite the narrowly defined social parameters of its composition, the nostalgic song held a lasting attraction for the Chinese.

An Old Eight Changes Song

North winds in early autumn come
Blowing round my Chang-hua Terrace.
Floating clouds, many tinged with twilight,
Seem to come from Yen-tzu hills.
Withered mulberry groans in deep woods,
Crickets echo on bare steps.
Whirling tumbleweed marches on.
Bitterly a wanderer pines.
His old village nowhere in sight,
Eternal gazing starts from this time on.

The two placenames, Chang-hua Terrace and Yen-tzu hills, link this song with the region of Ch'u. The terrace was built by a king of Ch'u in the Spring and Autumn era of the Chou. Yen-tzu is mentioned in 'Encountering Sorrow' of the *Songs of Ch'u*. It was the mythical place where the sun set.[4] Despite these specific names of the historical and mythological past, the song is marked by indeterminacy of character, time, and situation. The link with Ch'u is developed through other echoes from *Songs of Ch'u*. The solitary figure wandering in a bleak landscape derives from the pathetic mode of Ch'u elegiac verse.[5]

An Old Song

Autumn winds sough and sigh, sad enough to kill.
I go out so sad,
I come in so sad.
At the feast what men are they
Who do not harbour grief?
It makes me white-haired.
In the land of the Huns constant whirlwinds,
Trees how they toss, toss!
I left home, each day hastening further,
Robe and belt each day quickly slackening.
Thoughts of love I cannot tell.
In my guts carriage wheels turning, rolling.

The second half of the song tells the story. A man left home to do border duty in the north far from his native place. His longing to return makes him pine and become thin and grow prematurely white-haired. It is autumn. There is a feast, but instead of revelry, everyone is obsessed with nostalgia. The theme of returning home predominates, but there are several sub-themes: war, *carpe diem*, love. Familiar balladic devices are used: the binome 'sough, sigh', which is reinforced by the visual pun in the first line of autumn (*ch'iu*), and sad (*ch'ou*), which is written with the character for autumn with a heart-emotion indicator. The binomes continue with 'toss, toss', and the repetitive phrase 'turning, rolling', the movements described contrasting with the enforced immobility of the soldier. There is also the device of repetition in the construction of lines 2 and 3, and in the pivotal expression of time, 'each day', in the penultimate couplet. The question and answer formula appears in lines 4–6. The most significant device in the song is commonplace expression. The last couplet, with its striking imagery and forthright phrase, 'In my guts', is exactly the same as the last couplet of 'The Sad Song Ballad' at the end of this chapter. It also shares several lines with the first poem of the 'Nineteen Old Poems'.[6] The song's line six is similar to that poem's line 13:

'Thinking of you makes one grow old'. The song's line nine is similar to the poem's line nine: 'Leaving you each day ever further'. The song's line ten is similar to the poem's line ten: 'Robe and belt each day ever slacker'. In other words, the song shares five of its lines with lines in two other pieces, an anonymous Han song and an anonymous Han old poem.[7]

A Long Song Ballad, no. 3

Tall, tall pavilion on the mountain,
White, white stars among the clouds.
Distant gazing makes his heart pine,
The wanderer longing for his birthplace.
Driving his carriage he leaves the north gates,
Stares far-off at Loyang city.
Soft winds blow long thorn trees,
Young, young boughs and leaves bend down.
Yellow birds give chase in flight,
Trill, trill, at play with sounds of music.
He halts to gaze at West River.
Tears fall and soak his silken capstring.

This song belongs to the set of three which was discussed in Chapter Three (pp. 68–9). My reason for presenting each of the songs in different chapters is that they each have quite different content and do not seem to belong as a set. This is the most literary of the set. The pavilion, Loyang city, West River (which contains an historical allusion), silken capstring, and the quatrain 'Soft winds . . . sounds of music' (which echoes a classical poem), all point to literary diction and themes. The classical allusion of the quatrain may or may not express the idea contained in poem no. 32 of the *Book of Poetry*, but it uses the images of that poem: the joyous south wind (*k'ai feng*), the thorn tree, the young branches, the yellow birds and their song. The classical poem tells of a mother who has seven grown-up sons, but none of them 'consoles the mother's heart'. The last couplet echoes lines from another poem, no. 28, from the classic anthology and introduces another allusion, this time to West River. In the Chou poem are the lines: 'I gaze after her, can no longer see her,/ I stand still and weep'.[8] The allusion to West River concerns a man named Wu Ch'i (d. 381 BC), who was born in Wei state. When he left home he told his mother he would never return to Wei unless he went back in glory as prime minister. Later, although his mother died, he did not go home. In due course he was appointed prefect of West River in another state named Wei. When he had to leave the region, due to slanderous accusations, he wept over West River, grieving that his lord had believed the slander. The reference to Loyang in line 6 suggests that the time of the song might be in the Latter Han. The historical allusion gives a narrative context to the song: an official had to leave the capital and say goodbye to his family. He took up a post at West River, but when the time came to leave he had grown attached to the place and felt sad. The two allusions together, the classical and the historical, indicate that the official is longing for his old home and the family he left behind.[9]

Mount Wu is High

Mount Wu is high,
High and vast.
Huai River is deep,
Hard and fast flowing.
I want to go back east.
Oh why don't I do it?
I just have no pole or oar.
Oh how the river seethes and churns!
I lean over the river, gaze far along.
Tears fall, soaking my robe.
The human heart on a far road longs for return.
What more is there to say?

The two placenames, Mount Wu and Huai River, set the song in the region of Ch'u. The wanderer's home is somewhere in the east. Nature bars his way home. It is possible that the wanderer is an official. The drenching tears reveal that he is a man of tender sensibilities. The more resolute last line rescues the song from the maudlin. The repetition of the epithet 'high' in the first couplet, the question and answer formula, and the final question are devices of the song repertoire.[10]

The Sad Song Ballad

Sad song may serve as weeping,
A far gaze may serve as going home.
With love I remember my old village,
Brooding love, looming memories.
I want to go back, but there's no one at home.
I want to ford the river, but there's no boat on the river.
Thoughts of love I cannot tell.
In my guts carriage wheels turning, rolling.

The opening couplet expresses a stoical attitude despite the turmoil aroused by nostalgia. Much of the song echoes with lines and phrases in other songs and poems of the Han, but it is none the less poignant for that.[11]

CHAPTER TEN

Love Songs

Love in its infinite variety is pictured in these songs. A lady greets her distant lord, lovers vow eternal fidelity, a widow grieves for her drowned lord, a seemingly innocent girl falls under suspicion, and several girls complain of desertion. Although the brief love vow and the longer narrative forms occur, most of these songs are cast in the form of a love plaint voiced by a woman. So, already in the Han, the trend for depicting a woman's doomed love was set in motion, culminating in the fashionable love poetry of the Southern Dynasties three centuries later.

Two of the songs deal with married love. Only three songs depict happy love. The most frequent theme is desertion. The typical character of the songs is a jilted girl. There is a considerable difference between the portrayal of love in the Chou *Book of Poetry* and in Han songs. Anonymous poets of the Chou usually limited their imaginative portrait of a wife to her happy hour as a bride going to her wedding, leaving the reader or audience to assume that the cherished dream of wedded bliss lasted into old age or death. A bride in the Chou anthology was euphemistically referred to as 'one to grow old with her lord'.[1] The Han singers generally reject the romantic dream of the wedding day, preferring to depict the darker side of marriage and love. In this respect they developed the plaintive strain in the Chou anthology, ignoring the happy marriage songs.

The social framework of these songs seems to reflect the upper-class way of life rather than the truly popular, or folk, style. The evidence lies in small details of luxury, such as a bed, silk curtains, a woman's sash, the high hall of the home, the terrace and gates of a mansion, and jewels, gold vessels, and wine. The opulent details scattered among the songs are quite different from the folk-use of hyperbole in passages describing luxury with all the zest of the admiring poor. The language of these songs moreover reflects at times a literary awareness in their use of classical allusions. A fishing rod and fishtail, for example, suggest folk idiom; in fact, the context in which those images are used shows that they are echoes from the *Book of Poetry*.

In this chapter we are fortunate to have two anonymous titles with different versions. In each case the longer version contrasts with the more laconic narrative of the shorter. The songs in general display an interesting variety of form and metre. Some are brief four-line pieces, some are several dozen lines long. 'Almighty on High!', 'I Lean from the High Terrace', and 'The One I Love' have irregular metres. The two versions of 'Along the Embankment' are almost completely regular pentasyllabic songs. 'The Harp Lay' is in the archaic tetrasyllabic metre of the *Book of Poetry* which was used in Han hymns. The other love songs in this selection are pentasyllabic.

Kuo Mao-ch'ien classified three of these songs as Han military songs. They are 'Almighty', 'I Lean', and 'The One I Love'. As one might expect, the more plangent of the songs, such as 'Along the Embankment' and 'The White Head Lament', Kuo classified as modal pieces, in the Clear-mode and Ch'u-mode, respectively.

Almighty on High!

Almighty on High!
I long to know my lord,
Let our love never fade or die
Till mountains have no peaks,
Or rivers run dry,
Till thunder roars in winter,
Or snow pours down in summer,
Till the skies merge with the ground—
Then may I die with my lord!

This song is a mock-serious oath to the supreme deity, Shang-ti. There are two small clues which together suggest that the speaker is female. The word *chün* in the second and last lines may be translated as 'you' of either gender and as 'lord'.[2] In the last line the word *kan* is a form of polite address from a subordinate to a superior. The speaker might, of course, be a youth addressing his male lover who is his social superior. I have taken the song to be by a girl to her male lover. The oath is a litany of descriptions of the end of the world, to the end of time. The last involves a myth: in the beginning chaos reigned, then came the act of creation when the sky separated from the earth and the universe came into being. When the sky and the earth merge again, the world will come to an end. The litany gives the song a certain arch humour.[3]

I Lean from the High Terrace

I lean from the high terrace balcony.
Below there are clear waters, clear and cool.
In the river there is sweet grass, my eyes hold orchis.
A brown goose flies high, how far off it soars!
An arched bow has shot the goose.
Oh let my lord live long, ten thousand years!

The tenor of the song is lyrical and courtly. The images suggest that the lady of a noble lord gazes from her high balcony in the direction her lord took when parting from her. She notes the signs of spring, a metaphor for renewed love: clear water, sweet grass, orchis, and a goose in flight. The tone of bucolic lyricism is interrupted by the image of the goose killed randomly by a hunter's bow. The lady prays that her lord, who perhaps is on a military expedition, will not suffer the same fate.[4] She prays that he will enjoy a long life—this felicitation closure is a commonplace expression. This early song on the theme of lovers' separation combines lyrical grace with courtly restraint. The analogy between the natural world and the human world is similar to that used in 'A Crow Bore Eight or Nine Chicks', but here it is successfully integrated into the song's structure. The three couplets may also form a ritual address by a retainer to his lord, ending with an offering of a dead goose.[5]

The One I Love

The one I love
Is south of the great lakes.
What shall I send you?
A tortoiseshell hatpin with twin pearls,
With jade I'll braid and plait it.
I hear that you have another love—
I will break it, smash and burn it,
Smash and burn it,
Face into the wind, scatter its ashes.
From this day on
Nevermore will I love you.
My love for you is severed.
Cocks crow, dogs bark.
My brother and his wife must find out.
Alas! Oh my!
Autumn winds sough, sough. Dawn Wind hastens.
The east at a blink whitening will find out!

The song begins with a simple, prosaic statement that a lover lives in the south apart from the speaker. The second couplet uses the question and answer formula to describe an elaborate love-token. The gift explains the relationship between the lovers. It is a hatpin worn by an official to secure his cap of office. We may surmise that he is a high-ranking young official on a tour of duty. He has been in the girl's district for a while and has had a liaison with her. Then he had to move away and continue his circuit in the south. The girl believes his love is true and is preparing to send him an expensive gift. These first five lines relate that part of the story prior to the present time of the song. The rest of the piece is a narrative of the girl's present dilemma and her anxiety about her future. She has just heard that her lover has acquired a new mistress down south. She instinctively destroys the gift which symbolized her love, hoping to stifle her passion for her false lover. Then she pauses to consider what will happen when her family find out about her romance. 'Cocks crow, dogs bark' echoes poem no. 23 of the *Book of Poetry*: 'Slowly! Gently!/ Do not move my kerchief;/ do not make the dog bark!' in which a girl 'like jade' flirts nervously with a strange man in the forest.[6] The metaphor denotes gossip which will travel fast in the community. The girl in the Han songs says she is afraid of her brother's reaction, for he will resent the fact that she has ruined her chances of a fine marriage which would have made the family prosper.[7] The song's closure refers to the swiftly approaching season of autumn: Dawn Wind is the peregrine falcon, a metaphor for the swift passage of time. My conjecture is that the season of autumn, poetically linked to spring in Chinese, hints that spring was the time when the girl's romance blossomed. Six months later in autumn she is pregnant and her condition is becoming all too apparent. Hence the repetition, 'must find out', 'will find out'. The gossip in the community will soon be supported by the proof.

If this conjecture is correct, the song becomes more than a simple plaint about a fickle lover.[8] The singer depicts the giddy romance of an impulsive, naive young girl of a well-to-do family (her jewelled gift), who believed that the attentions of a young official were serious. The song shows how such an impulse, at first private and personal, has later social implications which may affect the person and the family for a lifetime. This the song achieves without moral censure. The girl herself is left to voice her own dismay and guilt.[9]

The Harp Lay

'Lord, don't ford the river!'
My lord did ford the river,
Sank in the river and died.
What's to be done for my lord now?

Ts'ui Pao provides the earliest context for this song.[10] One morning, Tzu-kao, a Korean from Chin-tsu village, went to punt his boat when he saw a mad old man with his white hair hanging loose, holding up a wine-jar. Though the current was strong, the old man went to ford the river. His wife followed to try and stop him, but she was too late, and then he drowned. She took up her harp and sang a very sad song [the song-text], and then she threw herself into the river and also died. Tzu-kao returned home and told his wife, Li-yü, and she was so moved that she played her harp and recorded the tragic song. All who heard it were deeply moved. Then Li-yü taught it to a neighbouring woman.[11]

Along the Embankment

long version

Rushes grow in my pool,
Rushes grow in my pool,
Their leaves so thick and lush.
A perfect sense of decorum
No one can know so well as I.
Common gossip that melts yellow gold
Has forced you to live apart.

I remember when you left me,
I remember when you left me,
Alone I am sad, ever cruel my sorrow.
I imagine I see your face,
Feelings tangle, bruise my heart.
Now sad night after night never more will I sleep.

Don't through glory and renown,
Don't through glory and renown,
Reject one you loved before.
Don't because fish and meat are costly
Reject the leek and shallot.
Don't because hemp and jute are cheap
Reject straw and rushes.

Your doubly favoured one has now grown cruelly withered,
Your doubly favoured one has now grown cruelly withered.
Your moving boat ever cruelly vanishes.
Please set your mind at rest,
Take care not to be anxious.
I remember taking leave of you,
And when will the time come
When we'll sit together again and face each other?

I go out so cruelly sad,
I go out so cruelly sad,
I come in so cruelly sad.
Many the sad border winds,
Trees how they sough, sough.
Today let's be happy in our love.
May your years last one thousand autumns!

While the song is clearly a love plaint, its narrative background is unsure. The speaker is a girl who at first says that she has behaved correctly, but even so other people's malicious gossip has caused a rift between her lover and herself. She feels despair after their separation. She then accuses her lover of contemplating desertion for ambition's sake, and perhaps for another, more attractive girl. She then admits that she has lost her looks and that is the reason her lover left her. She wonders when they will meet again. Finally, she says that the reason for the separation is that her lover is on border duty. She still loves him and hopes he will survive the war. Four reasons are proffered for the man's departure: scandal, loss of feminine allure through aging, ambition, and border warfare. The reasons do not seem entirely compatible, but it is possible that all four maintain in the narrative. It is a further possibility that the girl is considering various reasons why the man might have left her.

The song, which exists in two similar versions, has attracted a number of putative authors and has been taken as the biographical account of an empress of the post-Han era. The authors to whom the song has been attributed are Ts'ao Ts'ao, Ts'ao P'ei, and Empress Chen of the late Han and early Wei. Ts'ao Ts'ao founded the Wei Dynasty but died before ascending the throne. He is known by his posthumous title, Emperor Wu of the Wei. A number of songs and ballads are attributed to him, many of them imitations of Han originals. His son, Ts'ao P'ei, became the first ruling emperor of the Wei with the title, Emperor Wen. It is the story of Ts'ao P'ei's first marriage, based on historial fact, which has become woven into the fabric of the interpretation of this anonymous Han song. When he was made heir apparent he took the Lady Chen as his consort. Later, when she had been promoted to the rank of empress, she was slandered at court by Empress Kuo, so Ts'ao P'ei made Empress Chen commit suicide. When she was near to death, so the legend goes, she composed a poem which was the text of this song. For centuries the tradition has persisted that she composed the piece. Equally strong is the alternative tradition that Ts'ao P'ei composed it himself.[12]

Let us consider the alleged biographical details in the song to determine whether it narrates a biographical episode in the lives of Ts'ao P'ei, the Wei Emperor Wen, and his consort, Empress Chen, or whether the song exhibits the typical stylistic features common to other anonymous Han songs and ballads and in its original form is innocent of the historical drama which later commentators attached to it.

The first stanza might well relate the circumstances of the historical royal couple, especially the combination of 'gossip' and 'yellow gold', and the enforced separation. It is possible to read the first stanza either abstractly as the plaint of an ill-fated palace lady who links her misfortune of disgrace and demotion to that of other palace ladies, notably Empress Ch'en of the Han, or specifically as the plaint of Empress Chen of the Wei who links her disgrace with that of her royal predecessor.[13] The latter interpretation, however, is based solely on inference; there is no hard biographical fact in the first stanza which proves the historical connection. Moreover, the link between the two empresses is tenuous; Empress Ch'en was demoted legally by Emperor Wu because she failed to produce a male heir, while Empress Chen was the victim of defamation.

The remaining stanzas, moreover, fail to corroborate the claim, already tenuous, that the first stanza may be biographical. Stanza two contains several conventional expressions. The first image of luxuriant leaves in the opening lines of the song and the trope of sleeplessness in the closing lines of this stanza derive from the *Book of Poetry*, but were poetic clichés by the Han.[14] The third stanza removes the song even further from the royal biography. It expresses in a repetitive manner a man's rejection of a humble wife because he is ambitious for a successful career and a better wife. Here the song is close in meaning and expression to such anonymous Han songs as 'East Gate' and the *carpe diem* song, 'The Whenever Ballad'. Moreover, the latter ballads introduce the concept of morality into their narrative just as this song does in its first stanza. Like the wife in 'East Gate', the girl in the 'Embankment' song rejects the lure of success at the expense of moral integrity. The domestic images of this third stanza recall the realism of the narratives of humble, impoverished families in the anonymous Han repertoire more than the portrayal of the life of a palace lady.

The fourth stanza again departs from the story of Empress Chen. There was no question of Empress Chen losing favour because she was old and losing her beauty, as this song laments. Moreover, Empress Chen's husband, the Emperor Wen, did not leave the capital by boat. This stanza follows the style of the Han popular song in its restrained, even lyrical narrative of departure and in its quiet, affectionate tone, reminiscent of the finale of 'East Gate', long version: 'Mind how you go'.

The last stanza provides final evidence that the song belongs to the tradition of the anonymous Han repertoire of popular song. The female persona narrates that her lover has left her for the border, where conventionally he will do corvée work or guard an outpost. Her plaintive narrative ends abruptly, however, with a felicitation formula in which she wishes their love will endure and that he will live long. This ending, taken together with the endings of stanza two, in which the girl complains of sleeplessness, and of stanza four, in which she hopes for a reunion, do not depict the situation of Empress Chen in the historical episode. These endings do not convey the emotions of an empress about to commit suicide, a suicide which the emperor has graciously allowed her to carry out.

The song is full of the sort of narrative inconsistencies and stanzaic looseness which typify other narratives in this anonymous selection from the Han. It is no doubt due to the mention of scandal and to imperial 'gold' that the song has lent itself to the allegorizing interpretation of which Chinese literary commentators have traditionally been so fond. The most prudent conclusion to be drawn is that the content of the song does not match the biographical facts of the royal Wei family, that it belongs to the anonymous Han repertoire, and that the attributions to the Ts'ao family or to Empress Chen are spurious.

Let us now summarize the elements in the song which characterize it as a typical Han popular song. The major trope is the repetition of lines and semantic patterns, besides the repetition of key words like 'remember', and of the vocabulary of departure and parting. There are echoes from the *Book of Poetry*, not conscious literary quotations but traditional borrowings of images and expressions which are skilfully integrated into the song. There are echoes, too, from other anonymous Han songs, with similar phrasing and parallel situations. The closure, especially, contains two commonplace expressions. It resembles the closure of 'Up the Mound', 'Song of Melancholy', and 'A *Yen* Song, The Whenever Ballad' (in Chapter Two), and 'The White Head Lament', long version. The first three lines of the last stanza of 'Along the Embankment' resemble lines 2–3 of 'An Old Song' in the previous chapter, while the next two lines, 'Many the sad border winds,/ Trees how they sough, sough', are similar to lines 7–8 of 'An Old Song'.[15]

Along the Embankment

short version

Rushes grow in my pool
Their leaves so thick and lush.
A perfect sense of morality
None knows so well as your wife.
Common gossip that melts yellow gold
Has forced you to live apart.
I remember when you left me,
Alone I am sad, ever cruel my sorrow.

I imagine I see your face,
Feelings tangle, bruise my heart.
I remember you, ever cruel my sorrow,
Night after night I cannot sleep.
Don't through glory and renown
Reject one you loved before.
Don't because fish and meat are cheap
Reject the leek and shallot.
Don't because hemp and jute are cheap
Reject straw and rushes.
I go out so cruelly sad,
I come in so cruelly sad.
Many the sad border winds,
Trees how they sough, sough.
May army life though lonely make you happy,
May your years last one thousand autumns.

A comparison between the previous long version and this short version of the song title is interesting for the light it sheds on the process of composition. Simple repetitions are omitted, thus lines 2, 9, 15, 22, and 30 of the long version are dropped. Stanza four of the long version is completely excised, reducing thereby the confusing mix of reasons for the man's departure. Just one vestige of that stanza is retained: the female persona's affectionate anxiety, 'Please set your mind at rest,/ Take care not to be anxious', is skilfully woven into the final part of the short version: 'May army life though lonely make you happy', a line which replaces the long version's commonplace expression, 'Today let's be happy in our love'. The contrasting epithet 'costly' in the fourth line of stanza three of the long version is smoothed over to bring it into line with the similar pattern ending that passage, so that 'cheap' is repeated. The indeterminacy of persona in the long version is amended in the short version, line 4, with the introduction of the self-deprecatory word *ch'ieh*, concubine, or myself (used by a female), which I have translated as 'wife', though that relationship might not be present or implied. As with other short versions of a song title, the stanzaic divisions are removed to form one continuous narrative. The monologue form of the narrative marks a departure from such narratives as 'The Orphan Boy', 'The Ailing Wife', and 'East Gate', but is similar to *carpe diem* pieces such as 'West Gate' and 'Song of Melancholy'. In general, however, despite the changes in the short version, the intent of both pieces remains the same. The changes reveal an editorial mind at work, marking a trend toward the prosaic and away from the long version's lyrical song idiom.[16]

The White Head Lament

long version

White as mountaintop snow,
White as the moon between clouds.
I hear you have two loves,
That's why you have broken from me.

When we lived together in the city
Did we ever have a keg of wine at a party?
Today a keg of wine at a party,
Tomorrow dawn the top of the canal.
I trudge along the royal canal,
Canal water east then westward flows.

By the east city wall and there's a fuel-gatherer.
By the west city wall and there's a fuel-gatherer.
The two fuel-gatherers urge each other on;
Without kin, for whom would they feel pride?

Bleak, bleak, always bleak, bleak.
A bride at her wedding will not weep.
She longs to get a man of one heart,
Till white-headed time he would not leave her.

Bamboo rod so supple, supple!
Fishtail so thick and glossy!
When a man wants to know you,
What need has he of dagger-coins?
Such a crackle, like horses snapping wicker!
On the river great lords make merry.
Today let's be happy together.
May your years last to ten thousand!

The title proclaims that this song is a love plaint. On reading through the piece, however, it turns out to comprise seemingly disparate elements which do not cohere. The final section, for example, far from being a lament is a joyful burst of high spirits. Problems of structure are evident in other long Han songs, but have been found to be amenable to some sort of solution despite their initial incoherence. The song's five stanzas consist of a girl's lament that her lover has proved to be fickle (lines 1–10), an interlude (lines 11–14), an idealized view of marriage from a girl's point of view (lines 15–18), and a final passage which comments on two types of love already depicted, failure and success, and which proposes a resolution of the problem of love.

154

The title of the song is taken from the last line of stanza four: 'Till white-headed time he would not leave her'. The trope itself derives from the *Book of Poetry*, in which a bride is called 'one to grow old with her lord', and where the refrain 'together with you I was to grow old' occurs in three poems on a broken marriage.[17] The song's opening couplet develops the colour imagery of the title's trope, which is a traditional metaphor for a happy wedded life. Although it might be construed as a joke to compare, the white thatch of two old people with the snow-capped mountain, the intent is quite serious. The whiteness of the metaphors also denotes purity and honesty. These qualities are negated in the second couplet.

Stanza two continues with the plaint of the persona, conventionally identified as a jilted girl. She walks like a waif along the canal, a setting which recalls the other Han song, 'Along the Embankment', in terms of persona, mood, and situation. Water is often ominous in such narratives, and some heroines commit suicide by drowning.[18] The girl dully watches the water's current flowing 'east then westward', a tidal motion symbolizing her indecision and time aimlessly passing, as she wonders where to go after she has been deserted. The water image leads into the next stanza's interlude through the repetition of 'east' and 'west'. This quatrain is enigmatic. Perhaps it is explained by the proverb in poem no. 254 of the *Book of Poetry*: 'Consult with the grass- and fuel-gatherers'.[19] The Han song may use this echo from the Chou classic to suggest that humble though they are, these workmen are serene and happy because they have their families. As such, they contrast with the solitary girl who may now have no home.

This quatrain in its turn points forward to the next vignette of a new character in the narrative, this time a bride who is contemplating her forthcoming marriage. She is as yet untouched by the failure of love. She hopes for a 'man of one heart', unaware that the fate of the first girl in the narrative is likely to be repeated in her own life. The 'one heart' will soon prove to be 'two loves'. This vignette poses an ideal view of marriage through the character of the innocent bride. Yet this ideal is prefaced with a mocking refrain: 'Bleak, bleak, always bleak, bleak', which recalls the first girl's brush with harsh reality. The contrast between the ideal and the real, subtly managed in the song, enhanced by proverbial wisdom and plaintive epithets, creates an irony which proves to be the song's structural motif.

There is a sharp break in tone with the last passage. The admiring first couplet, seemingly about fishing, derives from the *Book of Poetry*, perhaps, again, not a conscious quotation, but a traditional cliché. Many nuptial songs in the Chou classic contain fish imagery, especially those featuring the wedding of royalty and the nobility:

> Wherewith does she angle?
> Of silk is her fishing-line,
> This child of the Lord of Ch'i,
> Granddaughter of King P'ing.[20]

The meaning of the fishing imagery is sexual, the symbolism of fish denoting fertility, as the reference to the generations in the last couplet reveals. There is another passage in the classic which brings us closer to the meaning of the Han song:

> In the south there are lucky fish,
> In their multitudes they leap.
> Our lord has wine;
> His lucky guests shall feast and rejoice.[21]

The theme here is of the lord's feast, conveying the idea of plenty and success. The guests share in the lord's good fortune. The context of the Chou poem may provide the necessary link between the first part of the finale and the line, 'On the river great lords make merry', which leads into the felicitation closure.

Taking the diverse ideas of the finale in turn, the meaning might be construed in this way: the singer exclaims that a girl and a man are ready for love, that this love is born of mutual attraction and does not need to be purchased; this happy love is but part of a scene of great merriment as some noblemen enjoy a pleasure excursion on the river, in company with the girls of their choice. On this happy day the singer wishes everyone well, hoping that the lords will enjoy a long life. The echoes from the Chou classic underscore the interconnection between the themes of sexual pleasure and *carpe diem*.

The final passage, seen in relation to the preceding stanzas, appears to posit a resolution to the two contradictory forms of love depicted, the real and the ideal, failure and success. The singer puts forward his own, masculine point of view, against that of the two girls in the song's first part. He says that for him and for other men, love is a matter of sexual drive, sexual attraction, it is to be taken on the wing, it is a thing of the day.

The baffling juxtaposition of contradictory passages may therefore be clarified: first one female point of view on love is presented, then an opposing feminine point of view, and finally a third point of view is posited, the masculine, which rejects the first two in a vigorous, virile, self-confident show of bravado. The song combines two love plaints with a statement of the *carpe diem* theme. Its composition takes the form of a stylized argument.[22]

The White Head Lament

short version

White as mountaintop snow,
White as the moon between clouds.
I hear you have two loves,
That's why you have broken from me.
Today a keg of wine at a party,
Tomorrow dawn the top of the canal.
I trudge along the royal canal,
Canal water east then westward flows.
Bleak, bleak, ever bleak, bleak.
A bride at her wedding must not weep;
She longs to get a man of one heart,
Till white-headed time he would not leave her.
Bamboo rod so supple, supple!
Fishtail so glossy, glossy!
When a man prizes the spirit of love,
What need has he of dagger-coins?

According to the *Miscellany of the Western Capital*, which is attributed to an author of the first century AD and to an author of the early fourth century AD, 'The White Head Lament' was composed by the wife of the Han court rhapsodist, Ssu-ma Hsiang-ju (179– *c.* 117 BC). Her name was Cho Wen-chün. The poet had wooed her as a wealthy young widow against her father's wishes. They eloped and after suffering dire poverty and disgrace were taken back by her father and lived happily together. The anecdote in *Miscellany* relates how after they had been married for some time the poet wanted to take another wife. Cho Wen-chün is said to have composed 'The White Head Lament' as a plaint. Her husband abandoned the idea of bringing another wife home.[23] This spurious attribution and romantic context resembles the case of 'Along the Embankment'; though the personalities involved have a less exalted role in the annals of history, they share with the Ts'ao family a considerable literary aura.[24]

Again, the omissions in the short version are revealing. Excised from the longer narrative are the biographical story of the lovers' once happy life in the city, the archaic quatrain about the fuel-gatherers, the onomatopoeic line describing the horses' movement, the lords making merry on the river, and the felicitation closure. These parts represent just those elements in the song which were most difficult to reconcile with the piece as a whole. It may be presumed that whoever edited the long version to produce the short must have also thought these parts too baffling to be retained. It is interesting that the *carpe diem* theme with which the long version ended has been amended in the short version,

157

producing a more mercenary, cynical closure. The new word 'prizes' accentuates this new monetary value of love.[25]

A *Yen* Song, A Ballad

Flit, flit, swallows by the hall
Show winter hides, summer appears.
My brothers two or three
Rove and roam in another part.
Old clothes who must mend?
New clothes who must sew?
I'm lucky to have a just mistress,
She takes them to stitch for me.
Her husband through the gates comes,
Looks askance slyly from the northwest room.
I say to Master, 'Please don't look askance at me!
Water runs clear, pebbles show,
Pebbles show in heaps and heaps.
Going far is not as good as going home.'

This song is made up of a series of images and enigmatic statements which are difficult to interpret. I believe the puzzles are deliberate. Perhaps their purpose is to disguise a taboo topic.

The first image is slightly out of focus. Usually swallows are said to be the harbinger of spring, not summer. Here the season of spring has been elided deliberately as the singer skips from winter to summer. This elision is an important clue to the puzzle. Swallows have already announced the spring, they have built their nests and are raising their young. The home-builder image of swallows is present in the *Book of Poetry*; poem no. 28, for example, uses the image of swallows flying eagerly to denote a young bride going to her husband's home.[26] The swallow also features in the mythology of ancient China as the messenger of a deity which makes a beautiful young princess in a tower pregnant.[27] Present in literary and mythological echoes, therefore, is the idea of a young girl, love, marriage, and pregnancy.

The second couplet, however, reveals that there is something amiss with these connotations. Brothers in popular Han songs often portend trouble in the family, and that trouble centres on a sibling, most often a younger sister who is involved in a romantic entanglement. In this song the brothers are away from home. Recalling the narrative of 'The One I Love', the lacunae of this song may be filled in: while the attention of the irresponsible brothers has been diverted, the younger sister has imprudently indulged in a rash liaison with a man who has since left her.

The third couplet introduces a domestic image. Customarily a girl learned how to sew and tailor clothes at an early age. Without mentioning the persona of the song, the first three couplets archly suggest her presence. The indirect mode of presentation perfectly suits the song's content, wittily anticipating the gesture 'Looks askance slyly' in the final passage. The typical question and answer formula is carefully manipulated here; the answers are delayed, but they are not complete answers—they raise even more questions. This central passage suggests that the girl is living in someone else's home, where she is expected to do some work. She fails to do it, either because she cannot, or, more likely, is too lacking in energy to fulfil her daily tasks. The mistress of the house, luckily, sympathizes with the girl and relieves her of her task. The master, however, suspects some trouble and tries to find out what is going on. The girl fends him off, saying, through allusions, that she is as pure as pebbles lying on the bed of a clear stream. This metaphor derives from poem no. 116 of the *Book of Poetry*, which tells of a girl's guilty enjoyment of a secret assignation with her lover.[28] Perhaps realizing that the master will not catch the allusion, the girl tells him the truth opaquely, so that in the end he is none the wiser. He may even believe that she is referring to her brothers in the last line, hoping they will come home and collect her.

If the narrative of 'The One I Love' and the contexts of the Chou poem and myth are referred to as a guide to the elucidation of this Han song, the resultant story begins to have some measure of plausibility. The young brothers of a nubile girl have left home to amuse themselves, somewhat irresponsibly, in the city. Their young sister has been entrusted with a respectable family, perhaps distant relations through the mistress of the house, in the village. The girl is a refined young miss who is not used to performing menial tasks like mending and sewing. Meanwhile, she has dallied with a man and become pregnant. He leaves her for another district. The master of the house suspects that the girl is in trouble, but he has not been told the truth. The sympathetic response of the mistress suggests that she is aware of the girl's condition. The girl attempts to stop the master from being too inquisitive. If this reconstruction of the story of the song is correct, we are presented with the portrait of a wilful, clever young girl, related to the characterization of the girl of 'The One I Love', and to the girl of the Chou anthology.[29]

Heartache, A Ballad

Shine, shine, white bright moon,
Let gleaming rays lighten my bed.
One in despair cannot sleep,
Restless, restless nights so long.

Soft breezes blow the bedroom door,
Silk curtains unmoved flare and drift.
I take my robe trailing its long sash,
Slip into shoes, leave the high hall.
East, west, which way shall I go?
I hesitate and falter.
A spring bird soaring flies south,
Flutters, flutters, circling alone.
Sad its voice calling to its mate,
Mournful cries that wound my guts.
Moved by nature I long for my lover,
Sudden spilling tears drench my coat.
I stand still, spitting out loud sighs.
To soothe my rage I complain to the domed blue.

The setting, imagery, diction, and emotional tone set this song apart from the typical Han popular song. The setting is in a mansion, 'the high hall', where someone is in a silk furnished bedroom at night. Compared with the Han repertoire this setting is boldly innovative. The persona is wearing a robe with a long sash and shoes or slippers. The elegance contrasts markedly with the empty clothes-line of 'East Gate', the unclothed infants of 'The Ailing Wife', and the bare, scratched feet of 'The Orphan Boy'. The song is dominated by two natural images, the moon and a bird which has lost its mate. The sentimental phrasing is repetitive: 'in despair', 'sad its voice', 'mournful cries', 'wound', 'moved', 'sudden spilling tears', 'loud sighs', 'rage', and 'complain'. Line 15 relates that the persona is suffering pangs of love (intimated by the bedroom setting) while parted from his or her lover. Although the cause of the emotion is different, the emotional language derives from the Ch'u elegiac mode. The excess of grief is in contrast to the stoicism of the typical Han song. It anticipates the vogue in the late and post-Han for lacrymose sentiment.

The image of the moon became a refined trope in late Han lyricism. In this song only a few of its later connotations are present: it is a spring moon (line 11 specifies the season), it is very bright, a device which allows the singer to describe the room's interior. The image of the white moon also suggests purity of heart. The trope is decorative, linked as it is with the gentle motion of the bedroom door and the swaying of the silk curtains.

The second major image is a reflection of the narrative of 'Two White Swans', or some similar story of a bird which loses its mate. Here the pathos of the loss is accentuated. It represents not so much an analogy of human love as a visual scene before the persona, serving as a device to demonstrate the refined sensibility of the persona and the singer. The response to this scene is extraordinary: a flood of tears, spitting sighs, rage, and complaints. If the persona is female, the contrast between her characterization and that of the wife in 'East Gate' indicates that this song has moved away from portraying woman as a custodian of domestic virtues to woman as a luxury object of leisure.[30]

CHAPTER ELEVEN

The Ideal Home and Perfect Marriage

This last group of songs may at first appear to be in search of a coordinating theme. Yet they seem to me to possess one feature which the songs in other chapters are striving towards. They present different concepts of the ideal and in each case the home is the focal point.[1] 'Cocks Crow' seeks to persuade that peace and harmony among brothers leads to prosperity in the family which in turn enhances social stability and political unity.[2] Two other songs which draw their material from this song accentuate the glamour of an idealized family which enjoys wealth, success, and an elegant style of living. 'Mulberry on the Bank' presents an ideal of a happy marriage between a beautiful, witty, young, virtuous, magnificently attired wife and her handsome, richly dressed husband who has reached the pinnacle of success in his career. The last song, 'The Lunghsi Ballad', portrays the ideal of a virtuous wife who lives in a well-furnished home. The songs express the theme of the ideal home and marriage from diverse points of view: there is the solemnly didactic, the brashly mercenary, the audacious, and the ironic. In their use of forms similar to the *chanson d'aventure*, satire, and allegory, they reveal a sophisticated wit and artistry.[3]

Cocks Crow

Cocks crow on the crown of tall trees.
Dogs bark within the palace.
The vagrants, where have they gone?
Under Heaven all is now at peace.
Laws, punishments are not relaxed,
Mercy and order have rectified the babble of names.
Of yellow gold are my lord's gates,
Of green disk jade his balconied hall;
Upstairs there are twin flagons of wine
Served by Han-tan singers.
Jasper green tiles of Liu princes,

Their retinue appears, city wall princes.
Behind the lodge are square ponds,
In the ponds are pairs of mandarin ducks,
Mandarin ducks seventy-two,
Ranged to form set lines.
Their calls so sweet and low
Are heard from my hall's east chamber.
The brothers, four or five men,
Are all gentlemen-in-waiting;
Every fifth day they come home,
Spectators fill the roadsides.
Yellow gold fringes their horses' heads,
Glittering, how it sparkles, sparkles!
A peach tree grows above an open well,
A plum tree grows beside the peach.
Maggots come and gnaw the peach roots,
But plum instead of peach grows stiff and dies.
The tree offered itself for another,
But older and younger brothers neglect each other.

The diverse themes of this song have prompted some ingenious inter-
pretations. Citing Huang Chieh, who has reviewed them, J.-P. Diény
presents a few of them. One line of interpretation argues that the first
part of the song, from 'Cocks crow . . .' to 'Laws, punishments . . .,'
represents the virtuous beginning of the Han Dynasty, the next passage
to the end represents the dynasty in decline, epitomized by its excessive
show of luxury. Apart from this generalized view of the song as a
commentary on the decline of the Han, another line of criticism argues
that it specifically satirizes members of the royal family in the Han
known as the Five Marquises. Ennobled in 27 BC, they were the half-
brothers of the consort of Emperor Yüan. They were notorious for their
extravagance and luxurious style. Their half-sister, the emperor's
consort, was named Wang. Lines 11–12 of the song refer to Liu princes,
not marquises, though the link with royalty might be due to poetic
licence; the lines might also refer to the Wang clan. On the other hand,
the couplet is probably corrupt. Yet another interpretation is that the
song is a satire of the parvenu in the Han. The first six lines serve as a
warning, the central section describes the ostentation of the *nouveau-
riche*, and the finale describes the inevitable downfall of the parvenu. A
more recent critic, Yü Kuan-ying, posits the idea that the song is made up
of three fragmentary texts. Critics like Feng Wei-no of the Ming who
have not wished to impose a tendentious ethico-historical interpretation
on the song have concluded that the three sections have no relationship
with each other.[4]

I would argue that the song does exhibit an internal coherence and design, even if, as is the case with many Han songs in the selection, the transitions from one passage to another are, by modern standards, crudely managed. In my view, the song's import is tempered by an ethical point of view: the state will flourish as a political entity and social organism if it is at peace and if it is stable; its success depends on the family, a small replica of the state, and on harmonious relations within the family; the family, allegorized as a tree, will perish if the members are divided against each other. The moral lesson of the song, which has socio-political ramifications, is expressed in an attractive metaphor of wealth and luxury in the home. The warning of the evil of a house divided against itself is expressed as a metaphor of a diseased fruit tree; its roots, main and minor branches are symbolic of the extended family system.

The first six lines of the song contain a number of images which create the idea of harmony in the state and at home. The first couplet consists of an allusion to cocks crowing and dogs barking which is used in some pre-Han and Han texts to denote peace and harmony. For example, in the Taoist classic, *The Classic of the Way and Its Power*, an idealized picture of a utopia is presented in which people

'. . . will be content in their abode / And happy in the way they live. / Though adjoining states are within sight of one another, and the sound of dogs barking and cocks crowing in one state can be heard in another, yet the people of one state will grow old and die without having had any dealings with those of another.'[5]

The dual images of cocks and dogs is also used, but this time expressed in negative terms, in a prophecy circulating in Emperor Wu's reign, foretelling the decline and fall of the Han Dynasty:

Thrice seventy, at the end of our era,
Cocks will not crow,
Nor will dogs bark.
At home a mad tangle of bramble and thorn,
While in public we'll see nine tigers fight for the crown.[6]

The Taoist classic uses the dual images of cocks and dogs positively to denote a Utopia. The Han prophecy uses them negatively to denote anarchy. The allusion in the Han song has a didactic function.

The third line of this initial passage is enigmatic. The 'vagrants' (*tang-tzu*) means in some contexts a libertine, in others a vagabond. In 'Light in the East', for example, the tautological compound term *yu-tang-tzu* is used to describe the makeshift army which was mustered to fight in

Ts'ang-wu. It is possible that this military connotation is present in 'Cocks Crow', since the next line states that the country is now at peace.

The phrase 'babble of names' at the end of this first passage refers to the ancient philosophical concept of the 'rectification of names'. In a passing in the *Analects* the Confucian expression of this is as follows:

'If names are not rectified, then language will not be in accord with truth. If language is not in accord with truth, then things cannot be accomplished. If things cannot be accomplished, then ceremonies and music will not flourish. If ceremonies and music do not flourish, then punishment will not be just. If punishments are not just, then the people will not know how to move hand or foot.'[7]

It is significant that in this well-known passage the rectification of names is linked with appropriate punishment, which in turn relates to the people's correct understanding of what is right and wrong. In its allusions, imagery, and diction, therefore, this opening passage of the song posits the idea of harmony in the state.

The next passage of eighteen lines shifts the focus to the family, the microcosm of the state. This kind of argument by analogy, from the larger entity to the smaller organism, or vice versa, typifies late Chou and Han philosophical disputation. This section of the song projects the idea that harmony springs from cohesion in the family and this in turn leads to material success. The ideal family is shown to have enormous wealth, successful careers, and to be the envy of the district: 'Spectators fill the roadsides'. Wealth is emphasized by the litany of different jewels and by their repetition: 'yellow gold' in lines 7 and 23–24, and varieties of green jade, from the fabled 'disk jade' once used only as an emblem of high office in the Chou, to the finest jasper used for mere tiles. The concept of harmony is developed through images of the feast: wine, beautiful women, and music. The song of the female singers from Han-tan continues in the chorus of mandarin ducks, symbolizing happy married love. The ducks also develop the theme of harmony through their perfect formation, denoting order and symmetry. The couplet of lines 11–12 may be corrupt, or may be the result of an unwieldy elision of a longer passage interpolated into this descriptive section of the song. Huang Chieh and Sawaguchi Takeo suggest that the 'Liu princes' denote the royal family of the Han, while the 'city wall princes' denote non-royal princes, that is, not members of the Liu clan.[8] The couplet may be taken literally as a reference to the Han palace, or it may be taken as hyperbole, the family described in the song having such wealth as only royalty possess. Hyperbole characterizes the whole of this eighteen-line passage.

The song then goes on to narrate the worldly success of the brothers of the family. This recalls the *carpe diem* song 'A *Yen* Song, The Whenever

Ballad' in which the singer projects the picture of a wealthy, successful family of three brothers 'robed in sable furs', who keep company with 'prince, lord, high official'. The presentation of this worldly success differs in each song: whereas the *carpe diem* singer's point of view is that of the outsider looking on with envy at the family's prosperity, the singer of 'Cocks Crow' distances himself by describing the family's glamorous attraction through the eyes of a crowd of onlookers in the family's neighbourhood.

Thus far the song has projected an image of peace and harmony in the state and an idealized image of prosperity in the home. The two are linked by the idea that the one is a refracted image of the other. Having presented this image of success, culminating in the line 'Glittering, how it sparkles, sparkles!' the song suddenly changes its tone. The theme of the family and brothers is continued, but this time it is developed through the allegory of a tree. The intent of the finale of the song is to warn that if the brothers in a family do not stand united, their house will no longer prosper. The intimation may also be that the dynasty will similarly decline and fall.[9]

They Met, A Ballad

> They met in a narrow alley,
> A path so tight would not admit carriages.
> Young men, I don't know who,
> Hubs wedged, one asks, 'And your lord's house?'
> 'My lord's house is very easy to recognize,
> Easy to recognize and hard to forget.
> Of yellow gold are my lord's gates,
> Of white jade my lord's hall:
> Up in the hall stand flagons of wine
> Served by Han-tan singers.
> In the middle court grow cassia trees,
> Flowery lamps how they blaze!
> The brothers, two or three men,
> The middle son is a gentleman-in-waiting,
> One in five days he comes home:
> On the road appears a brilliant light,
> Yellow gold fringes his horses' heads,
> Spectators crowd the waysides.
> Enter the gates and look left:
> All you see are pairs of mandarin ducks,
> Mandarin ducks seventy-two,
> Ranged to form set lines.
> Their chant so harmonious,

Storks sing on east and west houses.
The eldest's wife weaves silk fine and sheer,
The middle wife weaves flowing yellow,
The youngest's wife has nothing to do;
Clasping her zither she goes up the high hall:
"Husband, please sit still,
My tuning is not midway!" '

The main part of this song, from lines 7 to 24, closely resembles the central section of 'Cocks Crow', also lines 7–24. The enigmatic, archaic passages at the opening and close of 'Cocks Crow' have been omitted, resulting in three main changes: the socio-ethical tone is deleted, the masculine orientation is modified, and the song is presented from a well-defined narrative perspective. In ideological terms, 'They Met' has lost its Confucian framework. In literary terms it has lost its allegorical closure. The new song is characterized more as a narrative ballad than a didactic song.

The song opens with the narrator's introduction of two characters who chat while their carriages are being unhitched after getting stuck in a narrow lane. The new characters are young men, identified only in one case as someone attached to a lord's mansion. After the scene is set and the device of the encounter presented, the ballad introduces a question and answer formula. The question is put by one young man asking the other to describe his lord's house. The other man's answer constitutes the rest of the ballad. Although this section corresponds in most of its details to that of 'Cocks Crow', those details are rearranged. The most significant adjustment is the placement of the passage describing the brothers at the end of the passage describing the mansion. In 'Cocks Crow', the passage about the brothers was placed nearer the end of the song in order to provide a coherent link between the idealized family and the allegory of a family in decline. In 'They Met', since the intent is no longer to persuade the audience of the virtues of peace and harmony in the state and at home, the passage has been shifted. Instead, the emphasis is placed on the apartments of the married brothers, 'east and west houses', which in turn provides a new transition to the finale describing the elegant and refined wives of the brothers. This new finale is in accord with the appeal to luxury in the earlier hyperbolic passage describing the mansion. These changes, involving a new narrative introduction, a narrative formula of question and answer, a logical sequence from mansion to brothers, to garden, apartments, and finally to the graceful vignette of the wives, give the song a new coherence and narrative unity. At the same time, the song becomes a quite different work. It achieves a certain attractive glamour at the expense of more profound human values.[10]

In Ch'angan There is a Narrow Lane

In Ch'angan there is a narrow lane,
A narrow lane not admitting carriages.
By chance two youths meet:
Hubs wedged, one asks, 'And your lord's house?'
'My lord's house is near Newmarket,
Easy to recognize and hard to forget.
The oldest son is of two-thousand-bushel rank,
The middle son is a Filial-Pure aide,
The youngest son has no official post,
Capped and gowned he serves at Loyang.
The three sons enter the house together,
In the house appears a brilliant light.
The eldest's wife weaves silk fine and plain,
The middle wife weaves flowing yellow,
The youngest's wife has nothing to do;
Clasping her lute she goes up the high hall:
"Husband, hush, now hush!
My tuning, la! is not midway!" '

The narrative impulse in this version of the song is strong. The setting is divided between the two Han capitals, Ch'angan and Loyang, with a fashionable part of Ch'angan featured as the locale of the lord's mansion. This version derives more closely from 'They Met' than from 'Cocks Crow'. The description of the mansion has been excised; no doubt, it is to be understood by reference to its earlier prototype. Two of the brothers' official posts are detailed.[11] The descriptive passages have been severely curtailed. Apart from the mansion, the triumphant procession of the successful brother to his mansion, and the garden and apartments have been omitted. The passage describing the three wives, however, which was totally absent from 'Cocks Crow' and introduced in 'They Met', now acquires a prominent position in the song, not because it has been expanded (it is still six lines long), but because it now constitutes one-third of the whole narrative. In 'They Met' it formed one-fifth of the song. The trend towards the graceful and elegant in the finale of 'They Met' becomes more pronounced in this shorter version of the song. I would date it as the latest of the three songs, which I would characterize as versions, although they have different titles.[12] The trend toward elegance and refinement in the descriptive vignette of the three wives marks a distinct development in literary taste during the late Han and post-Han era, culminating in the sub-genre of court love poetry fashionable in the Southern Dynasties.[13]

Mulberry on the Bank

Sunrise at the southeast corner
Shines on our Ch'in clan house.
The Ch'in clan has a fair daughter,
She is called Lo·fu.
Lo·fu loves silkworm mulberry,
She picks mulberry at the wall's south corner.
Of green silk her basket strap,
Of cassia her basket and pole.
On her head a twisting-fall hairdo,
At her ears bright moon pearls.
Of apricot silk her lower skirt,
Of purple silk her upper blouse.
Passersby see Lo·fu,
They drop their load, stroke their beard.
Young men see Lo·fu,
They take off caps, put on headbands.
The ploughman forgets his plough,
The hoer forgets his hoe.
They come home cross and angry,
All from seeing Lo·fu.

A prefect comes from the south,
His five horses paw the ground.
The prefect sends his sergeant forward:
'Ask, Whose is the pretty girl?'
'The Ch'in clan has a fair daughter,
She is called Lo·fu.'
'Lo·fu, how old is she?'
'Not yet quite twenty,
A bit more than fifteen.'
The prefect invites Lo·fu:
'Would you like to ride with me?'
Lo·fu comes forward and rejoins:
'The Prefect is so foolish!
The Prefect has his own wife,
Lo·fu has her own husband.

'In the east more than a thousand horsemen,
My bridegroom is in the lead.
How would you recognize my bridegroom?
His white horse follows jet-black colts,
Green silk plaits his horses' tails,
Yellow gold braids his horses' heads.
At his waist a Lu·lu dagger
Is worth maybe more than ten million cash.

169

At fifteen he was a county clerk,
At twenty a palace official,
At thirty a gentleman-in-waiting,
At forty lord of his own city.
As a man he has a pure white complexion,
Bushy whiskers on both cheeks.
Majestic he steps to the courthouse,
Solemn he strides to the courtroom,
Where several thousand in audience
All say my bridegroom is unique!'

This song is a fine example of Han balladic art. A clearly defined narrative is enlivened with colourful description. The characterization of the heroine is distinctive. The dialogue is forthright and amusing, revealing the opposing personalities of the prefect and the mulberry picker. In his monograph on the motif of the mulberry in Chinese myth, ritual, and literature, J.-P. Diény shows how it evolved from the profane mating song set among the mulberries to a sacred imperial rite, and later developed into a narrative verse form imbued with folkloric elements.[14] He perceptively compares this Han song with its European counterpart, the pastourelle, pointing out the particularities of the Chinese form and the similarities between the two traditions.[15] Whereas the European pastourelle features a knight and shepherdess, the Chinese song features an official on circuit and a mulberry picker. The heroines of the pastourelle and of 'Mulberry on the Bank' are both approached by a gentleman travelling along the road. They both respond to his attempt at seduction with a forthright refusal. Though they are somewhat flirtatious, they are virtuous in the end. They defeat the seducer with his own weapons, using irrefutable arguments with finesse. As Diény concludes, the two literary forms portray spirited, amusing heroines. In the Chinese case, the Han form did not evolve into a distinct literary tradition. 'Mulberry on the Bank' is unique. On the other hand, the heroine's independent, pert spirit lives on in the shorter songs known as *Ch'ing-Shang* during the Wei and Chin period.

The portrayal of the heroine, Ch'in Lo-fu, is ambiguous. At first she appears to be a peasant girl out in the mulberry grove beside the road one spring day. Her appearance, however, contradicts that rustic impression, for she is dressed like a fine lady and wears expensive jewels and has an elaborate court hair-style.[16] Moreover, she talks like a lady who is familiar with technical terms like 'Lu-lu dagger' and official ranks at court, and she knows the niceties of courteous discourse.[17] There is also a conflict between her sensual appearance, which sends the local men into a flutter, and her virtuous repudiation of the would-be seducer. Finally, it is never explained why Lo-fu is exposed to the public gaze, or why she is not with her husband, a rich lord, in his eastern city. These ambiguities make the song provocative and diverting.

Perhaps a consideration of the song's structure might help to explain these artistic ambiguities. In his 'Treatise on Music', Shen Yüeh divides the song-text into three stanzas (*chieh*), and places the title in the musical category of 'Major Pieces'. The first part of the song, two stanzas, was classified by him as a *yen*, for which the music was specified as prefatory, or an overture; the last part of the song, the last stanza, was classified as the *tsü* which had music appropriate for a finale passage.[18] It seems that the whole song may have been composed by piecing together at least two parts, the *yen* and *tsü*, or possibly three parts, two *yen*-passages conjoined. Connecting links may have been provided to create a new narrative structure of originally disparate material: a description of a pretty mulberry-picker, a *chanson d'aventure*, and a description of a handsome, successful official. The ambiguities may arise in part from the unintentional inconsistencies in the resulting composition, in part from a deliberate conflict in character portrayal.

The song displays a number of balladic features. The most noticeable of these is the device of repetition. The heroine's name is repeated ten times throughout the first two sections and her clan name, Ch'in, recurs three times. Prosodic patterns are repeated, such as 'Of green silk', 'Of cassia', and so forth. Much of the construction of the song depends on parallel couplets, such as lines 9–10, 17–18, and 50–51. The word 'Prefect' is repeated as a sarcastic refrain throughout the second section. The grammatical pattern of the metrical line is repeated to create a litany effect; for example, in lines 4, 7, 8, 11, 12, and 26, the verb *wei* (to be), occurs in the centre of the line in each case. The decorative description of Lo-fu is linked through colour imagery to that of her husband; her green silk basket strap is twinned with the ribbons decorating her husband's horses' tails.[19] The device of incremental repetition is used in the final section to narrate the swift rise to fame of Lo-fu's husband, whom she ambiguously refers to as 'my bridegroom' (perhaps another indication of the incomplete method of piecing disparate songs together to form this new narrative). Finally, the rebuttal of the official is expressed in a repetitive couplet, which conveys the pert wit of the so-called peasant girl: 'The Prefect has his own wife, / Lo-fu has her own husband.' She audaciously reminds the public figure of his private responsibilities.

Although the characterization of Lo-fu is unique among the extant popular songs of the Han, much of the material is commonplace expression. The clan name Ch'in occurs in 'A Crow Bore Eight or Nine Chicks', as the name of the mischievous boy who shoots the crow. The name Ch'in Lo-fu occurs in 'A Peacock Southeast Flew' as the name of the local girl a mother wants for her son in place of his existing wife. The degree to which the name Lo-fu became fashionable in the Han is evidenced by the fact that it was the name of the daughter of the Prince of Ch'ang-i, a descendant of Emperor Wu.[20] The description of Lo-fu recurs in other Han pieces, such as that of the wine-maid in 'The Imperial Guards Officer', ascribed to Hsin Yen-nien (2nd century AD), and is similar to that of Lan-chih in 'A Peacock', a much later narrative. The Lo-fu song itself may be dated as a Latter Han piece; the official rank of the prefect, *shih-chün*, originated in that period. The description of Lo-fu's husband's white horse, 'Yellow gold braids his horses' heads', is almost the same as line 23 of 'Cocks Crow', 'Yellow gold fringes their horses' heads'. The device of incremental repetition in the last section of 'Mulberry' is reproduced in the opening section of 'A Peacock' to describe the development of the heroine from childhood to a young adult. There are other echoes and borrowings in the song, too. They are skilfully interwoven into the fabric of the narrative so that it moves fairly smoothly and coherently to its grand finale. The impulse to diversity which so obscures some other Han songs is therefore not so apparent.

The narrative is a blend of descriptive passages and dialogue. The narrator opens the song with a familiar reference to 'our Ch'in clan', setting up at once a personal relationship between the heroine, the audience, and himself. The narrator continues his presentation of the heroine to the middle of the second stanza, when Lo-fu herself intervenes in the narrative, taking it to its conclusion. At this point the song employs a sophisticated variation on the technique of question and answer formula. The prefect propositions Lo-fu with a question, 'Would you like to ride with me?' which provokes an answer extending to the end of the song, and in its dénouement introduces a second example of the formula, 'How would you recognize my bridegroom?'[21] The song is enlivened by some realistic repartee from Lo-fu and some realistic dialogue between the sergeant and herself about her name and age. Hyperbole also appears, centering on the two descriptive passages about Lo-fu and her husband. These hyperbolic passages are, as Hans H. Frankel has observed, appropriately theatrical: 'The humble folk like to dress up their heroes and heroines, with the same disregard for verisimilitude that is often found in theatrical costuming.'[22] It is the juxtaposition of realism and hyperbole which makes the song so vivid and colourful. The paradoxical *mélange* also provides a necessary contrast in the presentation of a fairly long song.

Ts'ui Pao provides the earliest context for this song. He explains that it was based on an historical episode. A girl named Lo-fu was a daughter of a clansman of Han-tan, the capital of Chao state in the Chou era. She was married to Wang Jen who owned a city and possessed a thousand carriages. He became a minister in the royal household of the King of Chao. One day Lo-fu went out to pick mulberry on a bank. The

172

king went up to his terrace to watch her and he became amorous. He set out some wine intending to seduce her. Lo-fu was skilled at playing the harp, so she immediately composed the song 'Mulberry on the Bank' to explain her reaction to the king. The king desisted. It may be that the original song was composed in this way, but the extant version dates from the Han, not the Chou. Ts'ui Pao's story of the extant song is much closer to the traditional story of Ch'iu Hu and his wife than it is to the story of Lo-fu of Han-tan. Ch'iu Hu is an official who has to leave home for circuit duty shortly after his wedding. He has to depart alone. He returns five years later and on the road home he meets a pretty young woman picking mulberry. He offers her some gold if she will be his mistress, not realizing that the woman is his own wife. She virtuously refuses. Later that evening she returns home from the mulberry patch and the husband and wife come face to face. She is so mortified that her husband would have betrayed their marriage that she commits suicide by drowning.[23] The comparison between the Lo-fu story and the tale of Ch'iu Hu's wife is superficial, however, for the characterization of the two is quite different: Lo-fu defends herself with wit and intelligence, while Ch'iu Hu's wife has courage but lacks wit.[24]

The Lunghsi Ballad

Up in Heaven what is there?
Rows and rows of planted white elm.
Cassia trees lining the way are growing,
Green dragons face across road corners,
Male and female phoenix sing in harmony,
A hen leads her nine chicks.
And as I look back down on the world of men
There is a scene of joy quite unique!
A fair wife goes out to greet her guests,
Her face happy and cheerful.
Bending low, she kneels twice,
Asks the guests, 'Was your journey pleasant?'
She invites the guests up the north hall,
Seats the guests on woollen cushions.
Clear wine, white wine, for each a separate tankard,
Over the wine are set ornate ladles.
She pours the wine, hands it to the guests,
The guests say, 'Hostess, you have some.'
She declines, kneels down twice,
Then accepts one cup.
Before talk and laughter are ended
She looks left, orders the inner kitchen:

173

'Hurry up and prepare the coarse grain,
Mind you don't dilly-dally!'
Cordially she shows the guests out,
Majestic they stride to the courtroom.
Showing the guests out she doesn't go too far,
Her foot won't cross the gate pivot.
Taking a wife you might get one like this,
But even Ch'i Chiang was not as good.
A sound wife who keeps good house and home—
One is worth more than one husband!

The opening quatrain has been borrowed, with a minor line change in its last line, from 'Walking out of Hsia Gate', the fantasy on immortality in Chapter Three.[25] There it formed the song's closure, presenting an image of paradise where a holy man become immortal will dwell. In the 'Lunghsi' ballad the projection of paradise becomes a sophisticated device for introducing satire. The singer, who seems to be poised up in this paradise contemplating the world below, describes the ideal world of heaven and then describes a scene on earth, a scene of unusual goodness and virtue in the home. He drolly adds that such a scene of feminine virtue is 'quite unique!'. In other words, his song is a satirical hymn of praise to the perfect wife who does not exist. Her good points are litanized within the framework of a domestic narrative. Her perfect behaviour when guests visit is described in detail. The singer intends that his audience should invert the litany of praise so that it becomes a string of criticism. In real life, he implies, when the typical wife greets her guests she is not 'happy and cheerful', but flustered and cross. She forgets to bow politely and neglects to ask how the guests' journey has been. Instead of declining the wine which is laid out in tankards, in real life she swigs as fast as her male guests.[26] She is comically shown refusing several times and then reluctantly taking just 'one cup'. Then, in the inverted reading of the song, she usually gets so tiddly that she neglects to have the meal cooked on time. Finally, in reality, the typical wife will impertinently show herself at the front gate when the guests are being escorted out, so that the ordinary passersby can see her. The song is a sly joke at the expense of 'modern' Han wives who have become liberated from the social mores of their sterner Chou forbears. The singer is amused rather than outraged by contemporary mores.[27] His use of the quatrain from 'Hsia Gate' as a commonplace expression to mount his gentle satire reveals a sophisticated, knowing wit.[28]

Notes

Introduction

1 Arthur Waley, *The Analects of Confucius* (1938); *The Book of Songs* (1937); Burton Watson, *The Complete Works of Chuang Tzu* (1968); *Records of the Grand Historian of China*, 2 vols. (1961); *Courtier and Commoner in Ancient China* (1974); D. C. Lau, *Mencius* (1970); *Lao Tzu, Tao Te Ching* (1963); Angus C. Graham, *Later Mohist Logic, Ethics and Science* (1978); Wm. Theodore de Bary, Wing-tsit Chan, and Burton Watson, *Sources of Chinese Tradition*, 2 vols. (1960); Homer H. Dubs, *The History of the Former Han Dynasty*, 3 vols. (1938–55).

2 It would seem that many Chinese classical authors belonged to the lower ranks of the aristocracy, or, in the case of at least Mo Tzu, from the middle class. For a general study see Hsü Cho-yün, *Ancient China in Transition: An Analysis of Social Mobility, 722–222 BC* (1965).

3 Much of the material which appeared at exhibitions in the early 1970s is included in *Historical Relics Unearthed in New China* (1972).

4 Citing the felicitous phrase of Matthew Hodgart, ed., *The Faber Book of Ballads* (1965), p. 12.

5 Derk Bodde, *China's First Unifier, A Study of the Ch'in Dynasty as Seen in the Life of Li Ssu* (1938), provides a detailed account of the Ch'in.

6 Michael Loewe, 'The Grand Inquest—81 BC', pp. 91–112 of *Crisis and Conflict in Han China* (1974), and Esson M. Gale, *Discourses on Salt and Iron* (1931).

7 Jean Lévi, *Le grand empereur et ses automates* (1985), presents a semi-fictional account of the first emperor, Ch'in Shih Huang-ti.

8 Hans H. Bielenstein, 'The Restoration of the Han Dynasty', 3 vols. (1954–67), provides a valuable study of the reign of Emperor Kuang-wu.

9 This rhapsody appears in Burton Watson, trans., *Chinese Rhyme-prose* (1971), pp. 38–51, 'Sir Fantasy'. I have translated Shang-lin as Royal Forest in my texts. For an account of Emperor Wu's expansionist policies see Yü Ying-shih, *Trade and Expansion in Han China* (1967).

10 Michael Loewe, 'The Capital City of Ch'angan' in *Everyday Life in Early Imperial China* (1968), pp. 128–36.

11 *Id.*, 'Life in the Cities', pp. 137–51.

12 *Id.*, 'The Countryman and his Work', pp. 163–79; Hsü Cho-yün, *Han Agriculture, The Formation of Early Chinese Agrarian Economy* (1980); Francesca Bray, *Agriculture* (1984).

13 Jean-Pierre Diény, *Aux origines de la poésie classique en Chine* (1968), p. 95; Loewe, *Crisis*, pp. 208–10; Anne Birrell, 'Mythmaking and *Yüeh-fu*' (1989), pp. 224–32.

14 Pan Ku, *History of the Han* (*Han shu*), ch. 19, 'The Table of Officials', p. 731; Diény, *op. cit.*, p. 86; Loewe, *Crisis*, pp. 200, 310, Table 6.

15 Ssu-ma Ch'ien, *Historical Records* (*Shih chi*), ch. 24, 'History of Music', p. 1,177; the three emperors were Hui, Wen, and Ching.

16 *Op. cit., ch.* 22, p. 1,043: 'In the second year of Emperor Hui the Filial [194 BC] he ordered the Director of the Bureau of Music, Hsia-hou K'uan, to arrange string and wind accompaniment for it [the set of hymns], and renamed it "Music to Set the World at Ease".' Diény, *id.*, 'La carrière du Yue-fou', pp. 81–4, succinctly summarizes the statements concerning the founding of the Bureau in the historical texts.

17 *Op. cit.*, p. 1,045: 'At the time when Emperor Wu defined the ritual for suburban sacrifices, he sacrificed to T'ai-i at Kan-ch'üan ... and to Empress Earth at Fen-yin .... Then he established the Bureau of Music.'

18 *Ibid.*

19 *Op. cit., ch.* 93.3725.

20 Loewe, *Crisis*, p. 196, n. 11, explains that even this date is changed in different sections of the *History of the Han (Han shu), ch.* 6 and 22. For fuller references to the 'horse of heaven', see p. 183, nn. 41–45 below.

21 James Robert Hightower, *Topics in Chinese Literature* (1950), p. 49; Burton Watson, *Early Chinese Literature* (1962), p. 289; Hans H. Frankel, 'Yüeh-fu Poetry' (1974), p. 69; Sawaguchi Takeo, *Gafu* (1973), p. 35, argues that Li Yen-nien's sister, Lady Li, is supposed to have originally entered Emperor Wu's palace as an entertainer and then his harem in 121 BC. When Lady Li died in 120 BC, the Ch'i magician Shao-weng was commanded by the emperor to summon her soul. The magician lost favour, however, because his powers were unproven, and he was executed in 118 BC. Sawaguchi cites Pan Ku, *History of the Han, ch.* 97 and *Historical Records, ch.* 28 (see Watson, trans., *Courtier*, pp. 247–49, and *Records*, Vol. 2, pp. 41–2). Hellmut Wilhelm, 'The Bureau of Music in Western Han' (1978), p. 123. P'eng Li-t'ien, 'A Discussion of Whether the Bureau of Music Arose in the Reign of the Han Emperor Wu' (1937), p. 182.

22 *Crisis*, p. 196.

23 Gary Shelton Williams, 'A Study of the Oral Nature of the Han *Yüeh-fu*' (1973), p. 23.

24 *Op. cit.*, p. 84.

25 *Id.*, p. 25; Birrell, 'Mythmaking,' pp. 232–33.

26 Loewe, *Crisis*, p. 209, n. 59. For one set of figures for the Bureau's personnel in 7 BC, see Pan Ku, *id.*, 'Treatise on Rites and Music', pp. 1,073–74.

27 Shen Yüeh, *History of the Southern Sung (Sung shu), ch.* 100, p. 2,452. Although the traditional date for completion of his *History* is set at AD 488 (Shen, *id.*, p. 2,466), Shen admitted in his presentation address to the throne that the 'Treatises' section of his *History* had yet to be finalized and added to his main text (*id.*, p. 2,468), but the date for their final completion is not known, presumably some time between AD 488 and 512, the year of his death. *Anthology of Literature (Wen hsüan)*, Hsiao T'ung (AD 501–31) *et al.*, comp.; David R. Knechtges, trans., *Wen xuan, or Selections of Refined Literature* (1982), Vol. 1. p. 27, notes that *yüeh-fu* forms a sub-category of the *shih* lyric genre in the anthology (*ch.* 27–8); *New Songs from a Jade Terrace (Yü-t'ai hsin-yung)*, Hsü Ling (AD 507–583), comp. *c.* AD 545; Anne Birrell, trans. (1982), the genre of *yüeh-fu* first appears there in Vol. 1, 'Old *Yüeh-fu* Poems'. Vincent Yuchung Shih, trans., *The Literary Mind and the Carving of Dragons (Wen-hsin tiao-lung)* (1959, 1983), Chapter 7, 'Musical Poetry (*Yüeh-fu*)', pp. 77–87.

28 *Wen hsüan, SPTK* 28.37b, *Wen-hsin tiao-lung, SPTK* 2.5a; *Wen hsüan, SPTK* 45.26b; Kuo, *ch.* 58, p. 850, and *ch.* 84, p. 1,180; Birrell, *id.*, pp. 233–35.

29 For example, Pan Ku, *id.*, and *Record of Ritual (Li chi), ch.* 27, 'Record of Music', Séraphin Couvreur, trans., *Li Ki, ou Mémoires sur les bienséances et les cérémonies*, (1913), Vol. 1, pp. 45–114. See Walter Kaufman, *Musical References in the Chinese Classics* (1976). In Pan Ku's 'Treatise on Literature', 2 song titles are listed under the tenth of the 28 headings, mostly regional, of 314 *ko-shih* sung poems: 'Goosegate' (*Ying-men*) and 'Lunghsi', which may be the source of titles for the Han *yüeh-fu* pieces entitled

'The Ballad of the Prefect of Goosegate' and 'The Lungshi Ballad' in Chapters One and Eleven above. (*Han shu, c.* 30, p. 1,754.)

30 Alan Bold, *The Ballad* (1979), p. 6; I have amended his phrase 'hard covers' to [book form]. It is worth noting that in the main repository of *yüeh-fu* of the twelfth century, *Anthology of Yüeh-fu Poetry*, compiled by Kuo Mao-ch'ien in 100 chapters, the poets of Shen Yüeh's era (the Liang) predominate among the total of poets from the Han to the end of the Southern Dynasties era—there are 73 poets and 546 *yüeh-fu* compositions. Moreover, of these Liang poets Shen Yüeh himself was the most prolific with 119 *yüeh-fu* pieces. Masuda Kiyohide, *Research on the History of Yüeh-fu* (1975), pp. 441–42, presents a breakdown of the 5,290 *yüeh-fu* pieces in Kuo.

31 These 16 *ku-tz'u*, plus one wrong attribution, and the '18 Han Songs for the *Nao*-bell', 35 Han pieces in all, appear in his 'Treatise on Music', *ch.* 21–22 (see p. 206).

32 Masuda, *op. cit.*, pp. 434–36, summarizes Kuo's biographical data. Kuo Mao-ch'ien, comp., *Yüeh-fu shih chi (Anthology of Yüeh-fu Poetry)*, 100 *ch.* (Chung-hua ed., 1979).

33 See pp. 207–08, Appendix II.

34 A precise definition of such terms as *yin* or *hsing* or *tz'u* has yet to be determined. For a discussion of the term *hsing* in many *yüeh-fu* pieces, see Shimizu Shigeru, 'The Meaning of *hsing*' (*Ko no hongi*, 1984), in which he suggests that the term in *yüeh-fu* pieces may have originated in the 3-tone music of 'travelling bells' (*hsing chung*) used by nobles in the Warring States era. It is interesting to note that no. 5 of Pan Ku's 28 headings for *ko-shih* pieces reads: 'Songs for Travel, Royal Tours of Inspection, and Excursions' (*Ch'u-hsing hsün-shou chi yu ko-shih*), *Han shu, ch.* 30, p. 1,754.

35 Indicative of the confusion surrounding what constitutes a Han ballad is the controversy over the inclusion or non-inclusion of certain *ku-shih*, old poems, in the *yüeh-fu* repertoire. For example, 'Uphill I Picked Sweet Herbs', (known as the *mi-wu* poem), a *shih*, or *ku-shih*, and nos. 8 and 13 of the 'Nineteen Old Poems', also *ku-shih*, of which the last two poems appear in Kuo's *Anthology, ch.* 74 and 61, 'Song-texts for Miscellaneous Pieces'. Recognizing the value of Kuo's classification system, but viewing the corpus from a literary standpoint, Hans H. Frankel makes distinctions between the oral and the literary traditions, the hymns and the ballads, the different regions, and different periods. He proposes a concise system of five *yüeh-fu* headings: 1) ritual hymns of the Han, 2) a special class of ritual hymns from the Southern Dynasties, 3) anonymous ballads of the Han, 4) anonymous ballads of the Southern Dynasties and Northern Dynasties, and 5) ballads in the *yüeh-fu* style by men of letters from the Han to the end of the T'ang; '*Yüeh-fu* Poetry', pp. 71–2.

36 *Op cit.*, p. 19.

37 Gordon Hall Gerould, *The Ballad of Tradition* (1932), p. 11.

38 For the four categories of Emperor Ming's time see Chu Ch'ien-chih, 'A Discussion of *Yüeh-fu*', in *A History of Chinese Music in Literature* (1935), pp. 130–31. Wang Yün-hsi, *A General Discussion of Yüeh-fu Poetry* (1958), p. 65, points out that the last two categories represent popular music, in contrast to the serious, stately music of the first two. Shen Yüeh, *op. cit., ch.* 20, p. 565, gives Ts'ai Yung's categories, without questioning the attribution. The terms Grand Yü Music, Yellow Gate, and *nao*-bell may be summarized briefly as follows. The Grand Yü Music (*T'ai Yü Yüeh*) was the name of a government office which was originally named *T'ai Yüeh*, Grand Music (its title was changed in AD 60). Bielenstein, *The Bureaucracy of Han Times* (1980), p. 164, n. 75, suggests that the title change was probably in response 'to a prediction . . . [that] the Han dynasty would compose a music named Yü'. This office supervised the music for national festivals and important state banquets. The Yellow Gate (*Huang-men*) was an early Han office. In the reign of Emperor Wu and later it supervised court entertainment and major ceremonies, including various forms of musical entertainment. It seems that when the Bureau of Music was abolished in 7 BC, the

Yellow Gate office assumed some functions. It enjoyed great prestige among the government bureaus in charge of music since it was directly associated with the emperor. The Yellow Gate's Drumming and Blowing [Music] (*Huang-men ku-ch'ui*) was traditionally known as music accompanying banquets given by the Han emperor for his officials. The *nao*-bell was a hand-held, hollow, metal musical instrument, in a deep cup shape, emitting a clear musical sound when struck (it did not have a clapper). It was early on associated with military music.

39   Shen Yüeh, *id.*, *ch.* 19, p.549 and *ch.* 21, p. 603, where he further defined *hsiang-ho*: 'Hsiang-ho are old Han songs. Stringed instruments *hsiang-ho* [= play in concert] in turn, the one holding the rhythm-baton sings.' Shen's folk-song imitations appear in *New Songs*, Birrell, trans., pp. 136–43, 251, 275. In all he imitated 14 of the Han originals among his 119 *yüeh-fu*.

40   The term, *Ch'ing-Shang*, appeared in some ancient texts, sometimes signifying a government office. In the late Han and Wei (3rd century AD), it acquired the status of a sub-genre of popular song, signifying a style of clear (*Ch'ing*) singing in the *Shang* tone (*Shang* was one of the notes of the ancient pentatonic musical scale), which was associated with the season of autumn. After the Chinese court went into exile south of the Yangtse in AD 317, *Ch'ing-Shang* was influenced by anonymous love-songs of the southeast, known as 'Wu Music' (*Wu sheng*), and later by 'Western Melodic Pieces' (*Hsi ch'ü*) of the southwest, mainly the region of ancient Ch'u. The term *Ch'ing-Shang* became attached to the repertoire of popular Southern Dynasties love-songs, composed by anonymous folk-singers, and imitations of them by named court poets. This repertoire flourished in the 4th–6th centuries. It is important to distinguish between this usage of the term *Ch'ing-Shang*, and that understood by Shen Yüeh in his 'Treatise on Music'. His categorization of melodic pieces lists the term as a category after *Hsiang-ho*, or 'Concerted' pieces. Instead of taking *Ch'ing-Shang* as a category of songs and melodies dating from the Southern Dynasties, Shen includes Han pieces in it, relegating it to the same period as the Han *ku-tz'u* of the 'Concerted' category. Moreover, he assigns three modes to *Ch'ing-Shang*, whereas most medieval historians and later compilers separate the three modes and list them after 'Concerted' pieces. Although Shen was the earliest literary compiler of this song-text repertoire, it is impossible to determine whether his system of categorization is correct or misinformed.

41   Wu Ching, *Yüeh-fu ku t'i yao-chieh*, in *Chin-tai pi-shu*, *ch.* 34.

42   For a discussion of Wu Ching's nine categories of *yüeh-fu* in comparison with Kuo's twelve see Masuda, *op. cit.*, pp. 511–31, 443–4.

43   Masuda, *op. cit.*, pp. 445–6 briefly compares Tso's and Kuo's classification schemes. He points out, p. 14, that Tso traced the origin of *yüeh-fu* to the legendary Yellow Emperor. Feng Wei-no (d. AD 1572) compiled *Notes on Ancient Poetry (Ku shih chi)* in 156 chapters, a vast repository of traditional verse and songs. Shen Te-ch'ien (AD 1673–1769), *Sources of Ancient Poetry (Ku shih yüan)*. Ting Fu-pao (1874–1952), comp., *Complete Poetry of the Han, Three Kingdoms, Chin, and Northern and Southern Dynasties* (1916). Lu Ch'in-li (1911–1973), comp., *Poetry of the Ch'in, Han, Wei, Chin, and Northern and Southern Dynasties* in 135 chapters (1982). *The Four Sung Books* edited by Li Fang *et al.* in the tenth century AD include the two valuable repositories of literature, *Imperial Survey of the T'ai-p'ing Era (T'ai-p'ing yü-lan)* and *Prize Blooms from the Garden of Literature (Wen-yüan ying-hua)*, each in 1,000 chapters.

44   Masuda, *op. cit.*, pp. 468–510, lists a number of fragments of old *yüeh-fu* preserved in Li Fang's compilations and various pre-Sung collections.

45   See Nakatsuhama Wataru, *Research on and Concordance to the Yüeh-fu shih chi*, pp. 572–701.

46   Bold, *id.*, p. 3.

47 Diény, *op. cit.*, pp. 5–8, discusses these texts from *Discourses of the States (Kuo yü)*, *Record of Ritual, Historical Records*, and *History of the Han*.

48 Diény, *id.*, p. 6 (my translation from his French version), citing *The Kung-yang Commentary (Kung-yang chuan)*, SPPY 16.11a, commentary, 15th year of Duke Hsüan.

49 Among the four sections of the *Book of Poetry (Shih ching)* the first, entitled *Kuo feng*, is believed to mean 'Airs of the States', or, since *feng* is a pun for wind, custom, or admonition, 'Grievances of the States'. This section was traditionally believed to contain songs of the people. The poems in it are subdivided into regional categories, suggesting that they had indeed been collected from various parts of the Chou realm. Tradition also has it that the song titles classified under regional headings in Pan Ku, *op. cit.*, ch. 30, pp. 1,753–55, 'Treatise on Literature' (*I-wen chih*), are songs of the people collected from the different regions of the Han empire voicing their grievances. Also see Birrell, *op. cit.*, pp. 232–33.

50 The episode appears in Ssu-ma Ch'ien's official biography of Emperor Kao-tsu (*Shih chi*, ch. 8.389), Watson, trans., *Records*, Vol. 1, pp. 113–14. Diény, *op. cit.*, Chapter 3, 'Les conditions de l'essor de la póesie lyrique sous les Han', pp. 45–6, includes this song in an interesting list of examples of spontaneous improvization in the early Han.

51 See Chapter Four, pp. 89–93.

52 Kuo's method is to place these anonymous versions together. Sometimes he dates one version in the Han, the other in the Chin. But it is not always clear which version is the earlier, nor can a firm date be attached to them. In general, I have followed the hypothesis of J.-P. Diény that the long version is likely to be the earlier, the short the later; Diény, *op.cit.*, p. 138, and *Les dix-neuf poèmes anciens*, 136–40.

53 'The Relation between Narrator and Characters in *Yuèfu* Ballads' (1985), p. 107.

54 Gummere, *op.cit.*, pp. 90–1. The device is noted by Gary S. Williams, *op. cit.*, p. 96.

55 *Id.*, pp. 90, 95, 117–34.

56 Williams, *op.cit.*, p. 146, presents a figure of '. . . 85 percent half-lines occurring formulaically' for the ballad 'They Met'. The figures he presents in his statistical survey of a core group of 50 Han *yüeh-fu* are unreliable, for it is a smaller group than my own selection of 77 pieces, and it includes some pieces which are not anonymous, popular *yüeh-fu*, but *shih* or *ku-shih*. Moreover, his prime exhibit, 'Two White Swans', must be rejected because his claim for it that it '. . . does not appear to be a version of another song' is untenable; in fact, there are two versions of the song, one appearing in Kuo's *Anthology*, ch. 39, pp. 576–77, the other in *New Songs*, Vol. 1. Birrell, trans., p. 37.

57 See especially Milman Parry, 'Studies in the Epic Technique of Oral Verse–making: 1, Homer and Homeric Style' (1930), and Albert B. Lord, *The Singer of Tales* (1960).

58 Sir Walter Scott, *Minstrelsy of the Scottish Border* (1830, 1931), p. 505.

59 Bold, *id.*, p. 50, citing Child's category 81A. The earliest firm date for the poetic treatment of the *yu-hsia* theme in Chinese literature is Chang Heng's (AD 78–139) descriptive passage in his rhapsody, 'The Western Capital', cited in James J. Y. Liu, *The Chinese Knight-Errant* (1967), p. 56.

60 Bronson, *The Traditional Tunes of the Child Ballads*, 4 vols. (1959–72), Vol. 1, Introduction, p. ix.

61 *History of the Southern Sung (Sung shu)*, 'Treatise on Music', ch. 21.

62 *Id.*

63 Kuo provides this information in various prefaces to his twelve categories and some sub-sections of them.

64 In *Record of Things Ancient and Modern (Ku chin chu)*, SPTK 2.2b, Ts'ui Pao (*fl.* AD 290–306) notes that a 'Wu *tsü* piece is a native song of the people of Wu'. Lu Chi's (AD 261–303) 'Wu *tsü* Ballad' contains the lines: 'My audience, listen clearly!/ Listen

to me sing a Wu *tsü*./ The Wu *tsü* first arose from Ch'ang Gate.' (This was a gate in Wu's capital city). Tso Ssu (? AD 250–?306) refers in his 'Rhapsody on the Wu Capital' to 'the *yen* [songs] of Ching, dances of Ch'u,/ Wu *yü* [?glee songs] and Yüeh laments.' (Ching was an old name for Ch'u. Wu, Ch'u, and Yüeh were states of ancient Chou.) These citations of Lu and Tso are from *Anthology of Literature* (*Wen hsüan*), SPTK 28.15b and 5.33b. The extant text of the anonymous *Wu tsü hsing* (A Wu Coda, A Ballad), appears in Kuo, *ch.* 64, p. 934, between Lu Chi's piece and a sixth-century version.

65 In his essay 'Assemblage and Segmentation in *Yüeh-fu* Song-texts' (1947), Yü Kuan-ying suggests eight methods of composition, such as the combination of two songs to form one extended piece, the insertion of one or more existing songs into a composition, the insertion of a quatrain from another song's closure to form a song's opening, and the use of phrases from other pieces, such as the felicitation closure. Some of Yü's eight methods overlap. I do not fully accept all of them, partly because it is impossible to date the songs in terms of earlier or later pieces, partly because some so-called 'methods' do not constitute a *general* practice of composition, but are unique techniques used by creative song-makers in one particular song. Yü, *A Discussion of the Poetry of the Han, Wei, and Six Dynasties*, pp. 26–38. The occurrence of pentasyllabic sections among passages of extreme irregularity in the Han *yüeh-fu* repertoire may provide important clues concerning the unsolved question of the rise of formal pentasyllabic verse (*shih*) which was a predominant verse form from the end of the Han to the T'ang.

66 'The Relation between Narrator and Characters in *Yüèfú* Ballads', p. 126.

67 See n. 28, p. 176.

68 First recorded by Pan Ku, *Han shu*, *ch.* 97a, p. 3,951, trans. Watson, *Courtier*, p. 247. The octosyllabic line might also be metrically construed as two lines: 3- and 5-syllables.

69 For the official biography of Lady Li see Watson, *id.*, pp. 247–51; for that of Wei Tzu-fu, see Watson, *Records*, Vol. 1, pp. 389–91. There were various names for entertainer: *ch'ang-chia* (singer), *yüeh-chia* (musician), or *ou-che* (popular song singer).

70 *Aux origines*, pp. 41–6. A 'fuller list of such court songs, or songs sung by eminent people in the Han, appears in Suzuki, *Research*, pp. 11–42, with texts and critical comments. Most of these texts were recorded with their social contexts in the Han histories. Sixteen of the most important examples of court members are listed by Suzuki, with a total of 25 songs: Hsiang Yü (1), Kao-tsu (2), Wu-ti (6), Chao-ti (2), Yu, Prince Yu of Chao (1), Tan, Prince Tz'u of Yen (1), Li Ling (1), Hsü, Prince Li of Kuang-ling (1), Ch'ü, Prince of Kuang-ch'üan (2), Lady Ch'i (1), Li Yen-nien (1), Ssu-ma Hsiang-ju (2), Tung-fang Shuo (1), Chao Fei-yen (1), The Wu-sun Princess (1), and Lady Hua-jung (1).

71 Diény, *id.*, p.46. Royal patronage of music continued immediately after the Han with the Ts'ao family, rulers of the Wei Dynasty. Ts'ao Ts'ao is known to have been particularly fond of *tan-ko*, the unaccompanied singing of popular Han airs, and he, like his sons and grandson, was fascinated by the art of imitating Han *yüeh-fu* titles.

72 Diény, *id.*, p. 94, quotes Emperor Hsüan's edict; Watson, *op. cit.*, p. 390, translates the anecdote about Wei Tzu-fu.

73 Diény, *id.*, pp. 53, 52–4.

74 *Id.*, pp. 67–74.

75 Shen Yüeh, *op.cit.*, and Kuo, *Anthology*, form the main sources; in the former work anonymous Han songs or *yüeh-fu* are usually designated by the term *ku-tz'u*, old songs, in Kuo they are designated by the terms *ku-tz'u*, old words, or *pen-tz'u*, original words after their title.

76 Birrell, trans., Chapter 1.

1 His *ch.* 1, 8, and 12 contain Han hymns; *ch.* 1–12 contain hymns from the Chin to the T'ang Dynasties. These twelve chapters form a significant proportion of Kuo's opus.

2 *Hsieh-lü tu-wei: tu-wei* is a military title, similar to commandant; *hsieh-lü* is a technical term for euphony. Loewe, *Crisis*, p. 195, n. 9, translates this title as Master of Harmony. It might also be rendered as Master of Euphony.

3 See Map, Bureau of Music in Ch'angan.

4 The humble origins of Emperor Kao-tsu are recorded in his official biography and examples of his plebian traits appear in the account of his contest for the empire with Hsiang Yü in the latter's biography, Watson, *Records*, Vol. 1, pp. 37–119 (*Shih chi*, *ch.* 8 and 7).

5 Loewe, *Crisis*, pp. 51–5, lists the six principal consorts of Emperor Wu; Diény, *Aux origines*, p. 50, emphasizes the humble social origins of many consorts and courtiers in the reign of Emperor Wu. For biographies of Lady Li and Empress Wei, see Watson, *Courtier*, pp. 247–51 (Pan Ku, *History*, *ch.* 97), and Watson, *Records*, Vol. 1, pp. 389–92. In both cases it was Emperor Wu's sister, the Princess of P'ing-yang, who introduced the girls to him while in her employ as entertainers skilled in singing and dancing.

6 The accounts of Ssu-ma Ch'ien and Pan Ku differ concerning which of the Li family, the brother or the sister, introduced the other to the emperor. Ssu-ma Ch'ien states that after the emperor's sister, the Princess of P'ing-yang, had introduced the Li sister to the emperor he 'had her installed in the women's quarters of the palace, at the same time summoning Li Yen-nien to an audience and appointing him to a higher post [than kennel lad].' Watson, *Records*, Vol. 2, p. 466, 'The Emperors' Male Favorites', *Shih chi, ch.* 125, p. 3,195. Pan Ku states, however, that Emperor Wu befriended Li Yen-nien because of his fine singing, and that it was the Princess who suggested to the emperor that Li's young sister might be the 'one so lovely you'll never find again,' words from Li Yen-nien's love song performed in the presence of the emperor; Watson, *Courtier*, pp. 247–48.

7 For his biography and a discussion of his works see Yves Hervouet, *Un poète de cour sous les Han: Sseu-ma Siang-jou* (1964). For a translation of his biography by Ssu-ma Ch'ien, see Watson, *Records*, Vol. 2, pp. 297–342.

8 For General Li's campaigns see Loewe and Hulsewé, *China in Central Asia, The Early Stage* (1979), pp. 132–36. For Chang Ch'ien see Jeannette Mirsky, ed., *The Great Chinese Travelers* (1964), Chapter 2.

9 Ssu-ma Ch'ien, *Historical Records*, 130 *ch.*, Watson, *Records*, 2 vols., a translation of nearly all the Han chapters; Edouard Chavannes, *Les mémoires historiques de Se-ma Ts'ien*, 6 vols. (1895–1905), a translation of *ch.* 1–52. For Ssu-ma Ch'ien's auto-biographical account see J. R. Hightower, trans., 'Letter to Jen An (Shao-ch'ing)', in Cyril Birch, ed., *Anthology of Chinese Literature* (1965), pp. 95–102.

10 For a partial translation of his work and a discussion of his philosophy, see Fung Yu-lan, trans. from the Chinese by Derk Bodde, *A History of Chinese Philosophy*, Vol. 2, pp. 16–71, and de Bary, Chan, and Watson, eds., *Sources*, Vol. 1, pp. 160–69; also see above, pp. 39–40.

11 The biography of Tung-fang Shuo appears in Watson, *Courtier*, pp. 79-106. (Pan Ku, *id.*, *ch.* 65).

12 This conversation (of 111 BC) is recorded by Ssu-ma Ch'ien, 'History of the Feng and Shan Sacrifices', Watson, *Records*, Vol. 2, p. 55 (*Shih chi, ch.* 28, p. 1,396). *Feng* means a mound, to raise a mound, to sacrifice on a mound, and to enfeoff; *Shan* means to level ground, to sacrifice on level ground.

13 For a review of the problem of Ssu-ma Hsiang-ju's involvement in this event, see Introduction, pp. 6–8 above.

14 For a review of the problem of the date of this institution see Introduction, pp. 5–7 above. Prior to this appointment there had been other directors of music, notably Master Chih, a Ch'in official, Shu-sun T'ung (notorious for having 'served close to ten different masters'), who had revised Ch'in sacrificial ceremonies for the Han Emperor Hui, and Hsia-hou K'uan, who in 194 BC was commissioned to set the hymns of Emperor Kao-tsu's consort to string and wind accompaniment. Watson, *Records*, Vol. 1, pp. 291–98; Wilhelm, *op cit.*, pp. 124, 130, nn. 13–15. (*Shih chi, ch.* 99, pp. 2,720–26; *Han shu, ch.* 22, p. 1,043.)

15 Loewe, *Crisis*, p. 18.

16 This incident is described in the biography of Lady Li, Watson, *Courtier*, p.249 (Pan Ku, *ch.* 97, p. 3,952).

17 The fate of Luan Ta illustrates this; Watson, 'History of the Feng and Shan Sacrifices', p. 54.

18 These reforms are enumerated by Ssu-ma Ch'ien, Watson, *id.*, pp. 37–69; they are discussed by Loewe, *Crisis*, pp. 168–70.

19 Watson, *id.*, pp. 52–3.

20 For *Chou sung* see Bernhard Karlgren, trans., *The Book of Odes* (1974), nos. 266–305, 40 *sung* in all; Waley, *The Book of Songs* (using his 'Finding List', p. 355), and Waley, *T'ien Hsia* (Oct. 1936), pp. 245–48 for a discussion of nos. 291–305. For translations of the 'Nine Songs', see David Hawkes, *Ch'u Tz'u, The Songs of the South* (1959), pp. 36–44, and Waley, *The Nine Songs: A Study of Shamanism in Ancient China* (1956).

21 The earliest recording of the text of this set occurs in Pan Ku, *ch.* 22, 'Treatise on Rites and Music', pp. 1,046–51; it was originally entitled 'Music for Private Performance', a title dating from the Chou. The content of the set is discussed by Frankel, '*Yüeh-fu* Poetry', pp. 72–4. Suzuki Shūji has shown that it is odd that these hymns are referred to as being in the Ch'u style. Of the 17 hymns, 13 are in the tetrasyllabic metre of the *Book of Poetry*, while only 3 of the 17 are in the trisyllabic metre associated with the *Songs of Ch'u*. The language, however, is reminiscent of the latter. Suzuki, *Research on Han and Wei Poetry* (1967), pp. 5–7.

22 The earliest recording of the text of this set occurs in Pan Ku, *id.*, pp. 1,051–70. It has been translated in full by Chavannes, *op cit.*, Vol. 3, Appendix 1, pp. 612–29.

23 For a brief survey of these hymns see Loewe, *Crisis*, pp. 198–99. For the problem of the dating of the horse hymn, see n. 44 below.

24 Hawkes, *op. cit., Chiu ko*, pp. 36–7.

25 Similar to the Judaic number twelve; in Chinese legend the ruler Yü the Great possessed Nine Tripods, his realm was called the Nine Regions; *cf.* the 'Nine Songs'.

26 This cosmic dualism is explained at more length in the next hymn.

27 In the ancient Chinese pentatonic scale the Five Tones were *kung, shang, chüeh, chih,* and *yü*.

28 Eight Points, *i.e.* the four cardinal points and the half-cardinal points.

29 Green and yellow might also signify spring and autumn, and by extension, the four seasons. This hymn has been translated, apart from Chavannes, *op. cit.*, by James Legge, *The Chinese Classics*, Vol. 4, Pt. 1, *She king*, p. 119 (*Shih ching*), and his translation is reproduced in Loewe, *Chinese Ideas of Life and Death* (1982), pp. 128–30.

30 The text appears in Pan Ku, *op. cit.*, p. 1,052, and in Kuo, *Anthology, ch.* 1, 'Words for Suburban and Temple [Sacrifices], Han Songs for Suburban Sacrifices', p. 3. The metre is trisyllabic, or hexasyllabic, taking two trisyllabic units together.

31 Derk Bodde, *Festivals in Classical China, New Year and Other Annual Observances during The Han Dynasty 206 BC–AD 220* (1975), pp. 38 and 197, presents two tables of the correspondences, which I have partially combined. I have amended his translation of the song titles to fit my translation of them. It is undoubtedly due to Tsou Yen's association with the articulation of the Theory of the Five Elements and *Yin* and

Yang that the seasonal songs for spring, summer, autumn, and winter (translated above) are attributed to him, with the caption 'Master Tsou's Music', by Pan Ku and others. Tsou Yen was also renowned for using pitchpipes to warm the northern climate so that cereal seed would germinate. Joseph Needham and Wang Ling, *Science and Civilisation in China*, Vol. 4, Pt. 1, p. 29.

32 In ancient China the earth was conceived of as a square, bounded on four sides by four seas; the sky was thought of as a round canopy covering the earth above. 'Lord God Draws Nigh', Pan Ku, *id.*, p. 1,054; Kuo, *ibid.*; tetrasyllabic.

33 D. C. Lau, trans., *Lao Tzu, Tao Te Ching*, XXV, p. 82, VI, p. 62; the text dates *c.* 300 BC.

34 *Id.*, IV, p. 60.

35 *Id.*, XIX, p. 75.

36 Lau, trans., *Mencius*, Book IV, Pt.A.9, pp. 121–22; 'The people turn to the benevolent as water flows downwards or as animals head for the wilds.' Citing *Meng Tzu, SSC* 7B.1a, a Confucian philosopher (*c.* fourth century BC).

37 The texts appear in Pan Ku, *id.*, pp. 1,054–56, and Kuo, *id.*, pp. 3–4; tetrasyllabic.

38 In his translation of this hymn, Chavannes, *op. cit.*, p. 617, VII, and n.1, renders *T'ai-yüan* as 'la majestueuse primitivité', glossing it as 'Le Ciel'; and in his study *Le T'ai chan* (1910), Appendix, pp. 521–25, he notes that the female earth deity is often linked with the male heavenly deity. Also see p. 35 above: 'Empress Earth is the rich Old Woman'.

39 Fung, *op cit.*, pp. 7–71; de Bary, Chan, and Watson,. *op. cit.*, pp. 162–65.

40 The text appears in Pan Ku, *id.*, p. 1,057, and Kuo, *id.*, p. 4. The metre is tetrasyllabic.

41 Loewe and Hulsewé, *op. cit.*, pp. 42 and 133.

42 *Id.*, pp. 132–33, 225–26, citing Pan Ku, *ch.* 96 and 61.

43 *Id.*, pp. 135 and 43.

44 The composition of the hymns is mentioned in Pan Ku's official biography of Emperor Wu, Dubs, *The History of the Former Han Dynasty*, Vol. 2, p. 75 and 102–03, citing Pan Ku, *ch.* 6. Loewe and Hulsewé, *op. cit.*, review the confusion surrounding the dates of the appearance of the horses, p. 133: the early dates of 121 BC or 120 BC are rejected in favour of 113 BC and 101 BC.

45 Loewe and Hulsewé, *id.*, p.134, n. 332. Waley, 'The Heavenly Horses of Ferghana, A New View', *History Today*, 5.2 (Feb. 1955), pp. 95–103. Also see 'The Blood-sweating Horses of Ferghana', in Dubs, *op. cit.*, Appendix 5, pp. 132–35, in which he explains that the 'crimson sweat' is a phenomenon caused by parasites embedded in the horse's skin.

46 T'ai-i was the deity especially honoured by Emperor Wu; in his mind the deity ranked higher than the traditional supreme deity, Shang-ti. It is not clear whether T'ai-i, Great Unity, is the same as *T'ai-yüan* of the hymn 'Lo! Holy Creator'. The words *T'ai*, *i*, and jade belong to the nomenclature of Taoism.

47 Loewe, *Ways to Paradise, The Chinese Quest for Immortality* (1979), pp. 47–50, refers to these guardian beasts as leopards in his interesting discussion of the artistic depiction of the Queen Mother of the West on a mortuary banner of the Former Han era.

48 Flowing Sands was the name of desert land west of China, which was also the region of Fountain River. Pan Ku states that the horses appeared from Wo-wei River (south of Tun-huang) and from Yü-wu (possibly in Shansi province), at the end of the first part of the hymn in this 'Treatise' and in his biography of Emperor Wu. Clearly, he was indulging in poetic license.

49 Chavannes, *Mémoires*, Vol. 3, Appendix I, p. 620, n. 2, notes that the Chih-hsü Star corresponds to *ch'en* in the series The Twelve Earthly Branches, and that its symbolic beast is the dragon, its direction east, and its colour green. The dragon in Chinese has equine attributes.

50 Wilhelm, 'The Bureau of Music in Western Han', pp. 132–33, n. 48, refers in another

connection to *Ch'ien* and *K'un*, the first two hexagrams of the classic, which are translated by Richard Wilhelm as 'Hidden dragon', and 'Flying dragon', with 'the perseverance of a mare', in his version of the commentaries of the hexagrams, *The I Ching, or Book of Changes* (1951, translated from Wilhelm's German by Cary F. Baynes), pp. 7–11.

51   The texts appear in Pan Ku, *ch.* 22, 'Treatise on Rites and Music', pp. 1,060–61, and Kuo, *id.*, pp. 5–6. The metre of both hymns is trisyllabic. In the 'History of Music' of Ssu-ma Ch'ien (*Shih chi, ch.* 24) different versions of the two hymns are given. They differ in metre and in wording, the latter quite significantly. The Ch'u trisyllabic metre in Pan Ku's versions is accentuated in Ssu-ma Ch'ien's versions by the presence of the sound carrier *hsi* between two sets of three characters. *Shih chi, ch.* 24, p. 1,178.

52   Cheng Kuo's feat is described in Ssu-ma Ch'ien, *Historical Records, ch.* 29, 'History of the Rivers and Drains', Watson, *Records*, Vol. 2, pp. 71–2, reproduced with a commentary in Hsü Cho-yün, *Han Agriculture*, pp. 257–58. In the historical account it is clear that Cheng Kuo's original motive had more to do with military strategy than a humanitarian agrarian policy.

53   The account of Lord Pai's extension of the ditch appears in Pan Ku, *History*, 'Treatise on Canals and Ditches', *ch.* 29, p. 1,685, where he also presents the text of the hymn, minus the fourth couplet. The text with the couplet appears in Kuo, *id., ch.* 83, 'Words for Miscellaneous Ditties, Part 1, Song-texts, Part 1', p. 1,172. The metre is tetrasyllabic. See David R. Knechtges' review article, 1990, p. 313.

54   Goosegate is a natural pass in Shansi, so named because when geese migrated from the north to south China they seemed to fly through the 'gate' of the pass. It was a military outpost. Lord Wang of Loyang had nothing to do with this part of China; he was from I-chou, modern Szechwan. Lord Wang's name was Wang Huan. In his youth he memorized the *Confucian Classics*, that is, *Poetry, History, Ritual, Changes*, and *Spring and Autumn Annals*, and knew the *Analects*, the recorded sayings of Confucius and his disciples. His biography appears in Fan Yeh (AD 398–446), *History of the Latter Han, ch.* 76.

55   In the reign of Emperor Huan of the Han (AD 147–167) many cults were proscribed due to the emperor's preference for Taoism; nevertheless the cult of Lord Wang was one of the few non-Taoist cults allowed to continue.

56   The hymn has been translated, annotated, and discussed by Diény, *op. cit.*, pp. 150–54. The text appears in Kuo, *ch.* 39, 'Words for Concerted Songs, Zither-mode Pieces, Part 4', p. 574. The earliest recording of the text appears in Shen Yüeh, 'Treatise on Music', *ch.* 21, 'Major Pieces' category, p. 622, under the title 'The Ballad of Loyang'. Another title for the hymn is 'The Governor of Loyang'. The metre is irregular. The first stanza has lines of 5, 3, and 8 syllables; the second stanza has one 6-syllable line, the rest are tetrasyllabic; the third is tetrasyllabic throughout; the fourth is a mix of 3, 6, 5, and 4 syllable lines; the fifth is tetrasyllabic except line 5; stanzas six to eight are tetrasyllabic.

Chapter Two

1   The extant edition of Aesop is much later, that of Maximus Planudes of the 14th century AD, based on texts of Aesop, transcribed with an unknown degree of fidelity by Demetrius of Phalerum of the 4th century BC. A. Lytton Sells, 'Fable in Verse' (1965), p. 269.

2   Watson, trans., *Chuang Tzu*; W. K. Liao, trans., *Han Fei Tzu*, 2 vols. (1959); Graham, trans., *Lieh Tzu* (1960).

3   As Kuo points out in his preface to this section, this kind of music is military. The

images of the ibis (connected with a drum) and of the pheasant may be related to military exercise through the sport of hunting, a possibility suggested to me by the remarks on the hunt in the Han in Bodde, *Festivals*, p. 381.

4   Other fables appear in sources outside Kuo's *Anthology*, without musical categories, which are indicated in the final note to my discussion of each piece.

5   Even in that monument to genre studies, *Anthology of Literature* (*Wen hsüan*) of the sixth century AD, no fable genre or verse fable genre exists.

6   Lu K'an-ju, *A Study of Old Yüeh-fu Texts* (*Yüeh-fu ku-tz'u k'ao*), p. 59, citing K'ung (AD 574–648), a noted scholar who wrote commentaries on the *Confucian Classics.*

7   Yang Shen (AD 1488–1529), author of a philological treatise and a miscellany.

8   Ch'en Hang, *Notes on Poetic Figures* (*Shih pi-hsing chien*), p. 12.

9   Bielenstein, 'An Interpretation of the Portents in the *Ts'ien-Han-shu*' (1950), pp. 127–43.

10 Compare the marriage songs of the *Book of Poetry*, Waley, trans., *The Book of Songs*, Chapter 2, nos. 85, 86.

11 These titles appear in Chapter Six below. The ibis and the drum are linked in three poems of the *Book of Poetry*: no. 136 has a dancer holding an ibis feather and beating a drum; no. 278 has guests flocking to a banquet like ibis and a speaker says, 'there, there is nothing to dislike,/ here, there is nothing to disrelish;' and no. 298 has flocking ibis linked to the sound of drums booming, again in the context of dance and guests at a banquet. Karlgren, *The Book of Odes*, pp. 87, 244, and 254 (he renders *lu* as egret rather than ibis). No. 136 is a love poem.

12 The metre is mainly trisyllabic, except for the first line of two syllables and the last line of four. The text appears in Shen Yüeh, 'Treatise on Music', ch. 22, 'Han Songs for the *Nao*-bell' category, p. 640, and in Kuo, *ch.* 16, 'Words for Drumming and Blowing Pieces, Han Songs for the *Nao*-bell', p. 226.

13 The metre is in regular pentasyllabics. Its structure is irregular, being a unit of seven lines. The song may be divided either into two parts, the first three lines and the last four, or, as Kuo, *ch.* 26, p. 384, citing a T'ang critic, indicates, it may divide into five stanzas of three lines each, made up of the first couplet and one of the 'Fish play' lines in sequence. This would suit its song style very well. The text appears in Shen, *ch.* 21, 'Concerted' category, pp. 604–5, and in Kuo, *ch.* 26, 'Words for Concerted Songs, Part 1, Concerted Pieces, Part 1', p. 384.

14 Yü, *Anthology of Yüeh-fu Poetry* (*Yüeh-fu shih hsüan*, 1950, rev. ed. 1954), p. 8.

15 The metre is irregular, with lines of between 2 and 7 syllables. The text is in Shen, *ch.* 22, 'Han Songs for the *Nao*-bell' category, pp. 642–43, and in Kuo, *ch.* 16, 'Words for Drumming and Blowing Pieces, Part 1, Han Songs for the *Nao*-bell', p. 231.

16 In these ballads a wealthy family is said to have four or five brothers and two or three brothers, respectively. See Chapter Eleven.

17 'Mulberry' appears in Chapter Eleven; 'Peacock' is translated in Birrell, *id.*, p. 53f.; the reference there to Ch'in Lo-fu is on p. 54. Diény, *Aux origines*, pp. 114–17, 108–14, and 128–36, discusses 'A Crow Bore Eight or Nine Chicks', 'Cocks Crow', and 'Mulberry on the Bank' (Lo-fu).

18 See poem nos. 166 and 172 of the *Book of Poetry*. South Mountain, *Nan-shan* or *Chung-nan-shan*, is south of Ch'angan; Royal Forest (*Shang-lin*) was south-west of Ch'angan.

19 *Shuo yüan SPTK* 9.4b-5a, attributed to Liu Hsiang (79–8 BC). The story is also in *Exoteric Commentary on the Han School Text of the Book of Poetry* (*Han shih wai chuan*), attributed to Han Ying (*fl.* 150 BC), Hightower, trans., *Han Shih Wai Chuan* (1952), *ch.* 10.21, pp. 341–42.

20 The metre is irregular, with lines of mostly uneven syllables: 2, 3, 5, 6, 7, 8, and 9 syllables. The text is in Shen, *ch.* 21, 'Concerted' category, p. 607, and in Kuo, *ch.* 28, 'Words for Concerted Songs, Part 3, Concerted Pieces, Part 3', p. 408.

21 The first of three stanzas, Karlgren, trans., *id.*, p. 67.

22 The metre is regular pentasyllabic. The text appears in Feng Wei-no, *SKCS* 3, *Notes on Ancient Poetry*, *ch.* 20.11b, and Shen Te-ch'ien, *Sources of Ancient Poetry*, *SPPY* 4.9a.

23 Wing-tsit Chan, trans., *Analects* (*Lun yü*), 18.6, *A Source Book in Chinese Philosophy* (1963), p. 48; Confucius (K'ung Fu Tzu, 551–479 BC).

24 The metre is regular, a pentasyllabic quatrain. The text appears in Li Shan's (d. AD 689) commentary on Lu Chi's imitation of the Han title in *Anthology of Literature* (*Wen hsüan*), *SPTK* 28.1a, and in Kuo's preface to Ts'ao P'ei's (AD 187–226) imitation of the Han title, *ch.* 31, p. 462. An extract is quoted elsewhere by Li Shan which might prove to be part of the quatrain 'The Fierce Tiger Ballad'. In his commentary on P'an Yüeh's (AD 247–300) 'Prose Poem on the Orphaned Wife' (*Wen hsüan*, *SPTK* 16.25a), Li cites a couplet which he says is part of the old 'Fierce Tiger Ballad': 'Young men are nervous and afraid,/ When friendless and alone they reach a different district.' It is not clear if Li means that the title to which he refers is the same as the Han piece, and if so where the couplet he cites fits, or whether he refers to a different old piece of the same title. The couplet, if it does belong to the Han quatrain, might fit at the end of it. Lu Ch'in-li, *Poetry of the Ch'in, Han . . .*, p. 288, presents the couplet separately from the Han quatrain as a second piece of the same title. In Li Shan's commentary on Shen Yüeh's 'Biographical Essay on Hsieh Ling-yün' (from Shen's *History of the Southern Sung*), Li cites another couplet attaching to the old 'Fierce Tiger Ballad': 'Natural endowment has its portion,/ Physical life has its timespan' (*Wen hsüan*, *SPTK* 50.15a). Perhaps this fragment opens the ballad.

25 'Peacock', Birrell, p. 53, lines 1–2, and p. 61, stanza 4, line 8, stanza 5, line 4.

26 The metre of the piece is regular pentasyllabic. The text appears in *New Songs from a Jade Terrace*, Ming rpr. ed., *ch.* 1.10–11, listed under 'Six Old Yüeh-fu Poems'.

27 Chien-an was a late Han reign-period, AD 196–200. For examples of post-Han lyrics on the theme of the neglected wife, see poems by Ts'ao poets translated in Birrell, *New Songs*, Chapter 2, pp. 64–72. For a translation and discussion of 'A Yen Song, The Whenever Ballad', with notes, see Diény, *id.*, pp. 142–46.

28 Peking University, *Reference Materials for Han Literary History* (*Liang Han wen-hsüeh shih ts'an-k'ao tzu-liao*, 1959) p. 531, suggests that in this closure the singer directly addresses the audience, and notes that the first couplet of stanza 3 echoes the 'Nine Songs' of the *Songs of Ch'u*: 'No sorrow is greater than the parting of the living;/ No happiness greater than making new friendships.' Hawkes, *id.*, 'The Lesser Master of Fate', p. 41, lines 13–14.

29 See n. 45, Introduction, above.

30 The metre is pentasyllabic except for tetrasyllabic lines 3-5; 4 quatrains and coda. The text appears in Shen, *ch.* 21, 'Major Pieces' category, p. 618, and in Kuo, *ch.* 39, 'Words for Concerted Songs, Part 14, Zither-mode Pieces, Part 4', pp. 576–77.

31 It is difficult to discuss metre in a text which is so corrupt that different editors divide the lines to produce various metrical patterns. The pattern as I have translated the piece is 7, 9, 5, 8, 7, 3, 6, and 8 syllables. The full text appears in Kuo, *ch.* 61, 'Song-texts for Miscellaneous Pieces, Part 1', p. 885. A fragment, the first three lines, with several variants, appears in Hsü Chien (AD 659–729) *et al.* comp., *Notes for Beginning Students* (*Ch'u hsüeh chi*), Chung-hua ed., *ch.* 30, p. 750.

32 The metre is pentasyllabic. The text appears in Kuo, *ch.* 74, 'Song-texts for Miscellaneous Pieces, Part 14', p. 1,044.

33 Yü Kuan-ying, *op. cit.*, p. 53.

34 Karlgren, *id.*, p. 4.

35 The metre is pentasyllabic. The text appears in full in Li Shan's commentary on P'an Yüeh's 'Prose Poem on the Reed-organ', *Anthology of Literature* (*Wen hsüan*), *SPTK* 18.33b, and in Kuo's preface to Hsiao Kang's (AD 503–551) imitation of the Han

song with the title 'Under the Date-tree What Bunches, Bunches!', *ch.* 74, p. 1,045. Hsiao Kang's piece is translated in John Marney, *Beyond the Mulberries* (1982), poem no. 16. The word for date, or jujube, *tsao,* is a pun for 'soon.'

36 *Chuang Tzu* (*c.*369–*c.*286 BC), *SPPY* 7/20.8b (my translation). Also see the translations of Watson, p. 209 and Graham, p. 121.

37 For South Mountain see n. 18. Poem 166 of the *Book of Poetry* ends with a series of eternity symbols, including South Mountain, pine and cypress. Loyang (line 5) was the capital of the Latter Han, and had been an important city from Chou times. See Hans H. Bielenstein, 'Loyang in Later Han Times' (1976). Master Shu and Pan of Lu state (line 14) are in fact one and the same man, Master Shu, Pan of Lu state; see Yü Kuan-ying, *A Discussion of the Poetry of the Han, Wei, and Six Dynasties* (*Han Wei Liu-ch'ao shih lun-ts'ung,* 1953), pp. 48–53. The mistaken double identity appears in such classical texts as *The Annals of Mr Lü* (*Lü-shih ch'un-ch'iu*), attributed to Lü Pu-wei (d. 235 BC), *SPTK* 21.9a, and *Huai-nan Tzu,* comp. *c.* 140 BC under the direction of Liu An, King of Huai-nan (d. 122 BC), *SPPY* 19.4a. Lines 13–14, the Han song's last passage, are a commonplace expression which occurs in an old poem in *New Songs,* Birrell, p. 32, lines 9–10.

38 The metre is pentasyllabic. The text is in *Compendium of Literature* (*I-wen lei-chü*), Ou-yang Hsün comp. (AD 557–641), Chung-hua ed. (1965), *ch.* 88.1516, entitled 'An Old *Yen* Song'. It is also in Kuo, *ch.* 39, 'Words for Concerted Songs, Part 14, Zither-mode Pieces, Part 4', pp. 579–80. Although the Han song goes by the title 'A *Yen* Song', there is no indication in Kuo's text that it divides into a *yen* / *tsü* structure; it is possible to conjecture that the first twelve lines constitute the *yen,* the last six, with their commonplace expressions, the *tsü.*

39 Feng, *Notes, SKCS* 2, *ch.* 16.7b. Hsün Hsü (d. AD 289), *Hsün's Poetry Notes* (*Hsün shih lu*). Hsün's work survives mainly in Chih-chiang's (*c.* AD 568) citation of Wang Seng-ch'ien's (d. AD 485) non-extant work; Chih-chiang, *Record of Ancient and Modern Music* (*Ku chin yüeh lu*) in Han Wei i-shu ch'ao, *ch.* 52.15, cited by Kuo, *ch.* 34, p. 501.

40 *San-fu huang-t'u* (The Yellow Chart of the Three Metropolitan Districts), anon. (? 3rd century AD), *SPTK* 5.7b.

41 The metre of the intact lines is pentasyllabic, suggesting that the lines with lacunae are the same. The text appears in Kuo, *ch.* 34, 'Words for Concerted Songs, Part 9, Clear-mode Pieces, Part 2', p. 501. The first quatrain is cited in *Compendium, ch.* 89, pp. 1,532-33.

42 Hawkes, *id.,* 'The Nine Declarations', pp. 76–7.

43 The metre is pentasyllabic. The first quatrain of the text appears in *Compendium, ch.* 86, p. 1,477 (listed as a *ku-shih,* old poem) and in Li Shan's commentary on one of Liu Chen's (d. AD 217) imitative poems about a cassia tree; Li refers to the piece as an old poem, *ku-shih,* and that is how it is usually listed in anthologies; *Wen hsüan, SPTK* 31.15a. The full text appears in Feng, *Notes, SKCS* 3, *ch.* 20.7a.

Chapter Three

1 Graham, *Chuang-tzū,* pp. 221–23, discusses the representative philosopher of the Yangist or 'Nurture of Life School'. Yang Chu (*c.* 350 BC). Suzuki Shūji has an interesting discussion on this theme in some early *yüeh-fu,* 'Impermanence and Wandering Immortals', *Research on Han and Wei Poetry* (1967), pp. 415–19.

2 Graham, *id.,* p. 176.

3 *Ibid.* The Ch'in founder's dates are 259–209 BC, r. 221–209 BC.

4 Loewe, *Chinese Ideas of Life and Death,* p.29. The Ch'in capital was in northwest China, near the later Han capital Ch'angan, modern Sian.

5 *Ibid.*

6   Watson, 'The Feng and Shan Sacrifices', *Records*, Vol. 2, p. 39.

7   *Id.*, pp. 48–9. The hymn celebrating this good omen appears in translation in Chavannes, *Mémoires*, Vol. 3, Appendix 1, no. 12, pp. 622–24.

8   Watson, *op cit.*, p. 56.

9   For a translation of the amnesty see Loewe, *Chinese Ideas*, pp. 83–4, citing *Han shu, ch.* 6. For a translation of the hymn see Chavannes, *id.*, no. 13, p. 624. The hymns on the cauldron (n. 7) and the fungus belong to the set of 19 Han hymns discussed and translated in part in Chapter One above.

10 Graham, *op. cit.*, p. 176.

11 Burton Watson, *The Columbia Book of Chinese Poetry* (1984), p. 94, notes: 'One of the "Nineteen Old Poems" alludes to the frequency with which people poisoned themselves by imbibing such "immortality potions", which were usually concocted of highly toxic ingredients such as lead, arsenic, or mercury.'

12 See 'The Far-off Journey', Hawkes, *Ch'u Tz'u*, pp. 81–7, of which the translator notes, p. 81: '[It] could be described as a Taoist's answer to the *Li-sao*—the poem is full of references to yoga techniques and to the hagiography of Han Taoism . . . I think its date of composition is probably not much earlier than the beginning of the first century BC.'

13 Watson, 'The Feng and Shan Sacrifices', p. 54.

14 Watson, *Chinese Lyricism, Shih Poetry from the Second to the Twelfth Century* (1971), Chapter Five, pp. 68–89, 'The Poetry of Reclusion'.

15 Graham, *id.*, p. 176.

16 *Ibid.*

17 Kuo, *ch.* 16, p. 226, citing Shen Yüeh, *ch.* 19, p. 538.

18 Hawkes, *op. cit.*, p. 42, lines 3–5, 'Ho Po, The God of the Yellow River', no. 8 of the 'Nine Songs'.

19 This group of miracles is mentioned by Loewe, *Chinese Ideas*, p. 89, with his translation of an imperial edict declaring a general amnesty on the occasion, citing *Han shu, ch.* 8. Ch'en Heng also lists the miracles in his discussion, *Notes on Poetic Figures*, pp. 3–4.

20 The metre is irregular. The first eight lines are pentasyllabic. The next two lines are of four and three syllables (or perhaps they combine to form one 7-syllable line). The next line is trisyllabic, followed by a 6-syllable couplet, then lines of 4 and 5 syllables (which might combine to form a 9-syllable line). The next quatrain is trisyllabic, 'Magic fungus . . .', and the final quatrain returns to pentasyllabics. The text is in Shen Yüeh, *ch.* 22, 'Han Songs for the *Nao*-bell' category, p. 641, and in Kuo, *ch.* 16, 'Words for Drumming and Blowing Pieces, Part 1, Han Songs for the *Nao*-bell', p. 229.

21 Yen Yü (*fl.* AD 1180–1235), *Remarks on Poetry from Ts'ang-lang (Ts'ang-lang shih hua)*, Kuang-wen (1972), *ch.* 5.2a, rebukes Kuo for not seeing that song no. 3 is thematically a quite separate piece. The passage is translated by Günther Debon, *Ts'ang-lang's Gespräche über die Dichtung*, pp. 97–8, section 105.

22 Ts'ui Pao, *Record of Things Ancient and Modern*, SPTK 2.3b. The two *wan-ko* appear in Chapter Five below.

23 George A. Kennedy, 'Metrical "Irregularity" in the *Shih ching*' (1939), p. 11, found that 91% of the 305 poems in the *Book of Poetry* are tetrasyllabic. For tetrasyllabic Han hymns see Chapter One above.

24 For example, Ts'ao Ts'ao (AD 155–220), 'Two Short Song Ballads, in six stanzas', anthologised by Kuo Mao-ch'ien, *ch.* 30, pp. 446–47, which lament the brevity of human existence.

25 By the late Southern Dynasties era of the sixth century AD, the title 'A Long Song Ballad' was given to poems in longer metres than the original pentasyllabic.

26 In Ko Hung (AD 243–334), *Master Embracing-simplicity (Pao-p'u Tzu, nei-p'ien)*, *SPPY* 15.6b, Lao Tzu, the founder of Taoism, is said to have been nine feet tall, with eyebrows five inches long, and ears seven inches long.

27 The metre is pentasyllabic, except for the penultimate line which is (?erroneously) tetrasyllabic. The text, minus the second couplet, appears in Ou-yang Hsün *et al.*, *Compendium of Literature, ch.* 81.1381–82, under the title 'Old Poem'. The full text is in Kuo, *ch.* 30, 'Words for Concerted Songs, Part 5, Level-mode Pieces, Part 1', p. 442.

28 This scene has been represented in early art, especially on censers, such as the *Po-shan*, Po Mountain censer; see *Historical Relics*, fig. 98.

29 For the regenerative symbolism of the two creatures see Loewe, *Ways to Paradise*, pp. 52–5, 127–33; for Illusion Tree, *Jo-mu, id.*, p. 111.

30 Hightower, *Han Shih Wai Chuan, ch.* 10.15, p. 337, n. 2. Ts'ui Pao, *Record, SPTK* 2.4a, interprets *t'ao* as a pun for expel, describing Tung Cho's expulsion and extermination with the compound *T'ao-wang*.

31 Wu Ching, *Explanations of the Old Titles of Yüeh-fu*, Chin-tai pi-shu 34, *ch.* 1.4b.

32 *E.g.* a poem attributed to Sung Tzu-hou (2nd-3rd centuries AD) with the title *Tung Chiao-jao*, taken to be the name of someone, which deals with the contrast between the eternal cycle of return in nature and human mortality, Birrell, *New Songs*, pp. 43–4. In a later anonymous work of between the fourth and sixth centuries AD, *The Inner Biography of Emperor Wu (Han Wu nei chuan)*, a handmaid of the Queen Mother of the West was named Tung Shuang-ch'eng. Kristofer Schipper, *L'Empereur Wou des Han dans la légende taoiste* (1965), p. 74, n. 4.

33 The metre is irregular. Stanza one: 7–6–5–4–2–4–4. Stanza two: 3–3–4–5–4–9. Stanza three: 6–5–5–5–2–9. Stanza four: 6–7–9–7–7. Stanza five: 4–4–6–6–6–8. None of the stanzaic metres is the same. Diény, *Aux origines*, pp.119–22, has an annotated translation and discussion of the text. He translates only the Shen Yüeh text and divides the lines to form a different metrical pattern in stanza three. He points out that the final quatrain of the whole song is in the same rhyme and that it constitutes an envoi to the emperor's longevity. The text is in Shen, *ch.* 21, 'Ch'ing-Shang Song Poems in Three Modes: Clear-mode' category, p. 612, and in Kuo, *ch.* 34, p. 505, 'Words for Concerted Songs, part 9, Clear-mode Pieces, Part 2'. The text may have another couplet. In his commentary to Ts'ao Chih's 'The Harp Lay', *Anthology of Literature (Wen hsüan), SPTK* 27.27b, Li Shan cites this couplet from what he calls 'The Old Tung Flees Ballad' (and Li uses *t'ao* = flee, not *t'ao* = peach): 'My life gradually draws to a close,/ Sinks and goes home beneath the hills.' If it does belong to the text, I would suggest it be placed at the very beginning to open the song. This would make the persona someone contemplating his advancing years and seeking initiation into an immortality cult to prevent the aging process. Li Shan, *id., SPTK* 22.30a, repeats the first line of the same couplet in his commentary to Shen Yüeh's 'Resting in the East Garden', citing from 'The Old Tung Peach Ballad', this time using *t'ao* = peach! It is not clear whether he refers to a completely different song or ballad of the same title, but probably he had in mind 'I long to make a pilgrimage'.

34 Watson, *Records*, Vol. 1, p. 202, *Shih chi, ch.* 91.

35 The Han historian, Ssu-ma Ch'ien, a contemporary of Emperor Wu and Liu An, provides a different account in his *Historical Records, Shih-chi, ch.* 118. He portrays Liu An, who was enfeoffed as King of Huai-nan in 164 BC, as a rebel and traitor who plotted against the throne, and committed suicide when he was arrested. Watson, *Records*, Vol. 2, pp. 366–87.

36 Robert H. van Gulik, *Sexual Life in Ancient China* (1961, rpr, 1974), pp. 79–88, gives a general review of Taoist ideas on sexual practices linked to the cult of immortality.

37 For example, Yü Tan (late 5th to early 6th centuries AD), 'One night I dreamed I went home', Birrell, *New Songs*, p. 157.

38 Waley, *The Analects of Confucius*, XVIII.6, pp. 219–20.

39 Hawkes, *op. cit.*, '*Li sao*', p.34, lines 184–85.

40 That the mulberry and catalpa were revered is evident from poem no.197 of the *Book of Poetry*. By the late Chou mulberry was a part of celestial lore; *Fu-sang*, Leaning Mulberry, for example, was the tree of sunrise. Catalpa became known as the sacred tree in which birds of paradise perched, and in times of harmony among men, sang and danced over it.

41 The metre is irregular. The first half mixes 3 and 7-syllable lines: 3–3–7–7–7–3–3–7–7. The second half is: 7–8–3–3–4–4–7–7. Ts'ui Pao, *Record*, *SPTK* 2.2a, provides the earliest context for this piece. The text is in Shen Yüeh, *ch.* 22, 'Songs for the Sweeping Dance' category, p. 635, and in Kuo, *ch.* 54, 'Song-texts for Dance Pieces Part 3, Miscellaneous Dances, Part 2', p. 792.

42 Perhaps the first is the same deity as 'The Great One, Lord of the Eastern World' or 'The Lord of the East' whose praises are sung in the 'Nine Songs', nos. 1 and 7, Hawkes, *op. cit.*, pp. 36 and 41. For Queen Mother of the West see Loewe, *Ways to Paradise*, pp. 86–126.

43 *Explanations*, *ch.* 1.6a-b, where Wu lists the title 'Walking out of Hsia Gate', but gives the paraphrase of 'The Lunghsi Ballad'.

44 The metre is pentasyllabic. The text is in Kuo, *ch.* 37, 'Words for Concerted Songs, Part 12, Zither-mode Pieces, Part 2', p. 545.

45 Hawkes, *id.*, pp. 37 and 42.

46 The metre is pentasyllabic. The text appears in a fragmentary form in *Imperial Survey of the T'ai-p'ing Era* [AD 976–984], Li Fang (AD 925–996) *et al.* comp. (*T'ai-p'ing yü-lan*), *SPTK* 539.3b, which has lacunae of three characters at the end of line 2 and the last six lines of the piece *in toto*. The full text is in Chang Chih-hsiang (AD 1496–1577), *Garden of Old Poetic Genres* (*Ku shih lei yüan*), Yü Hsien-ch'ing ed., *ch.* 45.14a-b.

Chapter Four

1 Horace, *Odes*, 1.11, is the *locus classicus* of the phrase; *Odes* 3.29 explores the theme. Roger A. Hornsby, '*Carpe diem* '(1965), pp. 103–04.

2 Petronius, *The Satyricon*, Chapter 5, 'Dinner with Trimalchio', also uses the feast as the context for the *carpe diem* theme, although Petronius' ultimate aim is to satirize vulgar pleasure-seekers. Suzuki, *Research*, pp.405–14, discusses Han *yüeh-fu* from the perspective of 'Impermanence and Pleasure' (*Mujō to kyōraku*), but mars his discussion by the use of the pejorative label, 'decadence'.

3 Karlgren, *The Book of Odes*, poem no. 217, stanza 3, last quatrain, p.171.

4 *Id.*, poem no. 114, stanza 1, p. 74.

5 *Id.*, poem no. 216, the refrain of the four stanzas, p. 169, and poem no. 211, stanza 4, last couplet, p.166 (Karlgren's explanatory parentheses).

6 Yü Kuan-ying, *Anthology*, p. 22, notes that line 2 is based on a proverb which continues: 'I look up to Heaven and sigh'.

7 The biography of Wang-tzu Ch'iao, or Wang Tzu-ch'iao, or Wang Ch'iao, appears in *Biographies of Immortals* (*Lieh hsien chuan*), Ku chin i-shih 7, *ch.* 1.12b-13a. He is said there to have been the son of King Ling of Chou (571–545 BC), and to have disappeared on Mount Kou-shih. (*Wang-tzu* means heir apparent.) Max Kaltenmark, trans., *Le Lie-sien tchouan, Biographies légendaires des Immortels taoïstes de l'antiquité* (1953), pp. 109–10. He also appears in *Songs of Ch'u*. Hawkes, *Ch'u Tz'u*, p. 227, notes that Wang Ch'iao was a 'Chou prince who flew off on a great bird and became an Immortal.' Elsewhere, *id.*, p. 50, n. 5, he notes that Wang Tzu Ch'iao,

according to one version of the legend, '. . . changed into a rainbow-serpent, then into a shoe and finally into a great bird which flew away.'

8   The line reads: *chi pu chi ts'an*, Hunger not reach meal.

9   Diény, *Aux origines*, p. 124.

10 See Chapter Three, 'The King of Huai-nan Ballad'.

11 Hans H. Frankel, 'The Problem of Authenticity in Ts'ao Chih' (1982), p. 194, n. 39, notes that Li Shan cites this couplet as part of this song, which Li attributes to Ts'ao Chih. As with his other citations, Li does not indicate where the couplet fits in the song. Frankel suggests that it constitutes the closure, on the basis of such closures in numerous other folk-songs, and with this I concur.

12 Diény, *id.*, p. 125. His translation of the song followed by annotations and a discussion is on pp. 123–24.

13 Yü, *op. cit.*, p. 23. For examples of the sub-genre of feasting poems in the late Han see Fu Hsüan (AD 217–278), 'Past Autumn's Nine', and Ts'ao Chih (AD 192–232), 'My Sad Fate', Birrell, *New Songs*, pp. 237–39.

14 The metre is tetrasyllabic, and each stanza is a quatrain. The text is in Shen, *ch.* 21, '*Ch'ing-Shang* Song Poems in Three Modes: Zither-mode' category, p. 616, and in Kuo, *ch.* 36, 'Words for Concerted Songs, Part 11, Zither-mode Pieces, Part 1', pp. 535–36.

15 See Chapter Five below.

16 A slightly altered quotation from *Major Commentary on the Book of Documents* (*Shang shu ta chuan*), attributed to Fu Sheng (2nd cent. BC), *SPTK* 2.8b, 'Hsia Commentary, The Exploits of Yü'; Yü was the legendary founder of the Hsia Dynasty.

17 The metre is pentasyllabic. The text is in *Anthology of Literature* (*Wen hsüan*), *SPTK* 27.21b–22a. It is also in *Compendium of Literature*, *ch.* 42.752, and in Kuo, *ch.* 30, 'Words for Concerted Songs, Part 5, Level-mode Pieces, Part 1', p. 442.

18 Hsü Yu was a legendary figure. For Ch'ang Chü and Chieh Ni, see Chapter Three, n. 38.

19 The phrasing of this line is similar to line 21 of 'A *Yen* Song, The Whenever Ballad' in this chapter, which leads to a similar reference to the singer's family of infants.

20 Of Yen Hui, Confucius said: 'A handful of rice to eat, a gourdful of water to drink, living in a mean street—others would have found it unendurably depressing, but to Hui's cheerfulness it made no difference at all. Incomparable indeed was Hui!' Waley, *Analects*, VI.9, pp. 117–18.

21 Tzu-hsi may be an arcane reference to Yüeh Hsia-kung, a follower of Lao Tzu. The first couplet of this stanza is a faint echo of *Chuang Tzu, Inner Chapter* 3, 'The Great and Venerable Teacher', *SPPY* (*nei p'ien* 3), 6.4b.

22 Chan, *A Source Book in Chinese Philosophy*, Chapter 19, 'Neo-Taoism', pp. 314–35.

23 The translated version is in Shen, *ch.* 21, 'Major Pieces', pp. 620–21. Both versions are in Kuo, *ch.* 43, 'Words for Concerted Songs, Part 18, Major Pieces', pp. 636–37. There is some confusion about the category 'Major Pieces'. Kuo's category reads 'Major Pieces, 15 Pieces', yet only 'Song of Melancholy' is listed, in two versions. It seems he simply copied Shen Yüeh, who listed it among the 15 in 'Treatise on Music', *ch.* 21, pp. 620–21. Of the 15 pieces categorized as 'Major' by Shen, Kuo rearranged 14 among other categories, 'Zither-mode Pieces' for the most part. The metre of the translated version is irregular. Stanza one is tetrasyllabic except for pentasyllabic line 1; stanza two is the same; stanza three is tetrasyllabic except for pentasyllabic lines 1, 4, and 7; stanza four is tetrasyllabic except for pentasyllabic lines 1 and 4; the final passage is in a 6-4 metre, its first eight lines are tetrasyllabic (except for hexasyllabic line 3), the last six lines are hexasyllabic; 4 stanzas, and coda.

24 The 'two-thousand-bushel rank' (2,000 *shih*) of line 5 of the song was the third highest in the Han government. Originally, the different amounts of grain in rank titles

signified an annual salary in kind, but by the Han they came to designate official status. In the Han era official salaries were paid partly in cash, partly in grain. A grain payment was often better protected against inflation. Hans H. Bielenstein, 'The Bureaucracy of Han Times' (1980), pp. 4, 125, and 126. (1 *shih* = 64lbs 8.8oz *av*.)

25 This is the approach taken by Diény, *op. cit.*, pp. 149–50, in his translation and discussion of the song, although his conclusions are somewhat different from mine.

26 The metre is irregular, except for the tetrasyllabic fifth stanza. Stanza one: 3–3–5–3; stanza two: 6–5; stanza three: 6–4–7; stanza four: 7–6–4; stanza five: 4–4–4–4; last passage: 5–5–5–8–5–5–6–6–7–5. The last passage is a *tsü*. The text is in Shen, *ch.* 21, 'Major Pieces' category, p. 620, and in Kuo, *ch.* 39, 'Words for Concerted Songs, Part 14, Zither-mode Pieces, Part 4', p. 577. Kuo attributes the song to Ts'ao P'ei. Shen Yüeh lists it as an anonymous Han piece.

27 Karlgren, *op cit.*, p. 89, stanza 2. The full translation of poem no. 13 of the 'Nineteen Old Poems' is in Diény, *Les dix-neuf poèmes anciens*, p. 33, and Watson, *Chinese Lyricism*, p. 29.

28 The metre is irregular in the first part and fairly regular in the last. Stanza one: 3–3–5–4; stanza two: 3–5–6–5; stanza three: 3–3–5–5; stanza four: pentasyllabic; stanza five: heptasyllabic; stanza six: pentasyllabic. The text is in Shen, *ch.* 21, 'Major Pieces' category, p. 617, and in Kuo, *ch.* 37, 'Words for Concerted Songs, part 12, Zither-mode Pieces, Part 2', p. 549. Departing from his usual practice, Kuo lists this version as the later, but places it first. He puts the other version second, listing it as the original. As Diény observes, it is unlikely that the short version, the so-called 'original words', served as the model for the long version. Diény *Aux origines*, p. 138. He translates the long version there on pp. 137–38; he translates and discusses the short version in *Les dix-neuf poèmes anciens*, pp. 137–40.

29 The metre is similar to the preceding version. No stanzas are indicated in the text. Stanzas three and four of the preceding version are the same as the quatrains of lines 10–13 and 14–17 of the short version. The text is in Kuo, *ch.* 37, 'Words for Concerted Songs, Part 12, Zither-mode Pieces, Part 2', p. 549. Shen Yüeh cites the last couplet of this short version and refers to a version which may well be this text, *ch.* 21, pp. 617–18.

30 Diény, *Les dix-neuf poèmes anciens*, pp. 137–40. He compares the *ku-shih* specifically with the short version of 'West Gate'. I have presented my own translation of the *ku-shih* in order to preserve the correspondences between the poem and the two song versions.

Chapter Five

1 Karlgren, *The Book of Odes*, poem no. 156, stanza 1, lines 5–8, p. 101.

2 *Id.*, poem no. 248, stanza 4, lines 7–12, p. 204.

3 There is, however, one curious poem about a girl being seduced in which she is likened to a dead deer wrapped and hidden in white grass; poem no. 23, *id.*

4 James Robert Hightower, 'Ch'ü Yüan Studies' (1954), critically surveys the views of traditional Chinese commentators on the *Ch'u Tz'u*, dismissing much of their allegorizing.

5 Hawkes, *Ch'u Tz'u*, p. 34, line 187, and p. 24, n. 1.

6 *Id.*, 'The Spirits of the Fallen', p. 44, line 18.

7 *Id.*, p.104, lines 14–18 of 'The Summons of the Soul'; Hawkes discusses it with 'The Great Summons', pp. 101–03.

8 Watson, *Early Chinese Literature*, pp. 255–58.

9 Diény, *Les dix-neuf poèmes anciens*, nos. 13 and 14, pp. 33 and 35; Waley, *A Hundred*

and *Seventy Chinese Poems* (1918), pp. 45–46, renumbered by him as nos. 12 and 13, respectively.

10 Originally these songs were called *sang-ko*, funeral songs; later they were called *wan-ko*, hearse-pullers' songs.

11 James R. Hightower, 'The *Wen Hsüan* and Genre Theory' (1957), pp.152–63. The translations of the genres are his. He notes a discrepancy between the names of the 38 genres listed in that anthology's preface and the actual 37 in the body of the anthology.

12 A. R. Davis, *T'ao Yüan-ming (AD 365–427), His Works and Their Meaning*, 2 vols. (1983), Vol. 1, 'In Imitation of Burial Songs', pp. 165–73, discusses, translates, and annotates the two anonymous Han burial songs and their imitations by post-Han poets.

13 'In Response to the King of Ch'u's Questions', *Anthology of Literature (Wen hsüan)*, *SPTK* 45.1a–2a.

14 Ch'iao Chou (? AD 220–270), *Master Ch'iao's Legal Precepts (Ch'iao-tzu fa hsün)*, Yü-han shan-fang chi-i-shu 17, *ch.* 67.1b–2a. Also see Richard B. Mather, trans., *Shih-shuo hsin-yü, A New Account of Tales of the World* (1976), p. 388.

15 Ts'ui Pao, *Record of Things Ancient and Modern*, *SPTK* 2.3a–b.

16 Tu Yü (AD 222–284), wrote an influential commentary on the *Tso Commentary (Tso chuan)*. Tu's note on the *Yü-pin* occurs in the entry for Duke Ai of Lu, 11th year, *SSC* 5, *ch.* 58.23b, in the *Tso Commentary*; Séraphin Couvreur, trans., *Tch'ouen Ts'iou*, Vol. 3, p. 669. Tu Yü's note is cited by Wu Ching, *Explanations of the Old Titles of Yüeh-fu*, Chin-tai pi-shu 34, *ch.* 1.2a. In Kuo's preface to the song he cites Ts'ui Pao, Ch'iao Chou, Wu Ching, and Tu Yü, in that sequence.

17 Karlgren, *op. cit.*, p. 118; the poem is a drinking song.

18 Bodde, *Festivals in Classical China*, p. 302, citing 'Treatise on Ritual', by Ssu-ma Piao.

19 *Id.*, p. 303, n.46, paraphrasing and citing J. J. M. de Groot, *Fêtes annuellement célébrées à Emoui*, pp. 333–37. The metre of the song is irregular: 3–3–7–7. The earliest text of the song appears in Ts'ui Pao, *Record*, *SPTK*, 2.3a. The text also appears in Li Shan's commentary on the first of Lu Chi's 'Three Hearse-pullers' Songs', *Anthology of Literature*, *SPTK* 28.33b. It is also in Kuo, *ch.* 27, 'Words for Concerted Songs, Part 2, Concerted Pieces, Part 2', p. 396. These three sources show some interesting variants. In some texts of Ts'ui Pao's *Record*, the word *tzu* (thick, heavy) occurs, which I have amended to *ling* (drop). Li Shan's version in *ch.* 28 adds the word *ch'ao* to l. 1: 'On the shallot the *morning* dew'; whereas in his version in *ch.* 24 the word *ling* occurs in the same place instead of *ch'ao*: 'On the shallot *falls* the dew'. My translation is based on Kuo's text, which is generally accepted. For other translations and discussions of the song see Hans H. Frankel, *The Flowering Plum and the Palace Lady, Interpretations of Chinese Poetry* (1976), pp. 81–2, and Davis, *op. cit.*, pp. 165–66.

20 Artemisia Village, *Hao li*, is also the name of a mountain south of Mount T'ai in Shantung. *K'ao li*, Burial Village, is a name which suggests withered dryness, by virtue of a pun on the word *k'ao*.

21 Loewe, *Chinese Ideas of Life and Death*, pp. 18, 26, and 27. Another example of a different version of the belief in the soul in the Han is evident in the song 'A Crow Bore Eight or Nine Chicks' in Chapter Two above. The metre of the burial song is: 5–7–7–7. The earliest text appears in Ts'ui Pao, *Record*, *SPTK* 2.3a. The text also appears in Li Shan, *ibid.*, and Kuo, *ch.* 27, 'Words for Concerted Songs, Part 2, Concerted Pieces, Part 2', p. 398. For another translation and discussion of the song, see Davis, *ibid.*

22 Quotation from *Chuang Tzu*, *ch.* 30, 'Explaining Swords': 'This sword cleaves floating clouds up above, severs earth's cords down below.' Trans. Graham, *Chuang-*

tzŭ, p. 221; he dates this chapter on magical swords at the end of the third century BC.

23 The anecdote of the three heroes appears in *The Annals of Master Yen (Yen-tzu ch'un-ch'iu), SPTK* 2.20b–22a.

24 The metre is pentasyllabic. The text is in Kuo, *ch.* 41, 'Words for Concerted Songs, Part 16, Ch'u-mode Pieces, Part 1', p. 606. The song has traditionally been attributed to the famous military tactician and hero, Chu-ko Liang (AD 181–234), Prime Minister of Shu Kingdom in the Three Kingdoms era, and known as 'Chu-ko Liang's Lament of Liang-fu'. It has also been attributed to Tseng Tzu, a disciple of Confucius and paragon of filial piety. Both attributions are erroneous.

Chapter Six

1 Diény, *Aux origines*, p. 5 (my translation from his French), citing *Discourses of the States, Discourses of Chou State, SPPY* 1.5a. In his Chapter 1, 'Les collectes de chansons populaires', pp. 5–10, he provides an excellent survey of the main classical texts on this subject.

2 *Id.*, p. 5, citing *Discourses, SPPY* 1.5a.

3 *Id.*, citing *Record of Ritual, SPPY* 4.5a–b.

4 'Poetic omens' are *shih yao*; James J. Y. Liu, *Chinese Theories of Literature* (1975), p. 65.

5 *Ibid.*

6 *History of the Han (Han shu), ch.* 27.1,393–96.

7 The appendices of this classic, known as 'wings', dates from the late Chou or early Han.

8 Watson, *Early Chinese Literature*, pp. 64–6, discusses the use of prophecy in the *Tso Commentary*.

9 Loewe, *Chinese Ideas of Life and Death*, pp. 80–90.

10 Poetic omens, *shih yao*, do not feature as a term in the titles of the songs I have translated. These are called *yao-ko* (popular songs), or *t'ung-yao-ko* (children's popular songs). The word *t'ung* refers to children between about the age of six to twelve, up till adolescence. The word *yao* of *yao-ko* is probably a pun on the word *yao* = omen. Donald Holzman, 'Les premiers vers pentasyllabiques datés dans la poésie chinoise' (1974), p.113, referred to these songs as popular slogans and political satire: 'These slogans may be considered as *vox populi* par excellence.'

11 *History of the Han, ch.* 27.1395. Bodde, *Festivals in Classical China*, p. 55, notes that in the Han 'the five spirits of the household' were the Well and Hearth, besides the Impluvium, Gate and Door. Perhaps an additional connotation of desecration is implied in Pan Ku's critique.

12 Loewe, *Crisis and Conflict*, p. 303, explains that two views of the Five Elements Theory and dynastic change maintained in the Former Han. The Modernists held that each Power conquered its predecessor, while Tung Chung-shu and others held that each Power gave rise to the next.

13 *Id.*, Chapter 9, 'Support for Wang Mang—AD 9', pp. 286–306, gives a sympathetic account of the statesman's rise to power. Dubs, *The History*, Vol. 3, pp. 125–474, translates Pan Ku's 'Biography of Wang Mang' (*Han shu, ch.* 99).

14 The song's metre is trisyllabic. The text is in Pan Ku, 'Treatise on the Five Elements', *ch.* 27.1395, and in Kuo, *ch.* 88, 'Words for Miscellaneous Songs and Ditties, Part 6, Words of Ditties, Part 2', p. 1,234.

15 *History of the Han, ch.* 27.1396.

16 Birrell, *New Songs from a Jade Terrace*, p. 233 gives the other text and its preface in translation. Also see Chapter Six, pp. 105–07 above.

17 The metre is pentasyllabic.The text is in Pan Ku, *id.*, p. 1,396, and in Kuo, *ch.* 88, 'Words for Miscellaneous Ditties, Part 6, Words of Ditties, Part 2', p. 1,235.

18 Pan Ku, *op. cit.*, p. 1,395. For a translation of Pan Ku's biography of Chao Fei-yen, see Watson, *Courtier and Commoner*, pp. 265–77.

19 *Id.*, pp. 267–70 for the fate of Ts'ao Kung and her child; *id.*, pp. 270–71 for the fate of Lady Hsü.

20 *Id.*, p. 276.

21 Birrell, *New Songs*, p. 233.

22 After Emperor Ch'eng's death, Emperor Ai came to the throne. One of his first acts was to dismantle the Bureau of Music and make half its staff redundant.

23 The metre is a mix of 5- and 3-syllable lines: 5–3–3–5–3–3–3–3; or, taking the first pentasyllabic line as two lines, as I have in my translation, 2–3–3, etc. The text is in Pan Ku, *id.*, p. 1,395, and in Kuo, *ch.* 88, 'Words for Miscellaneous Songs and Ditties, Part 6, Words of Ditties, Part 2', p. 1,234.

24 Ts'ui Pao, *Record of Things Ancient and Modern, SPTK* 2.3a; Wu Ching, *Explanations of the Old Titles of Yüeh-fu*, Chin-tai pi-shu 34, *ch.* 1.3a.

25 Chai may also be pronounced Ti. The prime minister's name was Chai (or Ti) Fang-chin; his biography appears in Pan Ku, *History*, *ch.* 84.3411–42.

26 This is the view taken by Yü Kuan-ying, *Anthology*, p. 13, and by Diény, *Aux origines*, pp. 117–19, where he translates, annotates, and discusses the song, dismissing some of the more fanciful interpretations of it, based on Ts'ui Pao and Wu Ching.

27 The metre is irregular: 3–3–7–3–4–7–3–3–7–3–3–7. The text is in Shen Yüeh, 'Treatise on Music', *ch.* 21, 'Concerted' category, p. 607, and in Kuo, *ch.* 28, 'Words for Concerted Songs, Part 3, Concerted Pieces, Part 3', p. 410.

28 The metre is trisyllabic. The text is in Ssu-ma Piao, 'Treatise on the Five Elements', *ch.* 16.3281, and in Kuo, *ch.* 88, 'Words for Miscellaneous Ditties, Part 6, Words of Ditties, Part 2', p. 1,236.

29 Ssu-ma Piao, *op.cit.*, p. 3,281.

30 I am grateful to Dr. Michael Loewe of the University of Cambridge for his helpful comments on Ssu-ma Piao's interpretation.

31 The metre is a mix of 7- and 3-syllable lines: 7–7–7–3–3–7. The text is in Ssu-ma Piao, *op. cit.*, p. 3,281, and in Kuo, *ch.* 88, 'Words for Miscellaneous Ditties, Part 6, Words of Ditties, Part 2', p. 1,237. A variant text of this ditty appears in *New Songs*, Chapter 9, p. 234, of which line 1 reads: 'Tall wheat green, green, short wheat shrivelled', reversing the epithets 'Tall' and 'short'.

32 I am grateful to Dr. Loewe for his helpful comments on Ssu-ma Piao's interpretation.

33 *The Bureaucracy of Han Times*, p.129.

34 The metre is regular in the first part, irregular in the last: the first eight lines are trisyllabic, the last five 7–7–7–5–7. The text is in Ssu-ma Piao, *id.*, pp. 3,281–82, and in Kuo, *ch.* 88, 'Words for Miscellaneous Songs and Ditties, Part 6, Words for Ditties, Part 2', p. 1,238. A variant text of the song appears in *New Songs*, Chapter 9, p. 234; the main difference occurs in the last three lines: 'Over the door is ground millet,/ Under the millet there is a hanging drum./ I want to strike it, but the minister will be angry.' It is worth noting that the image of crows, like other images in politicized songs, permits a variety of interpretations. 'Crows on city walls' also forms the opening line of a political song celebrating a period of moral order; Diény, 'Chansons des Han' (1962), p. 271.

35 Ssu-ma Piao, *id.*, p. 3,284; Ts'ui Pao, *op. cit.*, *SPTK* 2.4a.

36 See Chapter Three, pp. 70–2 above. The metre of 'The Song Tung Flees!' is regular: the uneven line numbers are trisyllabic, the refrain is of two syllables. The text is in Ssu-ma Piao, *id.*, p. 3,284, and in Kuo, *ch.* 34, p. 505, in the preface to 'The

Ballad Tung Flees!' The *hsing*-ballad version in Shen and Kuo are classified under 'Clear-mode' of 'Concerted Songs', but this does not necessarily mean that the *ko*-song version is of the same category.

37   Frankel, *The Flowering Plum*, pp. 95–6, explains the origin of the custom in the Han.

38   The metre is pentasyllabic; 4 stanzas. Shen, *ch.* 21, 'Major Pieces' category, p. 618, and Kuo, *ch.* 37, 'Words for Concerted Songs, Part 12, Zither-mode Pieces, Part 2', p. 547. Diény, *op. cit.*, pp. 139–42, translates, annotates, and discusses this piece. Williams, 'A Study of the Oral Nature of the Han *Yüeh-fu*', pp. 204–07, and Sawaguchi, *Gafu*, pp. 80–3, translate and annotate the piece.

Chapter Seven

1   The last section of 'We Fought South of the City Wall' appears to reflect the old values, in which a vassal addresses his lord and the lord praises his loyal vassals who have sacrificed their lives for him. The song is so beset with problems, however, that this interpretation is conjectural.

2   Waley, *The Book of Songs*, Chapter 3, 'Warriors and Battles', and Karlgren, *The Book of Odes*, poem nos. 31, 36, 110, 156, 167, 181, 185, 204, 232, 234.

3   Hawkes, *Ch'u Tz'u*, 'The Nine Songs', 'The Spirits of the Fallen', pp. 43–4.

4   Waley, *op. cit.*, poem no. 31, Waley's no. 121, p. 112.

5   Hawkes, *id.*, p. 44, lines 17–8.

6   Tso K'o-ming, *Ancient Yüeh-fu, SKCS* 4.4b. Tung-kuang is in modern Hopei to the north, Ts'ang-wu is south in Kwangsi; Tso's version thus creates a spatial parallelism. Feng Wei-no, *Notes on Ancient Poetry, SKCS* 2, *ch.* 16.2a, retains the repetition of *hu*, while noting the variant *p'ing*.

7   Watson, *Records* (*Shih chi*, *ch.* 113), Vol. 2, p. 248.

8   *Id.*, (*Shih chi*, *ch.* 28), p. 54. Watson translates *Hou t'u* as 'Earth Lord', but I prefer Empress Earth, following Chavannes; see Chapter One, n. 38.

9   'Try and eat' belongs to the closure of 'Watering Horses at a Long Wall Hole', which is similar to the closure of no. 1 of the 'Nineteen Old Poems', Watson, *Chinese Lyricism*, p. 20. The Western quotation, attributed to Napoleon, probably derives from Las Cases, *Mémorial de Ste-Hélène*, 1816.

10   While not entirely dismissing the historical interpretation, Diény, *Aux origines*, p. 107, points to these general themes; he translates, annotates, and discusses the song, pp. 106–07. Chih-chiang, *Record of Ancient and Modern Music*, Han Wei i-shu ch'ao, *ch.* 52.12, cites Chang Yung, *Arts Record of the Correct Music of the Era AD 424–454*, to the effect that this song title was originally for unaccompanied strings with no vocal part, but that a Wei Dynasty composer provided a music accompaniment for it. The metre is pentasyllabic, except for the trisyllabic first line. The text is in Shen Yüeh, 'Treatise on Music', *ch.* 21, 'Concerted' category, p. 605, and in Kuo, *ch.* 27, 'Words for Concerted Songs, Part 2, Concerted Pieces, Part 2', pp. 394–95.

11   Quotation from Ts'ao Ts'ao, 'Graveyard Song', J. D. Frodsham and Ch'eng Hsi, trans., *An Anthology of Chinese Verse, Han Wei, Chin, and the Northern and Southern Dynasties* (1967), p. 29, line 13.

12   Yü, *Anthology*, p. 4; the custom is discussed in Hawkes, *op. cit.*, pp. 101–02.

13   A dialogue between the dead and the living is a technique used in *Chuang Tzu*, *ch.* 18, in which Chuang Tzu finds a skull and asks how it came to its sorry state. He uses the skull as a pillow and sleeps; then in a dream the skull tells him its life story. Graham, *Chuang-tzū*, pp. 124–5.

14 Yü, *id.*, p. 4; Watson, *The Columbia Book*, p. 79; Peking University, *Reference Materials*, pp. 505–06.

15 Karlgren, *op. cit.*, poem no. 167, stanza 3, last line, p. 112; Hawkes, *op. cit.*, 'The Spirits of the Fallen', p. 44, line 11.

16 The metre is irregular. The first passage to line 7 is: 3–3–7–4–4–5–7; the lyrical couplet, lines 8–9 is tetrasyllabic; lines 10–11 are pentasyllabic; the next quatrain is: 3–6–7–7; the final quatrain is: 4–5–4–4. This closure might be viewed as an envoi, which is usually metrically regular; if the redundant word 'truly' (*ch'eng*) were omitted, the closure would then be a typical tetrasyllabic *luan*-envoi. The text is in Shen, *ch.* 22, 'Han Songs for the *Nao*-bell' category, p. 641, and Kuo, *ch.* 16, 'Words for Drumming and Blowing Pieces, Part 1, Han Songs for the *Nao*-bell', p. 228.

17 This citation from a *min-ko* suggests that it belongs to a narrative. It closely resembles lines 21–4 of Ch'en Lin's (d. AD 217) imitation of the same *yüeh-fu*, 'Watering Horses at a Long Wall Hole'; Ch'en's narrative is presented from the husband's point of view. Birrell, *New Songs*, pp. 48–9.

18 Within this system the attributes of water belong to this set of correspondences: winter, north, cold, black, female, and *yin*.

19 Karlgren, *The Book of Odes*, p. 41, stanza 4, first 6 lines (translator's explanatory parentheses); the 'K'i' is Ch'i River of the ancient state of Wei (modern Honan).

20 Line 15 of the song ambiguously reads, *hu erh*, lit. 'call boy'; this might mean that the woman calls her servant boy to open the wooden box containing the letter, or it might mean that she calls her own children to read the letter to them. The word *hu* is used in the phrase *ch'uan hu* in 'The Ailing Wife', line 2, to mean call for, or send for someone to come to one; in this context the wife calls her husband to her bedside. In general, *hu* has a peremptory tone denoting an order to an inferior. The word *erh* is used in 'The Ailing Wife', line 6, 'East Gate', long version, lines 8 and 13, and 'East Gate', short version, lines 8 and 12, to mean children or infants. In 'Watering Horses', the woman might be calling for her children to come to her, but I have chosen a more conservative reading in my translation.

21 Watson, *The Columbia Book*, p. 102.

22 *Id.*, p. 96.

23 *Ibid.*

24 Birrell, *id.*, Chapter 1, pp. 47–8.

25 *Anthology of Literature (Wen hsüan)*, SPTK 27.19b–20b, *Compendium of Literature*, *ch.* 41.78.

26 Pentasyllabic. Kuo, *ch.* 38, 'Words for Concerted Songs, Part 13, Zither-mode Pieces, Part 3', p. 556.

27 E.g., Feng, *Notes on Ancient Poetry*, SKCS 3, *ch.* 20.7a–b.

28 Kuo places this piece among songs of the Liang Dynasty, but it is more usually assigned to the Han. The metre is pentasyllabic, including the extra prelude. The text is in Kuo, *ch.* 25, 'Words for Horizontal Flute Pieces, Part 5, Liang Pieces for Drumming, Horn, and Horizontal Flute', p. 365. Kuo's title for the whole 24-line piece with the prelude is 'Words for the Chestnut Roan Horse Song'.

Chapter Eight

1 Karlgren, *The Book of Odes*, poem nos. 156 and 207.

2 Watson, *Chinese Lyricism*, pp. 33–51, discusses this trend in 'Chien-an and the New Realism'.

3 Watson, *Chinese Rhyme-Prose*, pp. 21–4, translates 'The Wind', attributed to Sung Yü (3rd century BC), which is unusual in its long realistic passage describing the lives of the poor.

4 Watson, 'Chien-an and the New Realism', gives examples of literary *shih* in the Han.

5 For example, poem 26 in which a girl who loves someone who is not her brothers' choice says: 'when I go and complain,/ I meet with their anger.' Poem 223 states: 'but the bad brothers/ mutually do harm to each other.' Poem 189 prays: 'elder and younger brothers,/ may they love each other,/ and not plot against each other.' Karlgren, *op. cit.*, pp. 15, 177, and 130 (last line slightly abridged).

6 The love song is 'A *Yen* Song, A Ballad' in Chapter Ten.

7 The observance of the La festival in the Han is described by Bodde, *Festivals in Classical China*, pp. 54, 58, 60, and 72.

8 Chiu-chiang was in the region of modern Anhwei; Ch'i and Lu were the names of states in the Chou era, in the regions of modern Shantung and Honan.

9 Most of the analysis of this song is based on Frankel's illuminating discussion of it, which he also translates in *The Flowering Plum*, pp. 62–7.

10 The narrative text has no stanza divisions. At the end there is an envoi. The metre is very irregular, a mix of different syllabic line lengths in which the tetrasyllabic predominates: lines 1–22: 3–5–4–4–3–3–4–6–4–5–4–5–4–4–5–5–3–5–6–5–5–3; lines 23–26 are tetrasyllabic; line 27 is pentasyllabic, the break in the metrical pattern indicating an emotional line; lines 28–33 resume the tetrasyllabic metre; lines 34–36 are: 6–3–3; lines 37–47 resume the tetrasyllabic metre. The line indicating the envoi is disyllabic; the envoi quatrain is irregular: 6–5–6–6. The text is in Kuo, *ch.* 38, 'Words for Concerted Songs, Part 13, Zither-mode Pieces, Part 3', p. 567.

11 The metre is very irregular, with a few regular couplets scattered among the lines. The first 9 lines are: 6–7–6–8–7–6–6–4–4; the envoi: 2–4–4; the last passage: 4–5–4–5–7–8–8–6–3–8–5–4–5. The text is in Kuo, *ch.* 38, 'Words for Concerted Songs, Part 13, Zither-mode Pieces, Part 3', p. 566.

12 In his translation and discussion of this piece Diény comments that it is evident that the man's first attempt to leave failed, *Aux origines*, p.127.

13 Poem no. 40, first quatrain, my translation.

14 It is tempting to characterize the husband as a knight-errant, *yu-hsia*, one who gave his services altruistically to those in need. But this would contradict the spirit of this ballad, for his wife has condemned his departure as 'self-regard'. It is more in keeping with the meaning of the narrative to view the husband as a mercenary who will be paid for his military skills. Diény, *id.*, p. 128, views the husband as a *yu-hsia*.

15 The texts of Shen and Kuo diverge in the last line. Shen's text is *Wang wu kuei*, 'Watch for my return', whereas Kuo's reads *Wang chün kuei*, 'I'll watch for your return.' If Shen's text is followed, the last four lines constitute alternate lines spoken by the wife and husband; if Kuo's is accepted, the wife's gentle farewell softens the ending of the harsh domestic drama.

16 Both ballads appear in Birrell, *New Songs*, Chapter 1, p. 61: 'goes toward the clear lake', and Chapter 2, p. 78: 'goes to the long flow'. Ch'iu Hu's wife is idealized as a chaste woman in the 'Biographies of the Chaste' section of *Biographies of [Virtuous] Women (Lieh nu chuan)*, attributed to Liu Hsiang, *SPPY* 5.6b–7b.

17 For a study of Tou O, see Shih Chung-wen, *Injustice to Tou O: Tou Yüan, A Study and Translation* (1972); for a study of Li Wa, see Glen Dudbridge, *Tale of Li Wa: Study and Critical Edition of a Chinese Story from the Ninth Century* (1983). The metre of 'East Gate Ballad' is irregular. The first quatrain is trisyllabic; lines 5–6 of the first stanza are 5–7; the second stanza is: 5–5–6–7; stanza three: 3–6–6–4–4–4–3; the last stanza: 4–4–4–3–4–3–3. The text of the long version is arranged in four stanzas. The text is in Shen Yüeh, 'Treatise on Music', *ch.* 21, 'Major Pieces' category, p. 616, and in Kuo, *ch.* 37, 'Words for Concerted Songs, Part 12, Zither-mode Pieces, Part 2', p. 550. Although Kuo presents the long version of the song first, he lists the short version following it as the original, which Diény disputes, see Chapter Four, n. 28.

18　The metre is 3–3–3–3–6–7–5–7–6–7–6–7–2–2–4–7, the first quatrain matching that of the long version. The text is presented as one narrative sequence. The text is in Kuo, *ch.* 37, 'Words for Concerted Songs, Part 12, Zither-mode Pieces, Part 2', p. 550, with the words 'original words' tacked onto the end of the piece, a dating disputed by Diény, who feels in general that long versions precede the short, *Aux origines*, pp. 128 and 138.

19　Kuo cites this ballad in his preface to Ts'ao P'ei's imitation of the title, and quotes Ts'ui Pao, *Record of Things Ancient and Modern* (*SPTK* 2.4b).

20　Yü, *Anthology*, p. 33, cites this hexasyllabic song from the commentary of Li Shan on Lu Chi's imitation of 'The Yü-chang Ballad' in *Anthology of Literature* (*Wen hsüan*), *SPPY* 28.3a, of which the Ch'ing editor, Hu K'e-chia, amends the name of the gate from Shang-tu to Shang-liu, *ibid.*

21　The metre is pentasyllabic. The text is in Kuo, *ch.* 38, p. 563, in Kuo's preface to Ts'ao P'ei's imitation, citing Shen Chien of the Northern Sung, *Elaborations on Yüeh-fu Titles* (*Yüeh-fu kuang t'i*), who gives the text of the quatrain and notes that the composer was probably of the Han era.

Chapter Nine

1　Karlgren, *The Book of Odes*, poem no. 167, stanza 1, line 3, p. 111; also see his translation of poem no. 156.

2　Hawkes, *Ch'u Tz'u*, p. 34, line 184.

3　This prejudice was first propounded by Lord Shang, or Shang Yang (d. 330 BC), of the state of Ch'in, J. J. L. Duyvendak, trans., *The Book of Lord Shang* (1928, 1963), 'Agriculture and War', pp. 185–96. In the Ch'in Dynasty the frequent travels of merchants around and beyond state frontiers were particularly suspect because as a group they could not be supervized easily, they hoarded private wealth, and introduced news and information which might disturb the local population.

4　Said to be in the north-west, in the region of modern Kansu.

5　The metre is pentasyllabic. The text is in Chang Chih-hsiang, *Garden of Old Poetic Genres*, *ch.* 45.13a–b, as the only extant song of a hypothetical set entitled 'Nine Tunes for the Eight Changes'. It is not clear what the phrase 'Eight Changes' means in the title; it may refer to the music title. It may have something to do with the Eight Skilled Gentlemen (*Pa neng chih shih*), who in the Han were specialists in magical ceremonies at the Winter and Summer solstices held at the court, of which one was to harmonize (*tiao*) Yin and Yang and the Five Elements, besides harmonizing musical notes and compositions. Bodde, *Festivals in Classical China*, pp. 169–72, 178–85, and 292–93. The number eight was particularly associated with harmony, viz. the Eight Musical Instruments (*i.e.* the eight kinds of materials used in making musical instruments), the Eight Trigrams, and the Eight (Military) Formations. The first quatrain of the text, attributed to T'ang Hui-hsiu (5th century AD), appears in *Imperial Survey of the T'ai-p'ing Era*, *SPTK* 25.5b, entitled 'An Old Song, Eight Changes'.

6　Translated by Watson, *Chinese Lyricism*, p.20, and Birrell, *New Songs*, pp. 38–9, 'On, On, Ever On and On.'

7　The metre is irregular with some regular passages. The first three lines are: 7-3-3, followed by three tetrasyllabic lines, the last six lines are pentasyllabic. The text is in Chang Chih-hsiang, *Garden of Old Poetic Genres*, *ch.* 45.14a. A version of the song entitled 'An Old Yüeh-fu Song Poem' appears in *Imperial Survey of the T'ai-ping Era*, *SPTK* 25.4a, minus lines 4–6 and with minor variants in the central passage.

8　Karlgren, *op. cit.*, poem no. 32, p. 20, poem no. 28, p. 16.

9　The metre is pentasyllabic. The text is in Kuo, *ch.* 30, 'Words for Concerted Songs, Part 5, Level-mode Pieces, Part 1', p. 443. The first six lines of the 12-line piece are listed in *Compendium of Literature*, *ch.* 27, p. 484, under Ts'ao P'ei, said to have been composed by him when he travelled through Ming-chin (this section of the encyclopedia is called 'Travel'); the piece is designated as a *shih*-lyric poem. In line 6 the *Compendium* version has Ho-yang for the full version's Loyang.

10 The metre is irregular, except for the first quatrain which is trisyllabic. Lines 1–4: trisyllabic; lines 5–6 tetrasyllabic; lines 7–8: 5–7; lines 9–10 tetrasyllabic; last couplet: 7–3. Lines 6 and 8 contain the nonsense word *liang*. The modern punctuation of lines 7–8 of the song in the Chung-hua edition of Shen Yüeh, *History of the Southern Sung*, 'Treatise on Music', *ch.* 21, p. 641, is erratic; it seems to be based on a preference for a tetrasyllabic central passage instead of a 5–7 metre. Yü Kuan-ying, *Anthology*, p. 5, amends line 4 from 'Hard and fast flowing' to 'Deep and fast flowing', repeating the device of repetition in the first couplet. This is a plausible amendment, but I do not follow it. The text is in Kuo, *ch.* 16, 'Words for Drumming and Blowing Pieces, Part 1, Han Songs for the *Nao*-bell', p. 228. The earliest recording of the text is in Shen, *ch.* 22, 'Han Songs for the *Nao*-bell' category, p. 641.

11 The metre is composed of regular passages of different syllabic line lengths: 6–6–4–4–5–5–5–5. The text is in Kuo, *ch.* 62, 'Song-texts for Miscellaneous Pieces, Part 2', p. 898.

Chapter Ten

1 Karlgren, *The Book of Odes*, poem no. 47, stanza 1, line 1; for similar phrases see poem nos. 31, 45, and 58.

2 Ch'en Hang, *Notes on Poetic Figures*, p. 14, takes *chün* to mean 'lord', and interprets this vow as an allegory of a loyal minister professing his loyalty to the ruler who has wronged him.

3 The metre is irregular: 2–6–5–3–4–4–3–3–5. The text is amenable to other metrical divisions. The text is in Shen, *ch.* 22, 'Han Songs for the *Nao*-bell' category, p. 643, and in Kuo, *ch.* 16, 'Words for Drumming and Blowing Pieces, Part 1, Han Songs for the *Nao*-bell', p. 231.

4 Ch'en, *id.*, p.10, suggests that this song specifically describes the royal tour of the Han Emperor Wu when he went on a pleasure cruise on the Yangtse.

5 The metre is irregular with a central passage of heptasyllabic lines: 5–7–7–7–4–6. The text is in Shen, *ch.* 22, 'Han Songs for the *Nao*-bell' category, p. 643, and in Kuo, *ch.* 16, 'Words for Drumming and Blowing Pieces, Part 1, Han Songs for the *Nao*-bell', p. 231. See J. P. Diény's 1990 review article, p. 135.

6 Karlgren, *op. cit.*, p. 13. The usual referrent of the phrase is *The Classic of the Way and Its Power*, *ch.* 80: 'the sound of dogs barking and cocks crowing', denoting an arcadian utopia; see Lau, *Lao Tzu, Tao Te Ching*, p. 142, line 193c; but this Han song does not make this allusion.

7 Compare the system of fraternal authority in 'The Orphan Boy', and in 'A Peacock Southeast Flew', Birrell, *New Songs*, p. 58. For an earlier reference to this social system see poem no. 76 of the *Book of Poetry*, Karlgren, *id.*, p. 51, stanza 2, which voices a girl's fear that her brothers will find out about her illicit lover, Chung Tzu.

8 Ch'en, *id.*, p.15, says that this is a poem of a resentful and anguished minister who has met with misfortune and has gone into exile. He says that the piece is a text full of hidden meanings.

9 The metre is irregular with a passage of six pentasyllabic lines: 3–5–5–5–5–5–5–3–5–4–4–5–4–5–3–7–7. The text is in Shen, *ch.* 22, 'Han Songs for the *Nao*-bell' category, p. 642, and Kuo, *ch.* 16, 'Words for Drumming and Blowing Pieces, Part 1, Han Songs for the *Nao*-bell', p. 230. For other translations see Watson,

The Columbia Book, pp. 80–1, and Frankel, 'The Relation between Narrator and Characters in *Yuèfǔ* Ballads', p. 111.

10   *Record of Things Ancient and Modern*, SPTK 2.2b. See Joseph R. Allen, *In the Voice of Others* (1992), pp. 185–87.

11   The metre is tetrasyllabic. The text appears in Kuo, *ch.* 26, preface to Li Ho's (AD ?790–816) title 'The Harp Lay', p. 377. This is the only extant example of Han lay-*yin*.

12   The attribution of the song in *New Songs from a Jade Terrace*, *ch.* 2, is misleading; it is listed after two pieces by Ts'ao P'ei with the caption, 'Another *Yüeh-fu*, Along the Embankment', the designation 'Another', usually signifying that the piece is by the previously listed author; Wen-hsüeh ed., p. 24, Birrell, *id.*, pp. 64–5. Shen Yüeh, *ch.* 21, pp. 612–13, and Kuo, *ch.* 35, p. 522, attribute it to Ts'ao Ts'ao. Li Shan notes that some commentators attribute the song to Empress Chen, some to Ts'ao Ts'ao, and others to Ts'ao P'ei. While attributing the long version to Ts'ao, Kuo attributes the short version to an anonymous author of the Han, designating it as *pen-tz'u*, the original words. K. P. K. Whitaker, 'Tsaur Jyr's Luohshern Fuh' (1954), pp. 44–8, presents another context to the song, citing *Wen hsüan*, Basic Sinological Series, Vol. 2, *ch.* 19, pp. 401–02, commentary on 'Prose Poem on the Goddess of Lo River' (*Lo-shen fu*). Ts'ao Chih, Ts'ao P'ei's younger brother, had wanted the hand of Lady Chen in marriage, but Ts'ao Ts'ao gave her in marriage to Ts'ao P'ei. Following a slanderous accusation of Empress Kuo, Lady Chen, promoted to the rank of Empress Chen, committed suicide. Ts'ao Chih depicted Lady Chen in his erotic prose poem which he originally entitled 'Longing for Empress Chen'. Later, Ts'ao Jui, the son of Ts'ao P'ei and Empress Chen, saw this title and changed it to 'Prose Poem on the Goddess of Lo River'. Whitaker notes that Hu K'e-chia dismisses this tradition as a spurious interpolation by an unknown author.

13   For a résumé of the career of Empress Ch'en, the Han Emperor Wu's first empress, see Loewe, *Crisis and Conflict in Han China*, p. 51, and Table 2, facing p. 64.

14   The binome 'thick and lush' *li-li*, is used to describe ripe millet in poem no. 65, Karlgren, *id.*, p.45; it denotes ripeness and at the same time a drooping appearance, from which a psychological heaviness, a drooping despair is implied in that poem. Poem no. 30, Karlgren, *id.*, p. 18, is a girl's love plaint which ends with the lines: 'I keep awake and do not sleep;/ while longing, I keep yearning (for you.)' (Karlgren's explanatory parentheses.)

15   The metre is mostly pentasyllabic. Stanza one: pentasyllabic; stanza two: penta-syllabic except for heptasyllabic last line; stanza three: pentasyllabic; stanza four: first quatrain pentasyllabic, then 5–7–4–5; stanza five: pentasyllabic. The text is arranged in five stanzas of unequal length. The text is in Shen, *ch.* 21, 'Ch'ing-Shang Song Poems in Three Modes: Clear-mode' category, pp. 612–13, and in Kuo, *ch.* 35, 'Words for Concerted Songs, Part 10, Clear-mode Pieces, Part 3', p. 522. Kuo erroneously places this version in a post-Han category.

16   The metre is pentasyllabic, with no stanzaic divisions. The text is in Hsü Ling, *New Songs from a Jade Terrace*, Wen-hsüeh ed., *ch.* 2, p. 24, and in Kuo, *ch.* 35, 'Words for Concerted Songs, Part 10, Clear-mode Pieces, Part 3', pp. 522–23. Kuo dates this version as earlier than the long version, an error of judgement.

17   Karlgren, *id.*, poem no. 31, stanza 4, line 4, p. 19; poem no. 47, line 1, p. 31; poem no. 58, stanza 6, line 1, p. 41, for examples of the use of the expression.

18   Compare the woman in 'The Harp Lay', above, Lan-chih in 'A Peacock Southeast Flew' and the wife of Ch'iu Hu in the narrative by Fu Hsüan, Birrell, *New Songs*, pp. 61 and 78.

19   Karlgren, *id.*, p. 213, stanza 3, last line.

20   Waley, *The Book of Songs*, poem no. 24 (his no. 84), last stanza, p. 78.

21   Waley, *id.*, poem no. 171 (his no. 169), stanza 1, p. 178.

22 The metre is pentasyllabic, except for hexasyllabic line 23; 5 stanzas. Most editors delete 'five': 'Such a crackle, like five horses snapping wicker!' to make it pentasyllabic to follow the rest of the text, an amendment I have accepted. The text is in Shen Yüeh, *ch.* 21, 'Major Pieces' category, pp. 622–23, and in Kuo, *ch.* 41, 'Words for Concerted Songs, Part 16, Ch'u-mode Pieces, Part 1', p. 600. Kuo erroneously dates this text as later than the short version. Diény, *Aux origines*, pp. 155–61, translates, annotates, and discusses this version of the song. Yü Kuan-ying, *Anthology*, p. 44, takes the view that the final passage is a salutation from the musicians performing the piece for their host and patron.

23 (*Hsi ching tsa chi*), attributed to Liu Hsin (d. AD 23) and Ko Hung (*c.* AD 280–340), *SPTK* 3.5b. It is not clear to which version of the song title *Miscellany* refers.

24 In Hsü Ling, *New Songs from a Jade Terrace*, *ch.* 1, p.10 (Wen-hsüeh ed.), this version is listed anonymously under the general title, 'Six Old *Yüeh-fu* Poems', giving as its title the first line.

25 The metre is pentasyllabic. The text is in Hsü Ling, *op.cit.*, *ch.* 1, p.10 (Wen-hsüeh ed.), and in Kuo, *ch.* 41, 'Words for Concerted Songs, Part 16, Ch'u-mode Pieces, Part 1', p. 600. Kuo erroneously dates this text as the original Han version.

26 Karlgren, *id.*, pp. 16–7.

27 Hawkes, *Ch'u Tz'u*, 'Encountering Sorrow', p. 30, line 119, and n. 1. The girl was the daughter of the Lord of Sung who became the ancestress of the Shang, named Chien Ti. When Chien Ti was imprisoned in a tower, the God Ti K'u, the First Ancestor of the Shang, sent her a swallow and she became pregnant by eating its egg.

28 Karlgren, *id.*, p. 75, stanza 1: 'In the stirred waters / the white stones are (rinsed clean =) shining; / with white robe and red collar / I follow you to Wu; / when I have seen my lord, / how should I not be happy?' (Karlgren's interpretations.)

29 The metre is pentasyllabic. The text is in Hsü Ling, *id.*, *ch.* 1, p. 10 (Wen-hsüeh ed.), under the general title 'Six Old *Yüeh-fu* Poems', and in Kuo, *ch.* 39, 'Words for Concerted Songs, Part 14, Zither-mode Pieces, Part 4', p. 579. At the end of the text in Hsü Ling's anthology the title *Yen ko hsing*, 'A Yen Song, A Ballad', is appended— the same title as in Kuo. For a different interpretation, see Diény, *op. cit.*, p. 138.

30 The metre is pentasyllabic. The text is in *Anthology of Literature* (*Wen hsüan*), *SPTK* 27.21a–b, listed as an anonymous old text. It is also in *New Songs from a Jade Terrace*, *ch.* 2, p. 27 (Wen-hsüeh ed.), attributed to Ts'ao Jui, Emperor Ming of the Wei Dynasty (AD 204–239); and in Kuo, *ch.* 62, 'Song-texts for Miscellaneous Pieces, Part 2', p. 897, listed as an anonymous old (Han) text. The text in Hsü Ling's anthology omits the last couplet, which both *Wen hsüan* and Kuo retain. The text of the song is so similar to the pentasyllabic poem no. 19 of the 'Nineteen Old Poems' that it is worth reproducing that text here for comparison:

> Bright moon white, so white
> Shines on my silk bedcurtains.
> In sad despair I cannot sleep,
> I take my robe, get up and pace.
> To travel, they say, is pleasant,
> But not as good as soon going home.
> I go outside, stroll in solitude.
> My sad longing to whom can I tell?
> I lean forward, go back to my room,
> Tears fall soaking my robe.

(From Birrell, *id.*, p. 40; see the translation and discussion of this old poem in Diény, *Les dix-neuf poèmes anciens*, pp. 45, 154–57.)

Chapter Eleven

1   *Cf.* the 'seven pillars of Wisdom', *Proverbs* 9.

2   This theme is also present in the *Book of Poetry*, poem no. 164, and in poem no. 189, and to some extent in no. 223.

3   Two of the most important of the five songs in this chapter have been translated and discussed in detail by Diény, *Aux origines*, pp. 109–14, 128–36—'Cocks Crow' and 'Mulberry on the Bank'. The latter title (also known by the name of its heroine, Lo-fu) has also been explored thematically by him in *Pastourelles et Magnanarelles, Essai sur un thème littéraire chinois* (1977), Chapters 1–3. Frankel, '*Yüeh-fu* Poetry', pp. 79–93, translates the song and presents a literary analysis which summarizes many features of the genre.

4   Diény, *Aux origines*, pp. 110–12, discusses these different interpretations; he translates and analyses the song pp. 109–14.

5   Lau, *Lao Tzu, Tao Te Ching, ch.* LXXX, p. 142, line 193c.

6   Citing Diény, *id.* p. 113, from Ting Fu-pao's quotation of 'A Ditty from the Reign-period 104–100 BC of the Han Emperor Wu', in Ting, *Complete Poetry, ch.* 5.5a. Ting in turn cites Wang Tzu-nien (d. AD 390), *Record of Neglected Data (Shih i chi)*, Ku-chin i-shih 2, *ch.* 5.6b. I am indebted to Diény for his illuminating discussion of this song.

7   Trans. Chan, *A Source Book in Chinese Philosophy*, p. 40, citing *Analects* 13.3. The style of argument in this passage of the *Analects* suggests that it does not date from the middle Chou era of Confucius, but the late Chou or early Han.

8   Huang Chieh, *Notes on the Style of Han and Wei Yüeh-fu (Han Wei yüeh-fu feng-chien,* 1961), *ch.* 1.5b; Sawaguchi, *Gafu*, p. 44.

9   The metre is pentasyllabic, except for the hexasyllabic line 8, which is perhaps best amended to a pentasyllabic line, omitting either the word 'hall' or 'balconied'. The text is in Shen Yüeh, *ch.* 21, 'Concerted' category, p. 606, and in Kuo, *ch.* 28, 'Words for Concerted Songs, Part 3, Concerted Pieces, Part 3', p. 406.

10 The metre is pentasyllabic. The text is in Hsü Ling, *New Songs from a Jade Terrace, ch.* 1.9–10 (Wen-hsüeh ed.), listed under the general title 'Six Old *Yüeh-fu* Poems', with the first line as its title. It is in Kuo, *ch.* 34, 'Words for Concerted Songs, Part 9, Clear-mode Pieces, Part 2', p. 508.

11 For 'two-thousand-bushel rank' see Chapter Four, n. 24. The title 'Filial-Pure aide' (*hsiao-lien lang*) indicates an aspiring young man judged to be suitable for promotion to official rank at the junior level.

12 The metre is pentasyllabic. The text is in Kuo, *ch.* 35, 'Words for Concerted Songs, Part 10, Clear-mode Pieces, Part 3', p. 514.

13 Compare, for example, this version of the song's finale by the court poet Shen Yüeh, which stands as an independent imitative piece:

Three Wives, An Imitation

> The eldest's wife dusts her jade jewel box,
> The middle wife ties silk bed drapes,
> The youngest's wife alone has nothing to do;
> She faces the mirror painting moth eyebrows.
> 'Darling, come and lie down.
> All night long I'm left to myself.'

By Shen Yüeh's time the courtly interest lay in the frivolous activities of boudoir ladies. The high moral tone of 'Cocks Crow' and its essentially masculine orientation, reflecting Confucian values, has disappeared. The new courtly aesthetics evince a desire to please. Cited from Hsü Ling, *id.*, *ch.* 5.61, Birrell, *New Songs*, p. 142.

14 *Pastourelles et Magnanarelles*, especially Chapters 1–3.

15 Diény explores the comparison between the Lo-fu song and a pastourelle by Marcabru (AD 1140), *id.*, pp. 2–10.

16 Her fashionable hair-do, also called the 'falling-horse' style, was devised by Lady Ling (Sun Shou) in the second century AD; her husband's sister became the consort of the Han Emperor Shun.

17 Lo-fu's husband wears a dagger at his waist, the hilt of which is decorated with a well-pulley (Lu-lu) motif.

18 Shen, 'Treatise on Music', *ch.* 21, p. 617.

19 Diény, *Aux origines*, p. 136, lists a number of these devices of repetition, noting that they would have served as mnemonic aids to the reciter in the case of such a long song as this.

20 Sawaguchi, *op. cit.*, p. 53.

21 The husband's white complexion and bushy sideburns and whiskers were the standard attributes of a handsome, upper-class male in the Han; *cf.* the description of Ho Kuang (d. 68 BC) in Pan Ku, *History*, *ch.* 68, trans. Watson, *Courtier and Commoner*, p.124. It is an interesting social detail that Lo-fu is said to be half her husband's age.

22 'Yüeh-fu Poetry', p. 85; see *id.*, pp. 79–81 for Frankel's translation of the Lo-fu ballad.

23 Ts'ui Pao, *Record of Things Ancient and Modern*, *SPTK* 2.3b. The Ch'iu Hu story is told in *Biographies of [Virtuous] Ladies*, *SPPY* 5.6b–7b. A poem by Fu Hsüan entitled 'A Pure Wife' which is based on this story is in Hsü Ling, *id.*, trans. Birrell, *id.*, pp. 77–8.

24 Pentasyllabic. The text has 2 *yen* stanzas, and a coda; Shen, *ch.* 21, p. 617, entitled 'A Yen Song, The Ballad of Lo-fu', and classified as a 'Major Pieces' composition. It is also in the somewhat later anthology of Hsü Ling, *id.*, *ch.* 1.9, listed under the general title 'Six Old *Yüeh-fu* Poems', with the title 'The Ballad Sunrise at the Southeast Corner'. This text has slight changes in diction and variations in grammatical structure compared with Shen's text. The text is also in Kuo, *ch.* 28, 'Words for Concerted Songs, Part 3, Concerted Pieces, Part 3', pp. 410–11, entitled 'Mulberry on the Bank', the title by which Ts'ui Pao referred to the song. In his preface to the song, Kuo cites Chih-chiang, *Record of Ancient and Modern Music*, to the effect that the song is in the zither-mode, but Kuo does not follow this; Chih-chiang, Han Wei i-shu ch'ao 52, *ch.* 52.11b. The text in Kuo contains minor variations in lines 22 and 32 compared with Shen's. In his comparison of European and Han ballads Frankel, 'Yüeh-fu Poetry', p. 81, makes the sensible comment that the *yüeh-fu* pieces of the Han are no doubt '. . . created anew in each performance, and subject to constant changes. There is never a definitive version.' His translation and analysis of the song appear in that article, pp. 79–93.

25 See Chapter Three, pp. 75–6 above. In addition to the White Elm star, Cassia star, and the Green Dragon constellation, the Phoenix was also the name of a star. Ch'i Chiang was the daughter of Lord Ch'i; she married Duke Chuang of Wei, and later Duke Wen of Chin in the Chou era; she is cited as the exemplar of the perfect wife in the closure of the song.

26 For 'ornate ladles' in this passage Sawaguchi, *op. cit.*, p. 75, reads 'relish, appetisers'.

27 The two types of wife, the modest, traditional woman and the brazen, modern woman, are contrasted in the old poem, known as the *mi-wu* poem, which opens Hsü Ling's anthology, trans. Birrell, *id.*, p. 30; the two wives are styled 'the new one' and 'the old one'.

28 The metre is pentasyllabic. The text, with minor variations in diction, appears in Hsü Ling, *id.*, *ch.*, 1.10, under the general title 'Six Old *Yüeh-fu* Poems', with the title

'The Lungshi Ballad' placed at the end of the text. Two variants are worth mentioning: line 23 reads 'fine meal' instead of 'coarse grain', and the last line reads: 'Is worth more than one fine husband!', The text is in Kuo, *ch.* 37, 'Words for Concerted Songs, Part 12, Zither-mode Pieces, Part 2', pp. 542–43.

APPENDIX I

Shen Yüeh's Four Categories of Melodic Pieces

(from *History of the Southern Sung*, 'Treatise on Music')

I   SUBURBAN AND TEMPLE SONGS, AND FORMAL
     BANQUET PIECES, CHAPTER 20

II CONCERTED (PIECES), *HSIANG-HO*, CHAPTER 21
     South of the River; Light in the East; Cocks Crow; A Crow Bore Eight or
     Nine Chicks; East of Flat Mound
     CH'ING-SHANG SONGS IN THREE MODES
       Level-mode
       Clear-mode
         The Ballad Tung Peach (Flees!); Along the Embankment (long
         version, attrib. Ts'ao Ts'ao)
       Zither-mode
         How Wonderful! A Ballad
     MAJOR PIECES
         East Gate Ballad (long version); A *Yen* Song, The Lo-fu Ballad
         (Mulberry on the Bank); West Gate Ballad (long version); The Ballad
         of Breaking Willow; A *Yen* Song, Whenever (also called The Flying
         Swans Ballad, long version); A *Yen* Song, The Whenever Ballad;
         Ballad, Song of Melancholy; The Ballad of the Prefect of Goosegate;
         The White Head Lament (long version)
     CH'U-MODE

III BALLADS FOR CAVALRY DRUM DANCES, CHAPTER 22
     SONGS FOR DANCES TO THE CLAPPERBELL
     SONGS FOR THE SWEEPING DANCE
       The King of Huai-nan Piece (*p'ien*)
     SONGS FOR CUP AND TRAY DANCES
     SONGS FOR THE HEADCLOTH DANCE
     SONGS FOR THE WHITE HEMP DANCE
     SONG-TEXTS FOR DANCES TO SONGS OF THE LIU-SUNG
       REIGN-PERIOD AD 465–472
     MAJOR ODES FOR WHITE HEMP PIECES (*P'ien*)

IV HAN DRUMMING AND BLOWING SONGS FOR THE *NAO*-BELL,
     CHAPTER 22
     18 Han Songs for the *Nao*-bell
       Vermilion Ibis; We Fought South of the City Wall; Mount Wu is
       High; Up the Mound; The One I Love; Young Pheasant Fancy-
       plume; Almighty on High!; I Lean from the High Terrace
     DRUMMING AND BLOWING PIECES

APPENDIX II

Kuo Mao-ch'ien's Twelve Categories of *Yüeh-fu*

(from *Anthology of Yüeh-fu Poetry*)

I WORDS FOR SUBURBAN AND TEMPLE SONGS, CHAPTERS 1–12
(803 pieces)
    Chapter 1, Part 1, Han Songs for Suburban Sacrifices
    Songs for Suburban Sacrifice, in 19 Parts: We Have Chosen a Timely Day; Lord God Draws Nigh; Greening *Yang*; Scarlet Brilliance; West White-light; Darkness Obscure; Lo! Holy Creator; The Horse of Heaven

II WORDS FOR BANQUET AND ARCHERY SONGS, CHAPTERS 13–15
(166 pieces)

III WORDS FOR DRUMMING AND BLOWING PIECES, CHAPTERS 16–20
(256 pieces)
    Chapter 16, Part 1, 18 Han Songs for the *Nao*-bell
    Vermilion Ibis; We Fought South of the City Wall; Mount Wu is High; Up the Mound; The One I Love; Young Pheasant Fancy-plume; Almighty on High!; I Lean from the High Terrace

IV WORDS FOR HORIZONTAL FLUTE PIECES, CHAPTERS 21–25
(303 pieces)
    Chapter 25, Part 5, Liang Pieces for Drumming, Horn, and Horizontal Flute
    Words for the Chestnut Roan Horse Song (= At Fifteen I Joined the Army)

V WORDS FOR CONCERTED SONGS, CHAPTERS 26–43 (831 pieces)
    Chapter 26, Part 1, Six Concerted Lays
    The Harp Lay (appears only in preface to a T'ang lay)
    Chapter 26, Part 1, Concerted Pieces, Part 1
    South of the River
    Chapter 27, Part 2, Concerted Pieces, Part 2
    Light in the East; Dew on the Shallot; Artemisia Village
    Chapter 28, Part 3, Concerted Pieces, Part 3
    Cocks Crow; A Cock Bore Eight or Nine Chicks; East of Flat Mound; Mulberry on the Bank
    Chapter 29, Part 4, Lament Pieces (*yin* and *t'an*)
    Chapter 30, Part 5, Level-mode Pieces, Part 1
    A Long Song Ballad, nos. 1, 2, and 3.

APPENDIX III

Earliest Sources of Han *Yüeh-Fu* Cited

Pan Ku (AD 32–92), *Han shu* (History of the Han)
Chapter 22   Songs for Suburban Sacrifice, in 19 Parts: (8) The Horse of Heaven; We Have Chosen a Timely Day; Lord God Draws Nigh; Greening *Yang*; Scarlet Brilliance; West White-light; Darkness Obscure; Lo! Holy Creator
Chapter 27   Well-water Overflows; Crooked Paths; Swallow, Swallow
Chapter 29   The Song of Cheng-Pai Ditch
Ssu-ma Piao (AD 240–306), *Hsü Han shu* (Continuation of the History of the Han)
Chapter 16   Straight as a Bowstring; Short Wheat; Crows on City Walls; The Song Tung Flees!
Ts'ui Pao (*fl.* AD 290–306), *Ku chin chu* (Record of Things Ancient and Modern)
Chapter 2   Dew on the Shallot; Artemisia Village
Shen Yüeh (AD 441–512), *Sung shu* (History of the Southern Sung)
Chapter 21   South of the River; Light in the East; Cocks Crow; A Crow Bore Eight or Nine Chicks; East of Flat Mound; The Ballad Tung Peach (Flees!); Along the Embankment (long version, attrib. Ts'ao Ts'ao); How Wonderful! A Ballad; East Gate Ballad (long version); A *Yen* Song, The Lo-fu Ballad (Mulberry on the Bank); West Gate Ballad (long version); The Ballad of Breaking Willow; A *Yen* Song, Whenever (The Whenever Ballad, Swans); A *Yen* Song, The Whenever Ballad (Whenever Will I Be Quite Happy); Song of Melancholy (Ballad of); The Ballad of the Prefect of Goosegate; The White Head Lament (long version)
Chapter 22   The King of Huai-nan Ballad (*p'ien*); Vermilion Ibis; We Fought South of the City Wall; Mount Wu is High; Up the Mound; The One I Love; I Lean from the High Terrace
Hsiao T'ung (AD 501–531) *et al.*, *Wen hsüan* (Anthology of Literature)
Chapter 27   Watering Horses at a Long Wall Hole; Heartache, A Ballad; A Long Song Ballad (no. 1)
Hsü Ling (AD 507–583), *Yü-t'ai hsin-yung* (New Songs from a Jade Terrace)
Chapter 1   They Met (A Ballad); The Lunghsi Ballad; A *Yen* Song, A Ballad (Swallows); White as Mountaintop Snow (The White Head Lament, short version); Flying This Way Two White Swans (An Old Ballad, Two White Swans)

Chapter 2   Along the Embankment Ballad (attrib. Ts'ao P'ei or Empress Chen, short version)

Ou-yang Hsün (AD 557–641) *et al., I-wen lei-chü* (Compendium of Literature)
Chapter 27   A Long Song Ballad (no. 3, fragment)
Chapter 81   A Long Song Ballad (no. 2, incomplete)
Chapter 86   The Pomelo, An Old Poem (fragment)
Chapter 88   A *Yen* Song, A Ballad (On South Mountain's rocks sheer, sheer)
Chapter 89   The Yü-chang Ballad (fragment)

Li Shan (d. AD 689) *et al.*, Commentary on the *Wen hsüan, Anthology of Literature*
Chapter 18   The Old Song of Sighs (The Date-tree)
Chapter 28   The Old Fierce Tiger Ballad

Hsü Chien (AD 659–729) *et al., Ch'u hsüeh chi* (Notes for Beginning Students)
Chapter 30   The Butterfly (fragment)

Li Fang (AD 925–996) *et al., T'ai-p'ing yü-lan* (Imperial Survey of the T'ai-p'ing Era)
Chapter 25   An Old Song (Autumn winds sough and sigh, fragment); An Old Song, Eight Changes (fragment)

Kuo Mao-ch'ien (*fl.* AD 1084–1126), *Yüeh-fu shih chi* (Anthology of *Yüeh-fu* Poetry)
Chapter 25   At Fifteen
Chapter 26   The Harp Lay
Chapter 30   A Long Song Ballad (nos. 2 and 3)
Chapter 34   The Yü chang Ballad
Chapter 35   In Ch'angan There is a Narrow Lane
Chapter 37   Walking out of Hsia Gate, A Ballad; West Gate Ballad (short version); East Gate Ballad (short version)
Chapter 38   The Ballad of Shang-liu-t'ien; The Ballad of the Orphan Boy; The Ballad of the Ailing Wife
Chapter 41   The Lament of Liang-fu
Chapter 61   The Butterfly
Chapter 62   The Sad Song Ballad
Chapter 74   A Withered Fish

Feng Wei-no (d. AD 1572), *Ku shih chi* (Notes on Ancient Poetry)
Chapter 20   The Pomelo, An Old Poem; If in a High Field

Chang Chih-hsiang (AD 1496–1577), *Ku shih lei yüan* (Garden of Old Poetic Genres)
Chapter 45   An Old Eight Changes Song; An Old *Yen* Song; An Old Song

Note: Two excellent reference works identify the sources of old anonymous songs, Suzuki, *Research*, pp. 286–96, and Lu Ch'in-li, *Poetry of the Ch'in, Han*, etc., Vol. 1, *passim.* I have not always agreed with their citations.

Bibliography

Some works frequently referred to have been abbreviated as follows:

ch.	volume or chapter of a Chinese work
Hsü	Hsü Ling, *Yü-t'ai hsin-yung, New Songs from a Jade Terrace* (Wen-hsüeh ed., 1955 rpr. of 1633 Ming ed. based on 1215 Sung ed.)
Kuo	Kuo Mao-ch'ien, *Yüeh-fu shih chi, Anthology of Yüeh-fu Poetry* (Chung-hua, 1979, edited and supplemented by the Chung-hua editors, based on the Sung ed.)
Li Shan	his commentary on the *Wen hsüan, Anthology of Literature,* comp. Hsiao T'ung *et al.,* incorporated into most subsequent editions (especially *Liu-ch'en-chu Wen hsüan,* 13th century)
Pan Ku	*Han shu, History of the Han* (Chung-hua ed., 1962)
Shen	Shen Yüeh comp. *Sung shu, History of the Southern Sung, ch.* 19–22, 'Treatise on Music' (Chung-hua ed., 1974)
Ssu-ma Piao	author of independent treatises incorporated into the later history of Fan Yeh, *History of the Latter Han (Hou Han shu),* the treatises sometimes referred to as *Hsü Han shu, Continuation of the History of the Han* (Chung-hua ed., 1965)
SKCS	*Ssu-k'u ch'üan shu, Collectanea of Books in the Four Treasure-houses,* comp. 1773–1782 by Chi Yün *et al.,* (rpr. Commercial Press, Taipei)
SPPY	*Ssu-pu pei-yao, Essential Items in the Four Branches of Learning* (Chung-hua, 1927–35)
SPTK	*Ssu-pu ts'ung-k'an, Collected Reprints of the Four Branches of Learning* (photo-lithographic rpr. by Commercial Press, 1929–36)
SSC	*Shih-san Ching,* The Thirteen Classics, *chu shu,* with commentaries (facsimile of 1815 ed., rpr. Chubun, Kyoto, 1974)
TSCC	*Ts'ung-shu chi-ch'eng, The Complete Collectanea* (Commercial Press, 1935–37)

Primary Sources

Ch'en shu (History of the Ch'en Dynasty), Yao Ssu-lien comp. (*c.* AD 637), 36 *ch.,* Peking, Chung-hua, 1972, in 1 vol.

Chin shu (History of the Chin Dynasty), Fang Hsüan-ling (AD 578–648) *et al.* comp., commentary by Ho Chao (AD 747), 130 *ch.,* Peking, Chung-hua, 1974, in 3 vols.

Chiu T'ang shu (The Old History of the T'ang Dynasty), Liu Hsü (AD 887–946) *et al.* comp., 200 *ch.,* Peking, Chung-hua, 1975, in 6 vols.

Ch'u Tz'u (Songs of Ch'u), comprising works by authors of late Chou to Latter Han (*c.* 300 BC–2nd century AD), commentary by Wang I (d. AD 158) and Hung Hsing-tsu (AD 1090–1155), 17 *ch., SPTK* (photolith. rpr. of Ming rpr. of Sung ed.). Trans. David Hawkes.

Ch'un-ch'iu (Spring and Autumn Annals), one of the *Chinese Classics*, incorporated with *Tso chuan, q.v.*

Chuang Tzu (Master Chuang), by Chuang Chou (*c.* 369–*c.* 286 BC), commentary by Kuo Hsiang (d. AD 312), glosses by Lu Yüan-lang (d. AD 626), 10 *ch.*, *SPPY*. Trans. Burton Watson 1968, Angus C. Graham 1981.

Han Fei Tzu (Master Han Fei), by Han Fei Tzu *et al.* (d. 233 BC), commentary anon., 55 *ch.*, *SPPY* (rpr. from Wu Tzu's AD 1818 ed. from a Sung *c.* 1165 ed.). Trans. W. K. Liao.

Han shih wai chuan (Exoteric Commentary on the Han School Text of the *Book of Poetry*), by Han Ying (*fl.* 150 BC), Chou T'ing-ts'ai ed., 10 *ch.*, *TSCC*. Trans. James Robert Hightower 1952.

Han shu (History of the [Former, or Western] Han [Dynasty]), by Pan Ku (AD 32–92) *et al.*, commentary by Yen Shih-ku (AD 581–645), 100 *ch.*, Peking, Chung-hua, 1962, in 8 vols. Trans. Homer H. Dubs (*ch.* 1–12, 99), Burton Watson 1974 (*ch.* 54, 63, 65, 67–8, 71, 74, 78, 92, 97).

Hou Han shu (History of the Latter Han), by Fan Yeh (AD 398–446), commentary by Li Hsien (AD 657–684) *et al.*, 120 *ch*; 30 of these 130 *ch.* are treatises known as *Hsü Han shu* (Continuation of the History of the Han) by Ssu-ma Piao (AD 240–306), commentary by Liu Chao (6th century), Peking, Chung-hua, 1965, in 6 vols. Study of early Latter Han era by Hans H. Bielenstein 1954, 1959, 1967.

Hsi ching tsa chi (Miscellany of the Western Capital), attributed to Liu Hsin (d. AD 23) and to Ko Hung (*c.* AD 280–340), pseudonym Pao-p'u Tzu (Master Embracing-simplicity), 6 *ch.*, *SPTK* (photolith. rpr. of Ming 1552 ed.)

Hsin T'ang shu (The New History of the T'ang Dynasty), Ou-yang Hsiu (AD 1007–1072) and Sung Ch'i comp., 225 *ch.*, Peking, Chung-hua, 1975, in 7 vols.

Hsü Han shu, see Hou Han shu, Ssu-ma Piao.

Huai-nan Tzu (Master Huai-nan), Liu An, King of Huai-nan, comp. (d. 122 BC), commentary by Kao Yu (3rd century AD) and Hsü Shen (AD 30–124), 21 *ch.*, *SPPY* (rpr. of Ch'ing 1788 ed. of Chuang K'uei-chi). Trans. Evan Morgan.

I Ching (Classic of Change), one of the *Chinese Classics*, anon. *c.* 800–2nd century BC, commentary by Wang Pi (AD 226–249) and Han K'ang-po, 9 *ch.*, *SPPY* (*Chou I*, rpr. from Sung ed. of Yo K'o, AD 1173–1240). Trans. Richard Wilhelm.

Kung-yang chuan (The Kung-yang Commentary), one of the *Chinese Classics*, anon., commentary by Ho Hsiu (2nd century AD), 12 *ch.*, *SPPY* (*Ch'un-ch'iu Kung-yang chuan*, rpr. from Ming 1640 ed. Chin P'an and Ko Tzu).

Kuo yü (Discourses of the States), anon., *c.* 3rd century BC, commentary by Wei Chao (3rd century AD), 21 *ch.*, *SPPY* (rpr. from Ch'ing 1800 ed. of Shih-li-chü Huang-shih ts'ung-shu).

Li chi (Record of Ritual), one of the *Chinese Classics*, anon., *c.* 1st century BC, commentary by Cheng Hsüan (AD 127–200), glosses by Lu Yüan-lang (7th century), 46 *ch.*, *SPPY* (rpr. of Sung ed. of Yo K'o, 12th–13th centuries), *SSC* 4. Trans. James Legge 1885, Séraphin Couvreur 1928.

Lieh hsien chuan (Biographies of Immortals), attributed to Liu Hsiang (79–8 BC), 2 *ch.*, Ku-chin i-shih 7 (rpr. of Ming ed. of Wu Kuan *c.* 1571–76). Trans. Max Kaltenmark.

Lieh nü chuan (Biographies of [Virtuous] Ladies), attributed to Liu Hsiang (79–8 BC), 8 *ch.*, *SPPY* (chiao-chu, rpr. from Ch'ing ed. of Wang K'ang-nien, 19th century).

Lü-shih ch'un-ch'iu (Spring and Autumn Annals of Mr. Lü), attributed to Lü Pu-wei (d. 235 BC), commentary by Kao Yu (3rd century AD), 26 *ch.*, *SPTK* (photolith. rpr. from Ming ed.).

Lun yü (Analects), the teachings of K'ung Fu Tzu (Confucius, 479–551 BC) and his disciples, one of the *Chinese Classics*, commentary by Ho Yen (d. AD 249), 20 *ch.*, *SSC* (*Ssu shu*, The Four Books). Trans. Arthur Waley 1938, D. C. Lau 1979.

Meng Tzu (Master Meng, Mencius), by Meng K'e (?371–289 BC), one of the *Chinese Classics*, 6 *ch.*, *SSC* (*Ssu shu*, The Four Books). Trans. James Legge 1875, 1985, D. C. Lau 1970.

Nan-Ch'i shu (History of the Southern Ch'i Dynasty), Hsiao Tzu-hsien comp. (AD 489–537), 59 *ch.* (Peking, Chung-hua, 1972, in 1 vol.).

Pao-p'u Tzu (pseudonym, Master Embracing-simplicity), by Ko Hung (AD 254–334), *SPPY*.

Shang shu (The Ancient History), one of the *Chinese Classics*, see *Shu Ching*.

Shih chi (Historical Records), by Ssu-ma Ch'ien (*c.* 145–*c.* 86 BC), commentary by P'ei Yin (5th century AD) *et al.*, 130 *ch.* (Shanghai, Chung-hua, 1964, in 4 vols.) Trans. Edouard Chavannes 1895–1905 (*ch.* 1–52), Burton Watson 1961 (*ch.* relating to Han era).

Shih Ching (Classic of Poetry, Book of Poetry), one of the *Chinese Classics*, anon., *c.* 800–600 BC, commentary by Mao Heng (2nd century BC) and Cheng Hsüan (AD 127–200), 20 *ch.*, *SSC* 3–4. Trans. Arthur Waley 1937, Bernhard Karlgren 1950.

Shih-san Ching (The Thirteen Classics), the *Chinese Classics* (*Chu-shu fu chiao-k'an-chi*), annotated by Chao Ch'i (d. AD 201) and Sun Shih (AD 962–1033), (Sung ed. rpr. Ch'ing 1815 with critical notes by Juan Yüan, AD 1764–1849, facsimile Chubun, 1974); the 13 classics are: *Shu Ching, Shih Ching, Chou li, I li, Li chi, Ch'un-ch'iu Tso chuan, Ch'un-ch'iu Kung-yang chuan, Ch'un-ch'iu Ku-liang chuan, I Ching, Hsiao Ching, Lun yü, Erh ya, Meng Tzu.*

Shu Ching (Classic of History, or Book of Documents), one of the *Chinese Classics*, also known as *Shang shu* (The Ancient History), anon., *c.* 800–3rd century BC, commentary by K'ung An-kuo (*c.* 156–74 BC), 13 *ch.*, *SSC* 1. Trans. Bernhard Karlgren 1950.

Shuo yüan (Garden of Anecdotes), attributed to Liu Hsiang (79–8 BC), 20 *ch.* SPTK (photolith. rpr. of Ming MS).

Sui shu (History of the Sui Dynasty), Wei Cheng (AD 580–643) *et al.* comp., 85 *ch.* (Peking, Chung-hua, 1973, in 2 vols.)

Sung shu (History of the [Southern] Sung), Shen Yüeh comp. AD 488 (AD 441–512), 100 *ch.* (Peking, Chung-hua, 1974, in 4 vols.)

Tao Te Ching (Classic of the Way and Its Power), attributed to Lao Tzu or Lao Tan (*c.* 300 BC), also known as the *Lao Tzu* (Old Master), 81 *ch.*, *SPPY* (*Lao Tzu*, rpr. from Ming *c.* 1573 ed. of Chang Chih-hsiang). Trans. Arthur Waley 1934, D. C. Lau 1963.

Tso chuan (The Tso Commentary), one of the *Chinese Classics*, attributed to Tso Ch'iu-ming (*c.* 4th or 3rd century BC), commentary by Tu Yü (AD 222–284). Originally text was an independent chronicle, later rearranged under various chronological entries of the *Ch'un-ch'iu*; 60 *ch.*, *SSC* 5. Trans. James Legge 1872, Séraphin Couvreur 1914.

Wei shu (History of the Wei Dynasty), Wei Shou comp. (AD 506–572), 114 *ch.* (Peking, Chung-hua, 1974, in 4 vols.).

Yen Tzu Ch'un-ch'iu (Spring and Autumn Annals of Master Yen), by Yen Ying (d. 493 BC), 7 *ch.*, *SPTK* (photolith. rpr. of Ming movable type print). Trans. Alfred Forke 1923.

Secondary References, Chinese and Japanese

Chang Chih-hsiang comp. (AD 1496–1577), *Ku shih lei yüan* (Garden of Old Poetic Genres), 130 *ch.*, Yü Hsien-ch'ing *et al.*, ed., Shanghai, *c.* AD 1602.

Chang Yung (AD 410–475), *Yüan-chia cheng-sheng chi lu* (Arts Record of the Correct Music of the Era AD 424–454), also known as *Yüan-chia chi lu, Chi lu, Chang Yung lu*, and *Chang lu*; not extant, fragments cited in Chih-chiang's *Ku chin yüeh lu.*

Ch'en Hang (AD 1785–1826), *Shih pi-hsing chien* (Notes on Poetic Figures), postface AD 1883, Shanghai, Peking, Chung-hua, 1959.

Ch'en Pen-li (AD 1812), *Han yüeh-fu san ko chien chu* (Commentary on the Three Song Sets of Han *yüeh-fu*), Ch'en-shih ts'ung-shu ed. Ch'en Feng-heng in 10 vols., Yang-chou-fu,

Tu-sao-lou ts'ung-shu, 1811–43. (The song sets are: Lady T'ang-shan's set of 17 hymns, the 18 Han songs for the *nao*-bell, and the 19 hymns for suburban sacrifice.)

Cheng Ch'iao (AD 1104–1162), *T'ung chih* (Comprehensive Survey of Historical Writing), 200 *ch.*, Prince Hung-chou, Te-ling, *et al.*, ed. in AD 1749, [Yü-chih ch'ung-k'o] san-t'ung, in 47 vols.

Ch'iao Chou (AD 201–270), *Ch'iao Tzu fa hsün* (Master Ch'iao's Legal Precepts), 1 *ch.*, Yü-han shan-fang chi-i-shu 17, ed. Ma Kuo-han.

Chih-chiang (*c.* AD 568), *Ku chin yüeh lu* (Record of Ancient and Modern Music), originally in 13 *ch.*, extant in 1 *ch.*, Han Wei i-shu ch'ao 52, ed. (Ch'ing) Wang Mo.

Chiu Ch'iung-sun, *Li-tai yüeh-chih lü-chih chiao shih* (Comparative Analysis of Historical Treatises on Music), Vol. 1, Peking, Chung-hua, 1964.

Chu Ch'ien-chih, *Chung-kuo yin-yüeh wen-hsüeh shih* (A History of Chinese Music in Literature), facsimile of 1935 ed., Shanghai, Hong Kong, Commercial Press.

Chung-kuo yin-yüeh yüan (Dept. of Chinese Music), *Chung-kuo ku-tai yin-yüeh shu-mu* (A Bibliography of Ancient Chinese Music), Chung-kuo yin-yüeh yen-chiu, Peking, Music Publishers, 1962.

Feng Wei-no (d. AD 1572), *Ku shih chi*, or *Shih chi* (Notes on Ancient Poetry, or Notes on Poetry), 156 *ch.*, *SKCS* 4411–4432, in 22 vols.

Fu Sheng attrib. (2nd century BC), *Shang shu ta chuan* (Major Commentary on the Ancient History, or Classic of History), commentary by Cheng Hsüan, 5 *ch.*, *SPTK* (photolith. rpr. of ed. of Ch'en Shou-ch'i, AD 1771–1834).

Fujiwara Sosui, *Kanshi kayō gakufu rōei sen* (Anthology of Han Poetry, Popular Songs, and *Yüeh-fu*), 2 vols., Tokyo, Seishin, 1977–78.

Hsiao T'ung (AD 501–531) *et al.*, comp. *Wen hsüan* (Anthology of Literature), 60 *ch.*, commentary by Li Shan (d. AD 689) *et al.*, *Liu-ch'en-chu Wen hsüan*, *SPTK* (photolith. rpr. of late Southern Sung ed.); *SPPY* (rpr. from AD 1181 ed.) with Li Shan's commentary, ed. Hu K'e-chia (AD 1757–1816) in AD 1809. Trans. David R. Knechtges, Vol. 1 of 8 projected vols.

Hsü Chien (AD 659–729) *et al.* comp., *Ch'u hsüeh chi* (Notes for Beginning Students), 30 *ch.*, Peking, Chung-hua, 1962.

Hsü Ling (AD 507–583) comp., *Yü-t'ai hsin-yung* (New Songs from a Jade Terrace), 10 *ch.*, Peking, Wen-hsüeh ku chi, 1955 (photolith. rpr. from Ming 1633 ed. of Chao Chün from the 1215 Sung ed. of Ch'en Yü-fu). Trans. Anne Birrell.

Hsün Hsü (d. AD 289), *Hsün shih lu* (Hsün's Poetry Notes); not extant, fragments cited in Chih-chiang's *Ku chin yüeh lu.*

Huang Chieh (AD 1874–1935), *Han Wei yüeh-fu feng-chien* (Notes on the Style of Han and Wei *Yüeh-fu*), 1923, rpr. Hong Kong, Commercial Press, 1961.

Jang Chü (or Jang T'ien, or *Ssu-ma* Jang Chü, *fl. c.* 377–331 BC), *Ssu-ma fa* (The Marshal's Methods), 3 *ch.*, *SPTK* (photolith. rpr. of rpr. of Sung MS).

Ko lu (Record of Songs), anon., pre-T'ang, 1 *ch.*, originally 10 *ch.*, Han Wei i-shu ch'ao 57. (14 notes on *yüeh-fu* gleaned from *Wen hsüan* commentaries.)

Kuo Mao-ch'ien (*fl.* AD 1084–1126) comp., *Yüeh-fu shih chi* (Anthology of Yüeh-fu Poetry), 100 *ch.*, Sung ed., rpr. Shanghai, Wen-hsüeh ku-chi, 1955, in 4 vols.; *SPTK* ed., based on Yüan (13th century) eds., transmitted by Mao Chin; *Yüeh-fu shih chi*, ed. amended and supplemented, based on Sung eds., by Peking, Chung-hua, 1979, in 4 vols., Chung-kuo ku-tien wen-hsüeh ch'i-pen ts'ung-shu.

Li Fang (AD 925–996) *et al.* comp., *T'ai-p'ing yü-lan* (Imperial Survey of the T'ai-p'ing Era [AD 976–984]), 1,000 *ch.*, *SPTK.*

Li Fang, *id.*, *Wen-yüan ying-hua* (Prize Blooms from the Garden of Literature), 1,000 *ch.*, facsimile of Ming 1567 ed., Peking, Chung-hua, 1966, in 6 vols.

Liu Hsieh (d. *c.* AD 523), *Wen-hsin tiao-lung* (The Literary Mind and the Carving of Dragons), *SPTK*, photolith. rpr. of Ming ed. Trans. Vincent Y. Shih.

214

Liu Hsien (AD 434–489), *Ting chün li* (Procedures for Controlling the Army), also known as *Ssu-ma ping fa* (The Marshal's Military Methods); not extant, cited by Kuo Mao-ch'ien.

Liu I-ch'ing (AD 403–444), *Shih-shuo hsin-yü* (A New Account of Tales of the World), commentary by Liu Chün (AD 462–521), 3 *ch.*, *SPTK* (photolith. rpr. of Ming 1535 ed.). Trans. Richard B. Mather.

Lo Ken-tse, *Yüeh-fu wen-hsüeh shih* (A History of *Yüeh-fu* Literature), 1931, rpr. Taipei, Wen-shih che, 1972.

Lu Ch'in-li (1911–1973), comp., *Hsien Ch'in Han Wei Chin Nan-Pei-ch'ao shih* (Poetry of the Ch'in, Han, Wei, Chin, and Northern and Southern Dynasties), 135 *ch.*, Peking, Chung-hua, 1982, in 3 vols.

Lu K'an-ju, *Yüeh-fu ku-tz'u k'ao* (A Study of Old *Yüeh-fu* Texts), Shanghai, Commercial Press, 1926, in the series Kuo-hsüeh hsiao-ts'ung-shu.

Lu K'an-ju and Feng Yüan-chün, *Chung-kuo shih shih* (The History of Chinese Poetry), 3 vols., Peking, Tso-chia, 1956, Vol. 1, '*Yüeh-fu*'; pp. 157–252.

Ma Tuan-lin (late 13th century), *Wen hsien t'ung-k'ao* (Critical Survey of Written Knowledge), 348 *ch.*, Prince Hung-chou, Te-ling *et al.*, ed. in AD 1748 [Yü-chih ch'ung-k'o] san-t'ung, in 38 vols.

Masuda Kiyohide, *Gafu* (or *Le-fu*) *no rekishiteki kenkyū* (Research on the History of *Yüeh-fu*), Tōyōgaku sōsho 9, Tokyo, Sōbunsha, 1975.

Mei Ting-tso (Ming), *Ku yüeh yüan* (A Garden of Ancient Music), 52+3 *ch.*, Ssu-k'u ch'üan-shu chen-pen pa-chi 170 (preface dated AD 1781), vols. 3649–3656.

Nakatsuhama Wataru, *Gafu shishū no kenkyū soin* (Research on and Concordance to the *Yüeh-fu shih chi*), Tokyo, Kyūko shoin, 1970.

Ou-yang Hsün (AD 557–641), Ling-hu Te-fen (AD 583–666) *et al.* comp., *I-wen lei-chü* (Compendium of Literature), 100 *ch.*, Wang Shao-ying ed., Peking, Shanghai, Chung-hua, 1965, in 2 vols.

Peking University, Dept. of Chinese Literature, comp., *Liang Han wen-hsüeh shih ts'an-k'ao tzu-liao* (Reference Materials for Han Literary History), 1959, rpr. Peking, Chung-hua, 1962.

P'eng Li-t'ien, '*Yüeh-fu shih yü Han Wu-ti pien*' (A Discussion of Whether the Bureau of Music Arose in the Reign of the Han Emperor Wu'), in *Yü-yen yü wen-hsüeh* (Language and Literature), ed. by Tsinghua University, Dept. of Chinese Literature, Shanghai, Chung-hua, 1937, p. 180f.

San-fu huang-t'u (The Yellow Chart of the Three Metropolitan Districts), anon. (? 3rd century AD), 6 *ch.*, annotated by Chang Yüan-chi *SPTK* (rpr. of a Yüan ed.).

Sawaguchi Takeo, *Gafu* (or *Le-fu*), (*Yüeh-fu*), Chūgoku koten shinsho 15, Tokyo, Meitoku, 1973.

Shen Chien (Northern Sung), *Yüeh-fu kuang t'i* (Elaborations on *Yüeh-fu* Titles), not extant, fragments cited by Kuo Mao-ch'ien.

Shen Te-ch'ien (AD 1673–1769), comp., *Ku shih yüan* (Sources of Ancient Poetry), 14 *ch.*, *SPPY* (rpr. from original Ch'ing 1725 ed.).

Shimizu Shigeru, '*Kō no hongi*' (The Meaning of *Hsing*), in *Nihon Chūgoku gakkaihō*, 36, 1984, pp. 1–11.

Suzuki Shūji, *Kan Gi shi no kenkyū* (Research on Han and Wei Poetry), Tokyo, Daishūkan, 1967.

Ting Fu-pao (1874–1952), comp., *Ch'üan Han San-kuo Chin Nan-Pei-ch'ao shih* (Complete Poetry of the Han, Three Kingdoms, Chin, and Northern and Southern Dynasties), 6 *ch.*, preface dated 1916, rpr. Peking, 1959.

Ts'ai Yung (AD 133–192), ?comp., *Li yüeh chih* (Treatise on Ritual and Music), not extant, cited by miscellaneous authors.

Tso K'o-ming (14th century AD), *Ku yüeh-fu* (Ancient *Yüeh-fu*), 2 *ch.*, preface dated AD 1346, *SKCS* 4930.

Ts'ui Pao (*fl.* AD 290–306), *Ku chin chu* (Record of Things Ancient and Modern), 3 *ch.*, *SPTK* (*san pien*, ed. Chang Yüan-chi, rpr. of Sung 1220 ed.).

Tu Wen-lan (AD 1815–1881) and Liu Yü-sung comp., *Ku yao-yen* (Old Popular Songs), rev. by Chou Shao-liang, AD 1892, Peking, Chung-hua, 1958.

Tu Yu (AD 735–812), *T'ung tien* (Comprehensive Survey of Classical Learning), 200 *ch.*, ed. by Prince Hung-chou, Te-ling *et al.* in AD 1747 [Yü-chih ch'ung-k'o] san-t'ung, in 13 vols.

Tu Yü (AD 222–284), commentary on *Tso chuan*, *q.v.*

Tuan An-chieh (*fl. c.* AD 894), *Yüeh-fu tsa lu* (Miscellaneous Records of *Yüeh-fu*), 1 *ch.*, Ku chin i-shih 29. Trans. Martin Gimm.

Wang Hsien-ch'ien, *Han nao-ko shih wen chien-cheng* (A Critical Survey of Commentaries on Han Songs for the *Nao*-bell), facsimile of AD 1872 ed. of the Hsiu-shou-t'ang, Taipei, Wen-ch'ieh, ? 1966.

Wang Seng-ch'ien (AD 426–485) comp., *Ta-ming san-nien yen-yüeh chi lu* (Arts Record of Banquet Music of the Year AD 459), also known as *Yen-yüeh chi lu*; not extant, fragments cited in Chih-chiang, *Ku chin yüeh lu.*

Wang Tzu-nien (Wang Chia, d. AD 390), *Shih i chi* (Record of Neglected Data), originally in 10 *ch.*, fragments reconstituted by Hsiao Ch'i (6th century AD) in 1 *ch.*, Ku chin i-shih 2, Wu Kuan ed. *c.* 1571–76, Shanghai, Commercial Press, 1937.

Wang Yün-hsi *Yüeh-fu shih lun-ts'ung* (A General Discussion of *Yüeh-fu* Poetry), Shanghai, Ku-tien wen-hsüeh, 1958.

Wen I-to (1899–1946), '*Yüeh-fu chien*' (Notes on *Yüeh-fu*), appendix to (*Sung-pen*) *Yüeh-fu shih chi*, Shanghai, 1955, see Kuo Mao-ch'ien.

Wu Ching (AD 670–749), *Yüeh-fu ku t'i yao-chieh* (Explanations of the Old Titles of *Yüeh-fu*), also known as *Yüeh-fu chieh t'i*, 2 *ch.*, Chin-tai pi-shu 34, Shanghai, 1922.

Yen Yü (*fl.* AD 1180–1235), *Ts'ang-lang shih hua* (Remarks on Poetry from Ts'ang-lang), facsimile, preface dated AD 1881, ed. Hu Chien, Taipei, Kuang-wen, 1972. Trans. Günther Debon.

Yü Kuan-ying, *Han Wei Liu-ch'ao shih hsüan* (Anthology of the Poetry of the Han, Wei, and Six Dynasties), Peking, Jen-min wen-hsüeh, 1958.

Yü, *id.*, *Han Wei Liu-ch'ao shih lun-ts'ung* (A Discussion of the Poetry of the Han, Wei, and Six Dynasties), Chung-kuo ku-tien wen-hsüeh yen-chiu ts'ung-k'an, Shanghai, T'ang-ti, 1953. Chapter 10 constitutes an appendix, pp. 108–126, providing corrections to authors' names and attributions in Kuo Mao-ch'ien, *Yüeh-fu shih chi.*

Yü, *id.*, *Yüeh-fu shih hsüan* (Anthology of *Yüeh-fu* Poetry), 1950, rev. ed., Hong Kong, Shih-chieh, 1954.

Secondary References, Western

Allen, Joseph R., *In the Voice of Others: Chinese Music Bureau Poetry*, Michigan Monographs in Chinese Studies 63, Ann Arbor, Center for Chinese Studies, University of Michigan, 1992.

Bielenstein, Hans H., 'An Interpretation of the Portents in the *Ts'ien-Han-shu*', in *Bulletin of the Museum of Far Eastern Antiquities*, 22, 1950, pp. 127–43.

Bielenstein, Hans H., *The Bureaucracy of Han Times*, Cambridge Studies in Chinese History, Literature and Institutions, Cambridge, Cambridge Univ. Press, 1980.

Bielenstein, Hans H., 'Loyang in Later Han Times', in *Bulletin of the Museum of Far Eastern Antiquities*, 48, 1976, pp. 1–142.

Bielenstein, Hans H., 'The Restoration of the Han Dynasty', Vol. 1, 'Prolegomena on the Historiography of the Hou Han shu'; Vol. 2; 'The Civil War'; Vol. 3, 'The People', in *Bulletin of the Museum of Far Eastern Antiquities*, 26, 1954, pp. 1–209, 31, 1959, pp. 1–287, 39, 1967, pp. 1–198.

Birrell, Anne, 'Erotic Decor: A Study of Love Imagery in the Sixth Century AD

Anthology Yü-t'ai hsin-yung (New Poems from a Jade Terrace),' Columbia University dissertation, 1979.

Birrell, Anne, 'Mythmaking and Yüeh-fu: Popular Songs and Ballads of Early Imperial China,' in *Journal of the American Oriental Society*, 109.2, 1989, pp. 223–35.

Birrell, Anne, trans., *New Songs from a Jade Terrace*, London, George Allen & Unwin, 1982.

Bishop, John L., ed., *Studies in Chinese Literature*, Harvard-Yenching Institute Studies 21, Cambridge, Harvard Univ. Press, 1966.

Bodde, Derk, *China's First Unifier, A Study of the Ch'in Dynasty as Seen in the Life of Li Ssu*, 1938, rpr. Hong Kong, Hong Kong Univ. Press, 1967.

Bodde, Derk, *Festivals in Classical China, New Year and Other Annual Observances during the Han Dynasty, 206 BC–AD 220*, Princeton, Princeton Univ. Press, 1975.

Bold, Alan, *The Ballad*, The Critical Idiom, 41, London, Methuen, 1979.

Bray, Francesca, *Agriculture*, Joseph Needham ed., Science and Civilisation in China, Cambridge, Cambridge Univ. Press, 1984.

Bronson, Bertrand Harris, *The Ballad as Song*, Berkeley, Univ. of California Press, 1969.

Bronson, Bertrand Harris, *The Traditional Tunes of the Child Ballads* [English and Scottish Popular Ballads] *with their texts, according to the extant records of Great Britain and America*, 4 vols., Princeton, Princeton Univ. Press, 1959–72.

Chan, Wing-tsit, trans., *A Source Book in Chinese Philosophy*, Princeton, Princeton Univ. Press, 1963.

Chavannes, Edouard, *Le T'ai chan: Essai de monographie d'un culte chinois*, Annales du Musée Guimet, Bibliothèque d'études, 21, Paris, Leroux, 1910.

Chavannes, Edouard, trans., *Les mémoires historiques de Se-ma Ts'ien*, 6 vols., 1895–1905, rpr. Paris, Adrien-Maisonneuve, 1967.

Child, Francis James, ed., *The English and Scottish Popular Ballads*, 5 vols., 1882–98, New York, The Folklore Press and Pageant Book Co., 1957.

Ch'ü T'ung-tzu, *Han Social Structure*, Han Dynasty China, 1, Seattle, Univ. of Washington Press, 1982.

Couvreur, Séraphin, trans., *I Li: Cérémonial; texte chinois et traduction*, 2nd ed., Sien hsien, Mission Catholique, 1928.

Couvreur, Séraphin, trans., *Tch'ouen Ts'iou et Tso Tchouan; texte chinois avec traduction française*, 3 vols., Ho Kien fu, Mission Catholique, 1914.

Davis, A. R., trans., *T'ao Yüan-ming (A.D. 365–427), His Works and Their Meaning*, 2 vols., Cambridge Studies in Chinese History, Literature and Institutions, Cambridge, Cambridge Univ. Press, 1983.

de Bary, Wm. Theodore, Wing-tsit Chan, and Burton Watson, eds., *Sources of Chinese Tradition*, 2 vols., New York, Columbia Univ. Press, 1960.

Debon, Günther, trans., *Ts'ang-lang's Gespräche über die Dichtung; ein Beitrag zur chinesischen Poetik*, Wiesbaden, Harrassowitz, 1962.

Diény, Jean-Pierre, *Aux origines de la poésie classique en Chine, Etude sur la poésie lyrique à l'époque des Han*, Monographies du T'oung Pao, 6 Leiden, Brill, 1968.

Diény, Jean-Pierre, 'Chansons des Han', in *France Asie-Asia*, 173 (May–June), 1962, pp. 267–76.

Diény, Jean-Pierre, trans., *Les dix-neuf poèmes anciens*, Bulletin de la Maison Franco-Japonaise, n.s. 7.4, Paris, Presses Univ. de France, 1963.

Diény, Jean-Pierre, *Pastourelles et Magnanarelles, Essai sur un thème littéraire chinois*, Geneva, Librairie Droz, 1977.

Diény, Jean-Pierre, 'Anne Birrell, *Popular Songs and Ballads of Han China*' (review article), in *T'oung Pao*, 76.1–3, 1990, pp. 132–45.

Dubs, Homer H., trans., *The History of the Former Han Dynasty*, 3 vols., Baltimore, Waverly Press, 1938–55.

Dudbridge, Glen, ed., *Tale of Li Wa: Study and Critical Edition of a Chinese Story from the Ninth Century*, London, Ithaca Press, 1983.

Duyvendak, J. J. L., trans., *The Book of Lord Shang, A Classic of the Chinese School of Law*, 1928, Chicago, Univ. of Chicago Press, 1963.

Forke, Alfred, 'Yen Ying, Staatsmann und Philosoph und das *Yen-tse Tch'un-tch'iu'*, in *Asia Major*, 1, Hirth Anniversary Vol., 1923, pp. 101–44.

Frankel, Hans H., 'The Abduction, the War, and the Desperate Husband: Three Early Chinese Ballads', in *Ventures* 1.5, 1965, pp. 6–14.

Frankel, Hans H., *The Flowering Plum and the Palace Lady, Interpretations of Chinese Poetry*, New Haven, Yale Univ. Press, 1976.

Frankel, Hans H., 'The Formulaic Language of the Chinese Ballad "Southeast Fly the Peacocks",' in *Bulletin of the Institute of History and Philology*, 39, 1969, pp. 219–44.

Frankel, Hans H., 'The Problem of Authenticity in Ts'ao Chih', in Chan Ping-leung ed., *Essays in Commemoration of the Golden Jubilee of the Fung Ping Shan Library (1932–1982)*, Hong Kong, Fung Ping Shan Library, 1982, pp. 183–201.

Frankel, Hans H., 'The Relation between Narrator and Characters in *Yüefu* Ballads', *Chinoperl Papers*, 13, 1984–85, pp. 107–127.

Frankel, Hans H., '*Yüeh-fu* Poetry', in Cyril Birch, ed., *Studies*, pp. 69–107.

Friedman, Albert B., 'The Oral-Formulaic Theory of Balladry—A Rebuttal', in James Porter, ed., *The Ballad Image*, pp. 215–40.

Frodsham, J. D., and Ch'eng Hsi, trans., *An Anthology of Chinese Verse, Han, Wei, Chin and Northern and Southern Dynasties*, Oxford, Clarendon, 1967.

Fung Yu-lan, *A History of Chinese Philosophy*, 2 vols., trans. by Derk Bodde, 2nd ed., Princeton, Princeton Univ. Press, 1952.

Gale, Esson M., trans., [*Yen-t'ieh lun*] *Discourses on Salt and Iron, A Debate on State Control of Commerce and Industry in Ancient China, Chapters I–XIX*, Sinica Leidensia, 2, Leiden, Brill, 1931.

Gerould, Gordon Hall, *The Ballad of Tradition*, New York, Galaxy (1932), 1957.

Gimm, Martin, *Das Yüeh-fu tsa-lu des Tuan An-chieh, Studien zur Geschichte von Musik, Schauspiel und Tanz in der T'ang Dynastie*, Asiatische Forschungen, 19, Wiesbaden, Harrassowitz, 1966.

Graham, Angus C., trans., *Chuang-tzŭ, the Seven Inner Chapters and Other Writings from the Book Chuang-tzŭ*, London, George Allen & Unwin, 1981.

Graham, Angus C., *Later Mohist Logic, Ethics and Science*, Hong Kong, Chinese Univ. Press, 1978.

Graham, Angus C., trans., *The Book of Lieh Tzu*, London, John Murray, 1960.

Gummere, F. B., *The Popular Ballad, The Types of English Literature*, London, Constable, 1907.

Hawkes David, trans., *Ch'u Tz'u, The Songs of the South, An Ancient Chinese Anthology*, New York, Beacon (1959), 1962; rev. ed., Penguin Books, The Penguin Classics, 1985.

Hawkes, David, Review of J.-P. Diény, *Aux origines de la poésie classique en Chine*, in *T'oung Pao*, 55, 1969, pp. 151–57.

Hervouet, Yves, *Un poète de cour sous les Han, Sseu-ma Siang-jou*, Bibliothèque de l'Institut des Hautes Etudes Chinoises, 19, Paris, Presses Univ. de France, 1964.

Hightower, James Robert, 'Ch'ü Yüan Studies', in Kaizuka Shigeki, ed., *Silver Jubilee Volume of the Zinbun-Kagaku-Kenkyu-syo*, Kyoto Univ., 25.1, 1954, Kyoto, Tōhōgakuhō, 1954, pp. 192–223.

Hightower, James Robert, trans., *Han Shih Wai Chuan; Han Ying's Illustrations of the Didactic Application of the Classic of Songs*, Harvard-Yenching Institute Monograph Series, 11, Cambridge, Harvard Univ. Press, 1952.

Hightower, James Robert, trans., 'Letter to Jen An (Shao-ch'ing)', in Birch, ed., *Anthology of Chinese Literature*, pp. 95–102.

Hightower, James Robert, 'The *Wen Hsüan* and Genre Theory', in John L. Bishop, ed., *Studies,* pp. 142–63.

Hightower, James Robert, *Topics in Chinese Literature, Outlines and Bibliographies,* Harvard-Yenching Institute Studies, 3, Cambridge, Harvard Univ. Press (1950), 1953.

Historical Relics Unearthed in New China, Peking, Foreign Languages Press, 1972.

Hodgart, Matthew, *The Ballads,* London, Hutchinson, 1950.

Hodgart, Matthew, ed., *The Faber Book of Ballads,* London, Faber, 1965.

Horace, Horatius Flaccus (Quintus), *Odes.*

Holzman, Donald, 'Les premiers vers pentasyllabiques datés dans la poésie chinoise', in *Mélanges de Sinologie Offerts à Monsieur Paul Demiéville,* Vol. 2, Bibliothèque de l'Institut des Hautes Etudes Chinoises, 20, Paris, Presses Univ. de France, 1974, pp. 77–115.

Hornsby, Roger A., *'Carpe diem',* in Alex Preminger, ed., *Princeton Encyclopedia,* pp. 103–04.

Hsü Cho-yün, *Ancient China in Transition: An Analysis of Social Mobility, 722–222 BC,* Stanford Studies in the Civilizations of Eastern Asia, Stanford, Stanford Univ. Press, 1965.

Hsü Cho-yün, *Han Agriculture, The Formation of Early Chinese Agrarian Economy (206 BC–AD 220),* Han Dynasty China, 2, Seattle, Univ. of Washington Press, 1980.

Kaltenmark, Max, trans., *Le Lie-sien tchouan [Lieh hsien chuan], Biographies légendaires des Immortels taoïstes de l'antiquité,* Paris Univ., Peking, Chinese Research, 1953.

Kao, George, ed., *Chinese Wit and Humor,* New York, Discovery House, 1974.

Karlgren, Bernhard, trans., 'The Book of Documents', in *Bulletin of the Museum of Far Eastern Antiquities,* 22, 1950, pp. 1–81.

Karlgren, Bernhard, trans., *The Book of Odes,* Stockholm, Museum of Far Eastern Antiquities, 1974.

Kaufmann, Walter, *Musical References in the Chinese Classics,* Detroit Monographs in Musicology, 5, Detroit, Information Coordinators, 1976.

Kennedy, George A., *Selected Works of George A. Kennedy,* ed. Tien-yi Li, New Haven, Far Eastern Publications, Yale Univ., 1964.

Knechtges, David R., 'A New Study of Han *Yüeh-fu'* (review of Anne Birrell, *Popular Songs and Ballads of Han China,* 1988), in *Journal of the American Oriental Society,* 110.2, 1990, pp. 310–16.

Knechtges, David R., trans., *Wen xuan, or Selections of Refined Literature,* Vols. 1 and 2, Princeton Library of Asian Translations, Princeton, Princeton Univ. Press, 1982, 1987.

Lau, D. C., trans., *Confucius, The Analects,* The Penguin Classics, Harmondsworth, Penguin Books, 1979.

Lau, D. C., trans., *Lao Tzu, Tao Te Ching,* The Penguin Classics, Harmondsworth, Penguin Books, 1963.

Lau, D. C., trans., *Mencius,* The Penguin Classics, Harmondsworth, Penguin Books, 1970.

Legge, James, trans., *Li Ki, or Collection of Treatises on the Rules of Propriety or Ceremonial Usages,* Vols. 27–28 of F. Max Müller, ed., The Sacred Books of the East, 1885, rpr. Delhi, Motilal Banarsidass, 1964.

Legge, James, trans., *The Chinese Classics,* 7 vols., London, Trübner, 1861–72.

Legge, James, trans., *The She king,* Vol. 4, Pt. 1 of *The Chinese Classics.*

Liao, W. K., trans., *The Complete Works of Han Fei Tzu,* 2 vols., London, Arthur Probsthain, 1959.

Liu, James J. Y., *Chinese Theories of Literature,* Chicago, Univ. of Chicago Press, 1975.

Liu, James J. Y., *The Chinese Knight Errant,* Chicago, Univ. of Chicago Press, 1967.

Loewe, Michael, *Chinese Ideas of Life and Death: Faith, Myth and Reason in the Han Period (202 BC–AD 220),* London, George Allen & Unwin, 1982.

219

Loewe, Michael, *Crisis and Conflict in Han China, 104 BC to AD 9,* London, George Allen & Unwin, 1974.

Loewe, Michael, *Everyday Life in Early Imperial China during the Han Period 202 BC–AD 220,* London, Transworld Publishers (1968), 1973.

Loewe, Michael, *Ways to Paradise, The Chinese Quest for Immortality,* London, George Allen & Unwin, 1979.

Loewe, Michael, and Anthony F. P. Hulsewé, [*Han shu*] *China in Central Asia, The Early Stage: 125 B.C.–A.D. 23; An Annotated Translation of Chapters 61 and 96 of the History of the Former Han Dynasty,* Sinica Leidensia, 14, Leiden, Brill, 1979.

Lord, Albert, *The Singer of Tales,* Harvard Studies in Comparative Literature, 24, Cambridge, Harvard Univ. Press, 1960.

Marney, John, trans., *Beyond the Mulberries: An Anthology of Palace-style Poetry by Emperor Chien-wen of the Liang Dynasty,* Asian Library Series, 17, San Francisco, Chinese Materials Center, 1982.

Mather, Richard B., trans., *Shih-shuo hsin-yü, A New Account of Tales of the World by Liu I-ch'ing with Commentary by Liu Chün,* Minneapolis, Univ. of Minnesota Press, 1976.

Mirsky, Jeanette, ed., *The Great Chinese Travelers,* Phoenix Edition, Chicago, Univ. of Chicago Press (1964), 1974.

Morgan, Evan, trans., *Tao, The Great Luminant,* Shanghai, Kelly and Walsh, 1934.

Needham, Joseph and Wang Ling, *Science and Civilisation in China: Physics and Physical Technology,* Vol. 4, Pt. 1, Cambridge, Cambridge Univ. Press, 1962.

Parry, Milman, 'Studies in the Epic Technique of Oral Verse-making', Part 1: 'Homer and Homeric Style', Part 2: 'The Homeric Language as the Language of an Oral Poetry', in *The Making of Homeric Verse; the Collected Papers of Milman Parry,* ed. Adam Parry, 1930, 1932, rpr. Oxford, Clarendon, 1971, pp. 266–324, 325–64.

Petronius Arbiter, *Satyricon.*

Pound, Louise, *Poetic Origins and the Ballad,* New York, Macmillan, 1921.

Porter, James, ed., *The Ballad Image; Essays Presented to Bertrand Harris Bronson,* Los Angeles, Center for the Study of Comparative Folklore & Mythology, University of California, 1983.

Preminger, Alex, ed., *Princeton Encyclopedia of Poetry and Poetics,* Princeton, Princeton Univ. Press, 1965.

Sadie, Stanley, ed., *The New Grove Dictionary of Music and Musicians,* 20 vols., articles on Chinese music, pp. 252–79, London, Macmillan, 1980.

Scott, Walter (Sir), comp., *Minstrelsy of the Scottish Border, Historical and Romantic Ballads,* Thomas Henderson, ed. (1802, 1803, 1830), London, Harrap, 1931.

Sells, A. Lytton, 'Fable and Verse', in Alex Preminger, ed., *Princeton Encyclopedia,* pp. 269–70.

Schipper, Kristofer Marinus, trans., *L'Empereur Wou des Han dans la légende taoiste: Han Wou-ti-nei-tchouan,* Publications de l'Ecole Française d'Extrême-Orient, 58, Paris, Ecole Française d'Extrême-Orient, 1965.

Shih, Chung-wen, *Injustice to Tou O: Tou Yüan, A Study and Translation* (Princeton Cambridge Studies in Chinese Linguistics, 4) Cambridge, Hong Kong Press, 1972.

Shih, Vincent Yuchung, trans., *The Literary Mind and the Carving of Dragons (Wen-hsin tiao-lung)* (1959), rev. ed. Hong Kong, Chinese Univ. Press, 1983.

Waley, Arthur, trans., *A Hundred and Seventy Chinese Poems,* London, Constable, 1918.

Waley, Arthur, trans., *The Analects of Confucius,* London, George Allen & Unwin, 1938.

Waley, Arthur, trans., *The Book of Songs,* New York, Grove Press (1937), 1960.

Waley, Arthur, 'The Heavenly Horses of Ferghana, A New View', in *History Today,* 5.2 (Feb.), 1955, pp. 95–103.

Waley, Arthur, *The Nine Songs, A Study of Shamanism in Ancient China,* 1955, rpr. San Francisco, City Lights, 1973.

Waley, Arthur, trans., *The Way and Its Power: A Study of the Tao Te Ching and Its Place in Chinese Thought,* London, Allen & Unwin, 1934.

Waley, Arthur, *T'ien Hsia* (Oct.) 1936, pp. 245–48.

Wang Chung-shu, *Han Civilisation,* Early Chinese Civilisations, trans. from Chinese by K. C. Chang, *et al.,* New Haven, Yale Univ. Press, 1982.

Watson, Burton, *Chinese Lyricism, Shih Poetry from the Second to the Twelfth Century,* New York, Columbia Univ. Press, 1971.

Watson, Burton, trans., *Chinese Rhyme-Prose, Poems in the Fu Form from the Han and Six Dynasties Period,* New York, Columbia Univ. Press, 1971.

Watson, Burton, trans., *Courtier and Commoner in Ancient China, Selections from the History of the Former Han by Pan Ku* [*Han shu*], New York, Columbia Univ. Press, 1974.

Watson, Burton, *Early Chinese Literature,* New York, Columbia Univ. Press, 1962.

Watson, Burton, trans., *Records of the Grand Historian of China, Translated from the Shih chi of Ssu-ma Ch'ien,* 2 vols., New York, Columbia Univ. Press, 1961.

Watson, Burton, trans., *The Columbia Book of Chinese Poetry, from Early Times to the Thirteenth Century,* New York, Columbia Univ. Press, 1984.

Watson, Burton, trans., *The Complete Works of Chuang Tzu,* New York, Columbia Univ. Press, 1968.

Whitaker, K. P. K., 'Tsaur Jyr's Luohshern Fuh' [Ts'ao Chih, *Lo shen fu*], in *Asia Major,* n.s. 4, Pt. 1, 1954, pp. 36–56.

Wilhelm, Hellmut, 'The Bureau of Music in Western Han', in G. L. Ulmen, ed., *Society and History: Essays in Honor of Karl August Wittfogel,* The Hague, Mouton, 1978, pp. 123–35.

Wilhelm, Richard, trans., *The I Ching, or Book of Changes,* trans. from German into English by Carl F. Baynes, 1951, 3rd ed., London, Routledge and Kegan Paul, 1968.

Williams, Gary Shelton, 'A Study of the Oral Nature of the Han *Yüeh-fu',* Ph.D. Dissertation, Univ, of Washington, 1973.

Yü Ying-shih, *Trade and Expansion in Han China; A Study in the Structure of Sino-Barbarian Economic Relations,* Univ. of California Press, 1967.

Index

agriculture 4, 37

animal speech 19–20, 45–6, 49–50, 54, 56

Anthology of Literature (Wen hsüan) 7–8, 15, 28, 96, 125, 176 n. 27; 180 n. 64; 185 n. 5; 193 n. 19; 199 n. 20; 202 n. 30; 209, 210

Anthology of Yüeh-fu Poetry (Yüeh-fu shih chi) 8, 12–14, 28, 36, 45, 55, 75, 118, 119, 125, 126, 127, 177 nn. 30, 32; 179 nn. 56, 63; 180 n. 75; 191 n. 23; 207–8, 210

army 2, 4, 117, 118, 126, 164

ballad, suite (?hsing) 9, 71–2, 177 n. 34; 189 n. 33

banquet, feast 3, 4, 10, 13, 16, 18, 26, 33, 77, 78–9, 81–2, 141 , 156, 165, 185 n. 11; 190 n. 2

binome 21, 35, 49, 123, 141, 201 n. 14

Book of Poetry (Shih ching) 16, 21, 47, 52–3, 59, 69, 78–9, 90, 94, 97, 116–17, 124, 130, 135, 139, 142, 145–46, 148, 151, 152, 155–6, 158–9, 179 n. 49; 182 nn. 20, 21, 29; 185 nn. 10, 11, 18; 187 n. 37; 188 n. 23; 190 n. 40; 203 n. 2

brother 19, 20, 88–9, 129, 130–31, 137–8, 148, 158–9, 162–3, 166, 167, 168, 185 n. 16; 200 n. 7

Bureau of Music (*Yüeh-fu*) abolished 5, 7, 178 n. 38; founded 5–6, 176 nn. 16–17, 21; functions 6–7; personnel 7, 25, 26, 30, 176 nn. 16, 26; reorganized 10; revived 7, 29, 30; subsections 10

bureaucracy 2

burial song, *also see* hearse-pullers' song (*wan-ko*) 83, 94–9

carpe diem 4, 17, 68, 77, 78–93, 94, 96, 136, 141, 151, 153, 156–58, 166, 190 nn. 1–2

Central Asia 30, 51, 116

Chang Heng 179 n. 59

Chang Yung 15, 196 n. 10

Ch'angan xvii, 3, 29, 61, 67–8, 103, 107, 112, 168

chanson d'aventure 20, 162, 171

characterization 17, 18, 126, 127, 130, 134–6, 137, 139, 145, 155, 159, 161, 170, 171

Ch'en Lin 197 n. 17

Chia I 95

Chih-chiang 15, 187 n. 39; 196 n. 10

children's song or ditty (*t'ung-yao*) 16, 102–12, 194 n. 10; 208

Ch'in, balladic clan name 51, 171–2

Ch'in Dynasty 2, 5–6, 44, 116, 123, 175 n. 5; 182 n. 14; 199 n. 3

Ch'in Shih Huang-ti, *see* first Ch'in emperor

Ch'ing-Shang 12, 27, 170, 178 n. 40; 206, 208

choir 16, 30, 35, 73–4

Ch'u elegy (*tz'u, sao*) 7, 74, 85, 94–5, 141, 160

Ch'u mode (*Ch'u tiao*) 11–12, 146, 206, 208

Ch'u state 6, 16, 24, 32, 34, 77, 94–5, 115, 141, 180 n. 64

Ch'u Tz'u, see Songs of Ch'u

Chuang Tzu, *Chuang Tzu* 45, 46, 60, 86, 191 n. 21; 193–4 n. 22; 196 n. 13

city 1–5, 17, 21, 23, 26, 29, 35, 42, 61–2, 64, 68, 76, 90, 95, 102, 108, 110, 112, 120, 128, 135, 142, 157, 168, 171, 187 nn. 37, 4

Classic of the Way and Its Power (Tao Te ching) 37, 46, 164, 200 n. 6

clear-mode (*ch'ing tiao*) 11, 45, 146, 206, 208

collection of folk-songs (*yüeh-fu*), theory of 15–16

colloquialism 17, 57–8, 135

comedy 51, 58, 146, 174

commonplace expression 17, 20–1, 56, 67, 76, 89, 91, 125, 131, 136, 141–2, 147, 152, 153, 171–2, 174, 179 n. 56; 187 n. 37

community 16, 46, 48, 49, 54–5, 59, 127, 148

Compendium of Literature (I-wen lei-chü) 15, 28, 56, 125, 189 n. 27; 200 n. 9: 210

Concerted piece (*hsiango-ho*) 8, 10–12, 23, 45, 178 nn. 39–40; 206, 207

Confucianism 33, 37, 39, 45, 53, 86, 102, 167, 203 n. 13

Confucius 15–16, 53, 74, 86, 114, 165, 186 n. 23: 191 n. 20

conscription, corvée 2, 4, 109–10, 123, 140, 151

countryside, rural life 1, 4, 17, 46–7, 109, 126–27, 170

court 1, 3, 5–6, 10, 11, 13, 23, 25–6, 29–33, 64, 66, 70, 85, 100, 128, 178 n. 40; 180 n. 70; 199 n. 5

dance 1, 3, 6, 11, 12, 16, 26–7, 30, 32, 35, 36, 74–5, 78, 206, 208

death 4, 20, 31, 46, 50, 51–2, 58, 62, 65, 66–7, 69, 78, 80, 83, 90–1, 94–9, 104–7, 108, 111,

223

Ku, *Han shu* 22) 5, 7, 14, 36, 176 nn. 16–18, 26; 182 nn. 21–2; 209

Ts'ai Yung 10, 14, 28, 125

Ts'ao Chih 11, 96, 186 n. 27; 189 n. 33; 191 nn. 11, 13; 201 n. 12

Ts'ao Jui 11, 186 n. 27; 201 n. 12; 202 n. 30

Ts'ao P'ei 11, 96, 150, 186 nn. 24, 27; 199 nn. 21, 9; 201 n. 12

Ts'ao Ts'ao 11, 96, 150, 180 n. 71; 188 n. 24; 196 n. 11; 201 n. 12; 206

Tso K'o-ming 13, 118, 178 n. 43

Tso Ssu 180 n. 64

tsü (coda, finale) 24, 50, 87, 88–9, 171, 180 n. 64; 186 n. 30; 187 n. 38; 191 n. 23; 192 n. 26; 204 n. 24

Ts'ui Pao 14, 69, 97, 107, 112, 137, 149, 172, 179 n. 64; 189 n. 30; 190 n. 41; 199 n. 19; 209

tune 6, 23, 25

Tung Chung-shu 30, 39–40, 181 n. 10; 194 n. 12

twelve categories of Kuo Mao-ch'ien 9–10, 12–15, 23–4, 45, 177 n. 35; 178 nn. 42, 43; 179 n. 63; 207–8

version (variant text) 9, 13, 15, 16, 27, 54–6, 87, 89, 92, 134–7, 146, 149–58, 162–8, 179 nn. 52, 56; 192 nn. 28, 30; 193 n. 19; 195 nn. 31, 34; 198 nn. 15, 17; 199 nn. 18, 7, 9; 201 nn. 15, 16; 202 nn. 22, 23, 24, 25; 204 n. 24; 206, 209

vox populi, voice of the people (*min chih k'ou*) 15, 100–11, 194 n. 10

wandering knight (*yu-hsia*) 22, 179 n. 59; 198 n. 14

Wang Mang (Hsin) 102–6, 107, 194 n. 13

Wang Seng-ch'ien 15, 187 n. 39

Western ballads 8, 9, 15, 17–19, 21, 22, 23, 48, 130

wife 1, 18–20, 54, 123–5, 128, 132–7, 157, 161, 162, 167–8, 170–4, 198 nn. 14, 15; 204 n. 27

wine, *see* liquor

words for miscellaneous ditties (*tsa ko-yao tz'u*) 7, 9, 208

Wu Ching 10, 12, 15, 72, 76, 107, 178 nn. 41–2; 190 n. 43; 193 n. 16

Yang 3, 35, 36, 37, 40, 102–3, 183 n. 31; 199 n. 5

Yellow Gate (*Huang-men*) 10, 177 n. 38

yen (prelude) 24, 171, 180 n. 64; 187 n. 38; 204 n. 24

Yen Song (Yen-ko) 17, 24, 55, 88, 171, 187 n. 38

Yin 35, 36, 40, 102–3, 183 n. 31; 197 n. 18; 199 n. 5

yüeh-fu, genre of popular song, ballad 7–14, 16, 18–26, 29, 48, 49–50, 76, 96, 115, 125, 176 nn. 27, 29; 177 n. 35; 178 nn. 43, 44; 179 n. 56; 180 nn. 65, 75; 186 n. 26; 187 n. 1; 190 n. 2; 204 n. 24; 209

Yüeh-fu, institution, *see* Bureau of Music

zither-mode (*se-tiao*) 12, 45, 184 n. 57; 191 n. 23; 204 n. 24; 206, 208